They stare at her
Some eyes glazed over
Some overwhelmed
Some not understanding her words
But still they stare
And then she smiles
Each reassured
No good day or bad day
One by one
High five or hug
Each leaves feeling important
Knowing she cares

To my sister Jamie Stormont-Smith and to wonderful teachers like Jessica Bach and Deanna Bickel, who foster resilience every day.

Preface

Consider the following questions:

- Why do so many children fail in school?
- What are the characteristics of children in schools today and how prepared are schools to address the needs of diverse learners?
- As teachers of young children, what foundational strategies are essential to use for all children, including those vulnerable for failure?
- How can teachers use more focused assessments to guide their teaching?
- What additional strategies can teachers use to support social and academic success for children who struggle in school?
- Overall, what can teachers do to foster resilience in children who are at risk for failure?

Kindergarten and primary grade teachers enter the profession and learn firsthand that some children do not respond to conventional group-oriented approaches and need differentiated instruction. At present, many schoolchildren have characteristics that create vulnerability for failure. Risk factors include characteristics that are within the child, such as attention deficit/hyperactivity disorder, limited English language proficiency, limited early achievement, and challenging behavior patterns. Other characteristics that are present in early home and school environments, such as family adversity, poverty, poor instructional practices, and inappropriate guidance strategies, further contribute to risk for failure. Risk for failure does not mean children are destined to fail. However, it is important to understand characteristics that are associated with social and academic failure to be able to create classrooms that support children's success.

This book aims to guide teachers' understanding of early risk characteristics and of their importance and role in diverting children from a path of risk and in supporting a path of resilience. Therefore, I chose to focus on what teachers can do as

Fostering Resilience in Young Children At Risk for Failure

Strategies for Grades K-3

Melissa Stormont
University of Missouri-Columbia

PEARSON
Merrill
Prentice Hall

Upper Saddle River, New Jersey
Columbus, Ohio

Library of Congress Cataloging-in-Publication Data

Stormont, Melissa.
    Fostering Resilience in Young Children At Risk for Failure : Strategies
for Grades K-3 / Melissa Stormont.
        p.   cm.
    Includes bibliographical references and index.
    ISBN 0-13-170673-X
    1. Children with social disabilities—Education (Elementary)—United States.
2. Effective teaching—United States.   3. School failure—United States—Prevention.
I. Title.

LC4091.S715 2007
371.93—dc22

2006012023

Vice President and Executive Publisher: Jeffery W.
    Johnston
Publisher: Kevin M. Davis
Acquisitions Editor: Julie Peters
Editorial Assistant: Tiffany Bitzel
Senior Production Editor: Linda Hillis Bayma
Production Coordination: Shiny Rajesh, Integra
Design Coordinator: Diane C. Lorenzo

Photo Coordinator: Monica Merkel
Cover Designer: Candace Rowley
Cover image: Getty One
Production Manager: Laura Messerly
Director of Marketing: David Gesell
Marketing Manager: Amy Judd
Marketing Coordinator: Brian Mounts

This book was set in Garamond by Integra. It was printed and bound by R.R. Donnelley & Sons Company. The cover was printed by R.R. Donnelley & Sons Company.

Photo Credits: Laura Bolesta/Merrill, pp. 1, 261; Scott Cunningham/Merrill, pp. 142, 178, 302, 346; George Dodson/PH College, p. 333; Laima Druskis/PH College, p. 124; John Paul Endress/Silver Burdett Ginn, p. 218; Krista Greco/Merrill, pp. 314, 335; Ken Karp/PH College, pp. 35, 56, 98; Anthony Magnacca/Merrill, pp. 15, 83; Anne Vega/Merrill, pp. 14, 134; Todd Yarrington/Merrill, p. 104; Shirley Zeiberg/PH College, p. 201.

Pearson Education Ltd.
Pearson Education Singapore Pte. Ltd.
Pearson Education Canada, Ltd.
Pearson Education—Japan

Pearson Education Australia Pty. Limited
Pearson Education North Asia Ltd.
Pearson Educación de Mexico, S.A. de C.V.
Pearson Education Malaysia Pte. Ltd.

10 9 8 7 6 5 4 3 2 1
ISBN: 0-13-170673-X

individual agents of change. I believe the common catchphrase used to inspire teachers, "You can make a difference!," is true and I have tried to outline exactly how teachers can make a difference with children who have unique needs for support.

As a special educator and behavioral consultant, I have done an extensive amount of research in the areas of challenging behavior, ADHD, and homelessness. The purpose of my research has been to prepare general educators to be more understanding of children's differences and more willing and able to accommodate for such differences in their classrooms. My research has not focused on children with identified disabilities; rather I am passionate about trying to prevent children from developing more serious problems wherever possible. In every elementary classroom, teachers will have children who need more support to be successful.

Thus, the target population for this book includes teachers who work with children who are vulnerable. Such children have specific characteristics that have been associated with risk for failure and often fall between the cracks. I believe the content of this text is appropriate for preservice, novice, and master primary grade teachers. Further, other professionals who work with young children will also find this information valuable, including school psychologists, school counselors, special educators, administrators, and home–school coordinators.

Distinctive Features of This Text

Fostering Resilience in Young Children At Risk for Failure offers

- A context for understanding risk, written at a level that is appropriate for undergraduate students
- A specific focus on the role of teachers in supporting resilience
- Important strategies for all early childhood educators
- Research-based approaches for working with children who struggle in school
- A focus on common needs of children who are at risk for failure and concrete examples of assessment tools and strategies teachers can use to support them
- Strategies to increase parent involvement and to support for children's learning at home
- Figures, including classroom artifacts, and tables to illustrate main ideas, and to provide examples and templates teachers can use in their classrooms
- Case examples and guiding questions, which are included throughout the text, to keep readers engaged with the material

Format and Chapter Sequence

Fostering Resilience in Young Children At Risk for Failure includes a framework for understanding risk in young children, followed by a series of chapters on strategies to support children and create conditions where their risk is minimized and resilience is fostered.

In Chapter 1, systems theory is used to describe how various risk characteristics interact to create or magnify vulnerability in children. Within-child and environmental risk factors are discussed, with specific attention given to the interaction among risk factors and the role that schools play in fostering risk in children. Chapter 2 describes common characteristics of learners who are vulnerable for failure regardless of the underlying issues that create risk. The potential impact of specific risk factors on task completion and social behavior is addressed to help teachers connect children's characteristics to specific problems they may have in academic and social arenas.

The next six chapters are strategy-based chapters. Chapter 3 deals with effective teaching strategies for all children. More unique support needs of learners who have limited resources due to poverty and/or who have limited English proficiency are addressed in Chapter 4.

Chapter 5, the chapter on assessment, provides teachers with multiple ways they can use ongoing assessment to monitor children's progress and to inform their teaching. This chapter also provides extensive concrete examples to help teachers understand how they can apply the information. Strategies to support appropriate behavior in children are presented in Chapter 6. Research-based strategies, which can be used school-wide, classroom-wide, or on an individual basis with children are presented. Specific examples of how the information from Chapter 5 and 6 could be combined and used to support individual children are presented at the end of the chapter.

Chapter 7 presents information on how to provide support for each characteristic presented in Chapter 2 and how to differentiate curriculum and instruction for learners with unique learning needs. The chapter also includes other research-based strategies for supporting academic learning, including graphic organizers and peer-mediated instruction. In the final chapter, Chapter 8, systems theory is revisited to explain how teachers can use the content from the text to foster resilience in school. Specific strategies to use to build partnerships with families are presented, followed by ways to increase family involvement and to help families meet their basic needs.

Acknowledgments

I am deeply thankful for the support and assistance I have received throughout my life and career that has made this text possible. First, I would like to thank my immediate family, including my husband David and my children Taylor Faye, Samantha, Phillippe, Danielle, and Michael for providing me with the support, love, and time needed to complete this book. Additional family members who have encouraged me along the way include my mother Faye, sisters Jamie and Tricia, Aunt Joan and Uncle Jim, and my grandparents Edith and Robert. I also value my close friends, including Molly, Rebecca, Sharon, and Nancy.

Other people who have directly contributed to this text include my former advisor, Sydney Zentall, from whom I have learned a great deal and who also supported my early interest in young children who are vulnerable for failure. I also received substantial editorial support from Nancy Knipping and Susanne Carter. I would also like to thank the reviewers of this text: Joyce Chang, Central Missouri State University; Marjorie Kostelnik, University of Nebraska, Lincoln; James McCrory, Mary Baldwin College; Dawn Mollenkopf, University of Nebraska, Kearney; Robert Ortiz, California State University, Fullerton; Alicja Rieger, Utica College; Jane Diane Smith, University of North Carolina, Charlotte; Donald Unger, University of Delaware; Jo Ellen Vespo, Utica College; and Edyth Wheeler, Towson University.

Finally, I would like to thank two first-grade teachers, Jessica Bach and Deanna Bickel, for contributing children's work samples and examples from their instruction, and for being strong models of how teachers can support resilience in young children. I would also like to thank Julie Peters, my editor, for her thoughtful assistance in the preparation of this book.

Discover the Companion Website Accompanying This Book

The Prentice Hall Companion Website: A Virtual Learning Environment

Technology is a constantly growing and changing aspect of our field that is creating a need for content and resources. To address this emerging need, Prentice Hall has developed an online learning environment for students and professors alike—Companion Websites—to support our textbooks.

In creating a Companion Website, our goal is to build on and enhance what the textbook already offers. For this reason, the content for each user-friendly website is organized by topic and provides the professor and student with a variety of meaningful resources. Common features of a Companion Website include:

- **Introduction** – General information about the topic and how it is covered in the website.
- **Web Links** – A variety of websites related to topic areas.
- **Timely Articles** – Links to online articles that enable you to become more aware of important issues in early childhood.
- **Learn by Doing** – Put concepts into action, participate in activities, examine strategies, and more.
- **Visit a School** – Visit a school's website to see concepts, theories, and strategies in action.
- **For Teachers/Practitioners** – Access information you will need to know as an educator, including information on materials, activities, and lessons.
- **Observation Tools** – A collection of checklists and forms to print and use when observing and assessing children's development.
- **Current Policies and Standards** – Find out the latest early childhood policies from the government and various organizations, and view state, federal, and curriculum standards.
- **Resources and Organizations** – Discover tools to help you plan your classroom or center and organizations to provide current information and standards for each topic.
- **Electronic Bluebook** – Paperless method of completing homework or essays assigned by a professor. Finished work can be sent to the professor via email.

To take advantage of these and other resources, please visit Merrill Education's **Early Childhood Education Resources Website.** Go to **www.prenhall.com/stormont**, click on the book cover, and then click on "Enter" at the bottom of the next screen.

TEACHER PREP

MERRILL
PRENTICE HALL

Teacher Preparation Classroom

Your Class. Their Careers. Our Future. Will your students be prepared?

We invite you to explore our new, innovative and engaging website and all that it has to offer you, your course, and tomorrow's educators! Organized around the major courses pre-service teachers take, the Teacher Preparation site provides media, student/teacher artifacts, strategies, research articles, and other resources to equip your students with the quality tools needed to excel in their courses and prepare them for their first classroom.

This ultimate on-line education resource is available at no cost, when packaged with a Merrill text, and will provide you and your students access to:

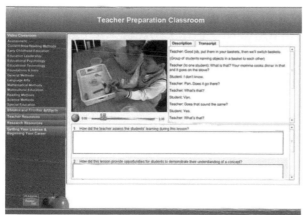

Online Video Library. More than 150 video clips—each tied to a course topic and framed by learning goals and Praxis-type questions—capture real teachers and students working in real classrooms, as well as in-depth interviews with both students and educators.

Student and Teacher Artifacts. More than 200 student and teacher classroom artifacts—each tied to a course topic and framed by learning goals and application questions—provide a wealth of materials and experiences to help make your study to become a professional teacher more concrete and hands-on.

Research Articles. Over 500 articles from ASCD's renowned journal *Educational Leadership.* The site also includes Research Navigator, a searchable database of additional educational journals.

Teaching Strategies. Over 500 strategies and lesson plans for you to use when you become a practicing professional.

Licensure and Career Tools. Resources devoted to helping you pass your licensure exam; learn standards, law, and public policies; plan a teaching portfolio; and succeed in your first year of teaching.

How to ORDER *Teacher Prep* for you and your students:

For students to receive a *Teacher Prep* Access Code with this text, instructors **must** provide a special value pack ISBN number on their textbook order form. To receive this special ISBN, please email: **Merrill.marketing@pearsoned.com** and provide the following information:

- Name and Affiliation
- Author/Title/Edition of Merrill text

Upon ordering *Teacher Prep* for their students, instructors will be given a lifetime *Teacher Prep* Access Code.

Brief Contents

Contents

Note: Every effort has been made to provide accurate and current Internet information in this book. However, the Internet and information posted on it are constantly changing, so it is inevitable that some of the Internet addresses listed in this textbook will change.

Fostering Resilience in Young Children At Risk for Failure

1

Children Vulnerable for Failure

David entered first grade as smoothly as he had entered kindergarten. On the first day of school he was out of his seat more than he was in it. He talked nonstop to anyone who would listen (and even to those who weren't listening). During the classroom sharing activities intended for community building, David interrupted each of his classmates and provided his own input even if it was off the topic. At one point, when David began to describe his mother's new bathrobe, his teacher decided to send him on an errand with another student so the class could finish. When he left the room, many of his classmates looked at each other, made faces, and sighed.

His first-grade teacher, Mrs. Williams, had been hand selected by the principal to work with David. Mrs. Williams had a reputation for being successful with children who were deemed "challenging" by different kindergarten teachers. However, she had no idea what to do with David and it was only 10 o'clock on the first day of school.

That evening she reviewed notes from the previous year that his kindergarten teacher had given her. She had not read them prior to the first day because she believed children deserved a "clean slate," and she did not want to have any biases against him. However, she knew she needed a lot more information on how to help David succeed in school. The notes from his kindergarten teacher were as follows:

"David was in my morning class. He has been my most challenging student this year. He is very immature and angers easily. He is not able to sit and listen for longer than two minutes, although he knows that is expected in my class. Over the course of the school year, I had to send him to the principal's office 45 times. David did not respond to time-out in the classroom and often did not even stay in the time-out area.

I met with his mother about twice a month to talk about ways that she could support my classroom expectations at home. David's mother is very nice and is young, single, and without a lot of resources at home. I asked her to get David evaluated for ADHD given his problems in school, but she did not want to have her child "labeled" with anything at such a young age.

David is a bright child, but he is already behind in some early literacy skills. He does not consistently identify different sounds associated with word beginnings and endings, and he does not know the names of any letters. I had David for only three hours a day and managed to figure out how to keep him somewhat occupied while the group was doing other things. For example, during group time I would let him go to the back of the room and work with Legos or color. I think he was listening to us while he was back there. I could not figure out how to include him in all of the activities that the other students were doing. David would work hard for me for about thirty minutes if I gave him a sticker or pencil.

His social problems are my biggest concern. He seems to want other children to like him, but all of his intense, disruptive, off-task, and aggressive behaviors cause other children to choose to avoid him whenever possible."

If you were David's teacher or an educational professional who was collaborating with David's teacher, would you know how to help David more fully participate academically and socially in school? To support your efforts, would you know what additional information needs to be obtained? Would you know how to assess his need areas?

Clearly teachers directly impact children's success or failure in school. Although most teachers go into the profession because they want to have a positive influence on children's lives, many leave the field due to feelings of disempowerment and dissatisfaction with what they were actually able to accomplish in the classroom. In schools today, there are many children who enter kindergarten without the skills needed to be successful (Graue & DiPerna, 2000; Stormont, Espinosa, Knipping, & McCathren, 2003; Walker, Ramsey, & Gresham, 2004). Teachers and other educational professionals need to be more prepared to support children who are vulnerable for failure in school. The need for such support is clear when we examine the characteristics that make children vulnerable for failure in school:

- Approximately 20% of children in the United States are limited in their English proficiency (Slavin & Cheung, 2003), and the number is growing (Bello, Fajet, Shaver, Toombs, & Schumm, 2003; Freund & Rich, 2005).

- Increases in poverty, stress, and other adversity in society, families, and schools are contributing to growing numbers of children with behavior problems (Espinosa & Laffey, 2003; Horner, Sugai, & Vincent, 2005; Kauffman, 2005; Stormont et al., 2003; Van Acker, Grant, & Henry, 1996). Yet, most teachers are not prepared to work with children who have challenging behaviors in their classrooms (Espinosa & Laffey, 2003; Gunter & Coutinho, 1997; Johnson & Pugach, 1990; Van Acker et al., 1996).

- The most common disorder you will see in children is attention deficit/hyperactivity disorder (ADHD). Approximately 3 to 5% of the school-age population show signs of ADHD, and most children with ADHD are in general education classrooms (Zentall, 2006).
- Many students underachieve in the primary grades. Children who fall behind early in school are at risk for having chronic underachievement (Mercer & Mercer, 2005).
- 27 million children live in poverty (Capuzzi & Gross, 2004). Poverty is associated with a number of conditions that create vulnerability in children (Kauffman, 2005; Stormont, 2004).
- Young children and their families represent 40% of the nation's homeless (Stormont, 2004).
- For many children, multiple risk factors interact to magnify their potential for failure and their needs for support:
  - Children from linguistically diverse backgrounds are three times more likely to be living in poverty than children from Euro-American backgrounds (Hodgkinson, 2003).
  - Children with ADHD are also at risk for being underachievers and for developing challenging behavior patterns (Stormont, 2001a; Zentall, 2006).
  - Children who live in impoverished conditions are at greater risk for developing challenging behavior problems and being low achievers (Kauffman, 2005).

Vulnerablity in Young Children

This book focuses on the primary grades because this time is incredibly important in children's lives. What children have been able to achieve by the end of third grade is highly predictive of their futures (Stormont et al., 2003; Walker et al., 2004). The fact that many children leave the primary grades with serious academic and behavioral concerns is unfortunate given that research has clearly paved the way for early intervention by illuminating early risk factors for academic and social failure (Campbell, 1998; Espinosa, 2005; Kauffman, 2005; Sanson, Smart, Prior, & Oberklaid, 1993; Stormont, 2001b, 2002; Walker et al., 2004; Webster-Stratton, 1997). Early intervention efforts can significantly improve children's success in school.

Understanding the Dynamic Nature of Risk in Children

More attention needs to be directed at integrating appropriate supports and educational practices for students who are at risk for social and/or academic failure. To this end, it is important to provide a framework for understanding vulnerability (or risk) in young children. The framework that this text will use to guide an understanding of risk is based on four premises supported by current research in this area:

1. Research has documented characteristics that are associated with serious academic and social problems in school.
2. Multiple characteristics interact to exacerbate or buffer children from risk.
3. Risk for failure does not mean failure is inevitable. Research has found characteristics associated with resiliency in children.
4. Children's characteristics should direct educational support needs.

Characteristics Associated with Significant Problems in School

The research has clearly documented specific within-child and environmental characteristics that are associated with significant school problems. Within-child characteristics that influence student success in school include the language they speak, their prior knowledge, and their behavioral patterns. Family characteristics with strong relationships to children's success in school include family stress, interaction patterns, and poverty. School factors that mediate children's risk for failure include, for example, the quality of instruction and behavioral management.

Figure 1-1 illustrates within-child and environmental characteristics that have been associated with children's risk for academic and/or social failure. This figure is not exhaustive of all characteristics associated with risk, but it includes the main areas that will be discussed in this text. It is important to understand the multitude of child, family, and school characteristics that contribute to problems in school in order to direct intervention efforts. This point was emphasized in a recent book about older children at risk:

> the concept of being at risk takes on new dimensions and places the emphasis on individual and systemic dynamics that may or may not lead to a wide range of destructive outcomes. Such a viewpoint emphasizes the vulnerability of all youth

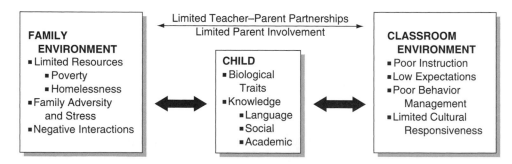

Figure 1-1
Characteristics Associated with Risk for Social and/or Academic Problems in School

> to be at risk and provides a strong rationale for the development of prevention programs directed toward stemming the negative impact of certain individual and systemic dynamics. (Capuzzi & Gross, 2006, pp. 6–7)

Research has clearly documented the potentially negative influence of specific characteristics on children's behavior in school. However, it is also important to view each child in context and to understand how individual characteristics that are within that child or within that child's environment may or may not influence each child's success in school (Pianta & Walsh, 1998; Rutter, 2000).

Interactions Among Risk Characteristics

Systems theory has been used to describe different influences on children's development and learning (Bronfenbrenner, 1979, 1989; Bronfenbrenner & Mahoney, 1975; Huitt, 2003; Pianta, 1999). According to Pianta (1999), children's development and learning are impacted by four levels and the systems that are present within each level. The culture and community level includes the systems of school, church, and neighborhood. The smaller social-group level includes the classroom, peers, and family systems, and the dyadic level includes interactions with teachers, friends, and parents. The fourth level is the child's biological and behavioral system. Each of these levels interacts in idiosyncratic ways. Essentially, Pianta emphasizes that children's learning must be viewed within a context that considers the characteristics of individual children (the behavioral and biological system), characteristics of specific environments (the school, classroom, peer, teacher systems), and interactions among characteristics (systems).

Similarly, Kauffman (2005) has used social cognitive theory to describe different contributing factors to the development of behavior problems in children. Kauffman stressed that social cognitive theory is the best theory for understanding the development and/or sustainment of problem behavior due to the theory's inclusiveness and usefulness for explaining behavior and the extensive research base that supports the theory's principles. Social cognitive theory emphasizes the importance of understanding the interactions between within-person and environmental variables when evaluating problem behavior.

I also believe that the best way to understand children's potential risk for academic and social behavior problems in school is to understand the multiple influences on their learning and development. Further, children, their families, and their school environments interact in unique ways to buffer children from risk or to further compound their risk (Kauffman, 2005; Pianta, 1999; Walker et al., 2004). Although communities and societal factors also contribute to risk and will be briefly discussed in this chapter (Kauffman, 2005; Pianta, 1999; Walker et al., 2004), these factors will not be given extensive attention in this text. Instead, this text will focus on environmental and individual factors that can be impacted greatly by primary grade teachers (refer to Figure 1-1).

Risk for Failure Does Not Mean Failure Is Inevitable

Risk for failure must be evaluated in context, and blanket assumptions of "risk" should not be made. Vulnerability for failure does not mean failure is inevitable. Some children have multiple factors in their lives that are associated with risk for failure but are successful in school. Research has been conducted to try to determine characteristics associated with resilience in children (Pianta & Walsh, 1998). Specifically, why are certain children living in adverse conditions able to adapt when other children in these same conditions fail? Children who are resilient typically have positive characteristics within them, such as strong social skills, and/or within their environments, such as positive relationships with adults (Merrell & Wolfe, 1998; Rutter, 2000; Werner, 1990). Characteristics that foster resilience in children are discussed throughout the text and include promoting positive and meaningful relationships, supporting children in developing social skills, and allocating resources early to support children deemed at risk and their families.

Although specific characteristics have been found to be correlated with resilience in children, researchers caution that viewing these characteristics in isolation is not appropriate (Pianta & Walsh, 1998). Just as it is important to understand risk in the context of interactions among multiple systems (child, family, school), it is also important to understand resilience in the same way (O'Donnell, Schwab-Stone, & Muyeed, 2002; Pianta & Walsh, 1998; Shumow, Vandell, & Posner, 1999). As a result, changing one characteristic in children's lives may have little impact on risk or resilience.

Focus on Supports to Lessen Risk

Information from the research on risk characteristics can help professionals determine children's needs for support. Promising educational supports have been documented for children with attention problems (Zentall, 2005, 2006), children with challenging behavior (Kaiser & Hester, 1997; Umbreit & Blair, 1997; Webster-Stratton, 1997), and children from culturally and linguistically diverse backgrounds (Espinosa, 2005).

Teachers can make a significant difference in young children's lives by furthering their understanding of conditions associated with failure in school and of strategies to lessen the impact of these characteristics. This chapter will set the groundwork for teachers in this process by illuminating the needs of children who are vulnerable due to specific characteristics that are within them, within their environments, or a combination of the two. Pianta and Walsh (1998) emphasize the importance of this area for primary grade professionals:

> There are two ways in which schools can respond earlier to the risk–outcome trajectory. The first involves early attention to vulnerable learners of any age; the second involves deliberate attention to the preschool–early elementary period. (p. 414)

Conditions Associated with Risk: Within-Child

Juan

Juan walks into his new elementary school with a tight grip on his mother's hand. He soon hears children talking and laughing as they line up and wait for their teachers to come and get them. Not one word sounds familiar to him. He feels as if he is having a bad dream. His mother finds his line and stands with him until his teacher comes. His teacher smiles at him and reaches for his hand. Juan turns to his mother with a look of fear and uncertainty. His mother gently takes his hand and places it in his teacher's hand.

Charles

Charles opens the book during reading time in his second-grade classroom and stares at the page. He does not know one word. Furthermore, he has no idea how to phonetically decode words and is completely lost when he is prompted to determine word possibilities using context clues. Lately, when it is time to read, he sits with the class and pretends to read. When the teacher calls on him to read, he says he has a headache. On other days he may say he can't see the board, or he will just begin to whine. If these tactics don't work, he will yell or cry. His behavior usually allows him to be dismissed from the activity. He has outstanding math skills and impeccable verbal skills. Charles just doesn't know where to begin when it comes to reading. It is almost the end of the second-grade school year and Charles has very limited reading skills.

John

John attempts to jump over a little girl in the hallway. She stands up before he has completely cleared her body and the two tumble into some lockers. His first-grade teacher hears the noise and speculates that the commotion is related to John. The teacher asks a peer to walk the little girl to the nurse's office and calmly confronts John about what has happened. John shouts, "You hate me!" He then throws himself on the floor and begins to cry.

Jamie

Jamie is in trouble again. Her third-grade teacher calls Jamie over to her desk to discuss her behavior. On her way to the teacher's desk, Jamie bops three children on the back with her pencil. When she arrives, Jamie asks if she can go to the bathroom. Her teacher says no and states that they need to talk about Jamie's behavioral choices. While her teacher is talking, Jamie notices her teacher's lips are moving and that she appears upset. However, Jamie is more interested in her

Children's characteristics profoundly affect engagement and success in learning.

teacher's new necklace. "Where did you get that cool necklace? I love it!" One of Jamie's friends walks by the classroom door, and Jamie jumps in the air and yells, "Sally! Hey Sally!" A classmate in the front row is staring at Jamie. Jamie says, "What are you looking at, four eyes?" Jamie is in trouble again.

These examples represent behaviors and characteristics that may place children at risk for failure in school. In some cases, if children's characteristics are understood and interventions or supports are put in place early, then they will not experience failure in school. However, in other cases, children's risk for failure due to within-child characteristics is greatly increased because they enter unresponsive school environments. We will discuss the many environmental factors that interact with children's behavior later in the chapter.

For the purposes of this book, four within-child characteristics were selected based on three main considerations. First, the specific within-child characteristics were chosen because they have been associated with significant failure in school. Second, within-child characteristics were selected according to the profiles of children who have historically fallen through the cracks due to inadequate resources to address their needs. Third, characteristics were selected based on their prevalence in primary grade settings. Based on these criteria, the four within-child characteristics addressed in this chapter include attention deficit/hyperactivity disorder, challenging behavior, limited English proficiency or English language learners,

Children's characteristics affect their ability to pay attention in school.

and low achievement. Each section includes a description of children's characteristics and their academic and social problems.

Attention Deficit Hyperactivity Disorder

The most prevalent disorder in children is attention deficit/hyperactivity disorder (ADHD) (Barkley, 1998; Zentall, 2006). Children with ADHD are most commonly identified in early elementary grades and are most often educated in the general education classroom (McKinley, 2003; Zentall, 2005, 2006). Although children can be identified as having a disability under specific learning disability, emotional disturbance, or other health impairments, at least half of children with ADHD are not identified as having a disability and do not receive any special services (McKinley, 2003; Zentall, 2006).

To be identified by a licensed psychologist or medical doctor as having one of three main types of attention deficit/hyperactivity disorder, children must manifest specific characteristics according to the revised fourth edition of the *Diagnostic and Statistical Manual of Mental Disorders* (*DSM-IV-TR;* American Psychological Association, 2000). According to the *DSM-IV-TR,* children can be diagnosed with Inattentive Type (ADHD-I) if they manifest at least six of the nine inattention characteristics, Hyperactive-Impulsive Type (ADHD-H) if they have at least six of the nine hyperactive and impulsive characteristics, or Combined Type (ADHD-C) if they meet the criteria for both Inattention and Hyperactivity-Impulsivity. Most school-age children have Combined Type ADHD (ADHD-C; Barkley, 1998; Zentall, 2006). Boys are at least two to three times more likely than girls to have ADHD (Raymond, 2004; Zentall, 2006). Children with ADHD typically have significant problems in school academically and socially.

Educational Characteristics

Children with ADHD are much more likely than peers with similar intelligence to experience failure in school (Barkley, 1998; Zentall, 1993). By the time these children reach the late elementary grades, many are years behind in several areas, and as many as one in three will have repeated a grade. Without early understanding and support, children with ADHD may continue on a course of failure in school upto 30% of children with ADHD will repeat a grade and 35% will drop out of high school (Barkley, 1998).

Children with ADHD typically have problems in attention, impulsivity, and hyperactivity that greatly affect their educational performance (American Psychological Association, 2000; Barkley, 1995, 1998; Lerner, Lowenthal, & Lerner, 1995; Zentall, 1993, 2005, 2006). Each of these characteristics interacts to make success in school very challenging for most children with ADHD. The following list describes the most common educational characteristics of children with ADHD (American Psychological Association, 2000; Barkley, 1995; 1998; Lerner et al., 1995; Zentall, 1993, 2005, 2006).

- ***Attention difficulties,*** including
  - Problems attending to what they should be attending to, according to the teacher, at any given time (selective attention).
  - Being easily pulled off-task to other more rewarding, fun, novel, or interesting activities.
  - Difficulty getting started on tasks.
  - Difficulty figuring out the important parts of tasks, activities, or assignments.
  - Problems seeing the "big picture" or main idea when it is accompanied by extensive detail.
  - Difficulty attending to tasks across a school day (problems more likely toward end of school day).
  - Difficulty with tasks that are long, or involve repetitious or rote responding, attention to detail, or handwriting.
  - Problems sustaining attention for very long to something that is not interesting. Children can be seen as having sustained *interest* problems rather than sustained *attention* problems.

- ***Activity needs,*** including
  - Problems refraining from activity for period of time (length of time depends on age).
  - A need to move more than peers when given a choice to do so (learning center, free play).
  - A need to talk more.

- ***Behavioral inhibition and internal organizational problems,*** including
  - Problems organizing actions according to rules.
  - Problems using past consequences to direct behavior.
  - Frequent impulsive and intense responses.
  - Tendency to do inconsistent work.

- Tendency to do sloppy work (often due to a desire to do something else).
- Problems delaying reinforcement. Need immediate reinforcement.

Finally, young children with ADHD need extensive adult assistance to complete activities (Barkley, 1995). By understanding the unique ways that children with ADHD perceive and interact with their environments, professionals can be better prepared to meet their needs in educational settings. Their unique characteristics also impact their social behavior.

Social Characteristics

Children with ADHD are more likely to have social problems, including negative social behavior, inadequate social knowledge, and negative interactions with peers (Stormont, 2001a). They are more likely than their peers to have more behavior problems, including aggression, disruptive behavior, off-task behavior, and oppositional behavior. Research has found that 62% of kindergarten children with ADHD characteristics had social problems according to their teachers as compared to only 12% of their kindergarten peers (Merrell & Wolfe, 1998). Children with hyperactive and aggressive types of behavior are at risk for being rejected by their peers as early as kindergarten, and this negative peer status lasts into the second grade (Vitaro, Tremblay, Gagnon, & Biovin, 1992; Vitaro, Tremblay, Gagnon, & Pelletier, 1994). The following list includes specific social characteristics of children with ADHD that influence their relationships with peers and adults (Bloomquist, August, Cohen, Doyle, & Everhart, 1997; Cunningham & Siegel, 1987; Diener & Milich, 1997; Grenell, Glass, & Katz, 1987; Hubbard & Newcomb, 1991; Landau & Milich, 1988; Landau & Moore, 1991):

- Limited social knowledge related to selecting good choices for specific social settings and connecting actions with consequences.
- Problems explaining why they selected certain behaviors.
- Tendency to propose aggressive solutions to problems.
- Difficulty adjusting social behavior to fit role-play situations.
- More negative interactions with peers (and negative ratings from peers), especially when the task is structured.
- Problems generating rules or an organizational structure to guide work or play activities.

Causal Myths and Factors

Many teachers have received inaccurate information regarding the causes of ADHD (Stormont & Stebbins, 2005). Perhaps the greatest myth regarding the cause of ADHD is that it is due to diet. In a summary of the myths related to ADHD, Barkley (1995) succinctly described how diet has been widely disseminated as a cause of ADHD. First, food additives were reported to be a primary cause of ADHD, and diets free of additives, such as the Feingold diet, were recommended for treatment. Despite the fact that no scientific research has supported the use of such a diet for treatment of ADHD, as late as the 1980s, well-known individuals, such as advice columnist Ann Landers, directed parents of children with ADHD to the Feingold Association. After much study, the validity and interest in food additives waned. However, sugar began to be linked to ADHD and continues to be a widespread dietary myth as a cause of ADHD. According to Barkley (1995),

> So widely accepted had this idea become that in January 1987 it was paired as the correct response to the statement "The major cause of ADHD in North America" on the popular game show *Jeopardy*. Not a single scientific study has been provided by proponents to support these claims. (p. 66)

Why is it important to dispel myths and clarify likely causes? For greater understanding of the disorder and the impact that its characteristics have on educational and social behavior, it is important to know causal factors. In addition, for treatment directions, professionals cannot fall into the trap of believing widely disseminated but not scientifically validated causes. For interventions to be successful, they need to be directed at the educational manifestations of the disorder, with an understanding of brain-based differences in learning. Simply assuming that a child had a doughnut for breakfast or candy at lunch and waiting for the behavior to subside is not an effective treatment for ADHD.

So what is the real cause of ADHD? ADHD can be seen as a brain-based difference that is usually the result of inherited traits. Most of these children have someone in their immediate family with similar characteristics. In cases where ADHD tendencies cannot be found in family members, and as a result a genetic link is not likely, the cause has been linked to injury to the brain before, during, and/or after birth (Barkley, 1995, 1998; Raymond, 2004).

Challenging Behavior

In this text, the within-child characteristic of challenging behavior includes children with significant behavior concerns who do not meet the criteria for an emotional disturbance under the Individuals with Disabilities Education Act, a federal law (Raymond, 2004). Thus, this within-child characteristic includes children with early challenging behavior who are at risk for developing stable behavior and academic problems. These problems may eventually lead to a referral for evaluation for special education and related services. However, with understanding and supports-many children can be diverted from this path (Horner et al., 2005).

Children with early behavior problems are vulnerable for social and academic problems. The most common types of challenging behavior patterns are externalizing behavior problems, including aggression, acting out, noncompliance, and oppositional behavior (Arnold, 1997; Walker et al., 2004). The majority of children with externalizing antisocial behavior patterns are boys (Kauffman, 2005). In the classroom, teachers may see such children having difficulty following directions, showing limited self-control, and requiring extensive need for teacher attention and direction. Children may also have attention problems, impulsivity, immaturity, and low self-confidence. They often have limited knowledge of how to get their needs met in socially appropriate ways and may use aggression to secure objects, to resolve conflicts, to escape certain settings, or to get attention from peers. Children with aggressive tendencies often have a difficult time generating alternative prosocial solutions to resolving conflicts (Bloomquist et al., 1997; Coie & Dodge, 1988; Stormont, 2001a; Walker et al., 2004). They are also at risk for significant academic problems (Arnold, 1997; Horner et al., 2005; Kauffman, 2005; Walker et al., 2004). When children have both challenging behavior and low achievement, their risk for continued and more serious problems is much greater (Arnold, 1997; Kauffman, 2005).

Sadly, children's risk for failure increases dramatically each year that their needs are not addressed. Children with challenging behavior patterns can be identified as early as age 4 (Stormont, 2001b; Walker et al., 2004). However, as a group, these children are not typically identified and, as a result, prevention efforts with young children with challenging behaviors are rare (Kaiser & Hester, 1997; Kauffman, 2005; Walker et al., 2004; Webster-Stratton, 1997). As previously noted, children who do not receive remediation and support for challenging behavior in the primary grades are vulnerable for developing very serious antisocial behavior problems. By the end of the fifth grade, researchers can accurately identify children who are at greatest risk for being arrested 5 years later (Walker, Colvin, & Ramsey, 1995).

Contributing Factors to Early Behavior Problems

Multiple factors contribute to the development and sustainment of challenging behavior in young children. It is critical that educational professionals increase their understanding of such characteristics as early as possible, and then use this understanding to inform intervention efforts.

In preschool, many children have behavior problems that they outgrow. However, if early behavior problems are severe, include multiple externalizing behaviors (hyperactivity and aggression), and are present across different environments, then children are more likely to continue to have problems (Campbell, 1998; Campbell & Ewing, 1990; Stormont, 2001b; Webster-Stratton, 1997). Each of the family characteristics presented in the next section has been documented to be associated with behavior problems in young children.

In early elementary school, young children with behavior problems are often met with inappropriate teacher expectations for social behavior and limited individualized help for their needs (Arnold, 1997; Espinosa & Laffey, 2003; Gunter & Coutinho, 1997; Van Acker et al., 1996). As discussed in the section about schools, teachers have rated social skills as more important than academic skills for kindergarten success (Graue & DiPerna, 2000; Piotrkowski, Botsko, & Matthews, 2000). When teacher expectations and children's inappropriate behavior collide, children often receive frequent negative attention from their teachers (Herring & Wahler, 2003). Children with challenging behavior may also experience negative attention from their peers and may be rejected as early as kindergarten (Olson, 2001; Stormont, 2002). Early peer rejection is a critical characteristic to consider for children's futures. Experts in this area note that after children are rejected by their same-age "normal" peers they gravitate toward each other. Once children with significant antisocial behavior find each other, often in later elementary grades, their risk for engaging in more serious antisocial behavior increases substantially (Walker et al., 1995). Overall, by the end of the elementary grades, many children with early behavior problems appear to be headed for the worst possible outcomes. Many societal conditions further compound children's risk for behavior problems.

Community and Societal Factors

Children today are faced with multiple additional risk factors that create environments where problem behavior is glorified and sometimes celebrated. Contributing community factors include living in an area with a high crime rate, gang influences, and limited opportunities to access prosocial recreation activities (Walker et al., 1995). Compounding these community factors, children today are exposed to excessive violence in the media (Kauffman, 2005; Walker et al., 2004). According to Lieberman, media violence is available for children 24 hours a day and should be viewed as a serious contributing factor for endorsing violent behavior:

> Hundreds of empirical studies have documented that exposure to media violence (video games, TV news, cartoons, children's programs, films, and daily television programs) desensitizes children to violent acts, makes them more likely to behave in an aggressive fashion, and increases the likelihood that they will commit violent acts themselves. (as cited in Walker et al., 2004, p. 46)

Violence is also readily available for children on the Internet.

Thus, children and youth are often sent a mixed message. The media floods children's lives with aggressive and irresponsible behavior and uses high-status models to do so. However, youth who engage in such behavior are often punished by the same society that supported its development (Kauffman, 2005; Walker et al., 2004). The children most likely to model the aggression they see in the media are children who are already vulnerable due to within-child and environmental risk factors (Kauffman, 2005; Stormont, 2002).

In summary, many factors contribute to the development of early problem behavior patterns. The combination of multiple within-child and environmental risk factors dramatically increases children's risk for continued problems. Essentially, young children who are the most vulnerable for continued behavior problems are those who "do not have either the internal resources or the external supports to help them overcome early difficulties with self-regulation and behavior control" (Campbell, Pierce, March, Ewing, & Szumowski, 1994, p. 837).

Limited English Proficiency

According to Espinosa (2005), "Children from different cultures and low-income households who enter school programs speaking little or no English are highly vulnerable to chronic academic underachievement and eventual school failure" (p. 837).

As many as 20% of children in the United States are limited in their English proficiency (Slavin & Cheung, 2003). Hispanic children represent the largest group of children in the United States (14%) who enter school with limited English (Espinosa, 2005; Freund & Rich, 2005). In the year 2000, 36% of children entering kindergarten in California were limited in their English proficiency, and the vast majority of these children spoke Spanish (Espinosa, 2005). According to recent demographic data, 85% of students who were English language learners in California in 2003–2004 spoke Spanish (California Department of Education, 2005).

The impact of entering school as an English language learner is influenced by the preparedness of schools and teachers to accommodate learner differences and to create an environment where children can be successful. The needs of children with limited English can be extensive as they may enter school already vulnerable for failure due to discrepancies between their skills and those of their peers. Further contributing to and in many cases mediating their risk for failure in school, children from Hispanic backgrounds are at higher risk than children from White or Asian backgrounds for living in poverty (Espinosa, 2005; Hodgkinson, 2003).

Children with a strong command of their primary language are more successful in school and have an easier time developing fluency in a second language (Freund & Rich, 2005). However, many students enter elementary school with borderline mastery of underlying concepts in their primary language and are then required to develop English language proficiency with this shaky foundation. Children who have limited English proficiency are at greatest risk for achievement problems when educational tasks rely heavily on language (English). When students with limited English proficiency were assessed in less language-based areas, such as mathematics, their scores were more comparable to their peers (Abedi, 2003).

The outcomes for children with limited English in the area of reading are of great concern. In a synthesis of the literature in the area of reading and English language learners, Slavin and Cheung (2003) noted that less than half of Latino children in the fourth grade (44%) met or exceeded a "basic" reading level on the National Assessment of Educational Progress exam. Children from "Anglo" backgrounds performed much better, with 75% meeting or exceeding a basic level of proficiency. As a result of their vulnerability for underachievement in reading, Slavin and Cheung (2003) stated that "The reading education of English language learners (ELLS) has become one of the most important issues in all of educational policy and practice" (p. 1). Strategies that teachers can use to support the unique needs of ELLs in the primary grades will be discussed in Chapter 4.

Low Achievement

Children with ADHD, challenging behavior, and limited English are all at risk for being low achievers. However, children may underachieve without these other characteristics. Low achievement does exacerbate children's risk for failure even if they do have other risk characteristics. It is important to discuss early underachievement as a risk factor for school failure in order to stress the need to initiate early systematic assessment and instruction. Early intervention for children with limited knowledge in specific areas is important. First, many students will respond to early intervention and be placed on a more even level with their peers in the primary grades. This initial success can foster future success, and such children will not be subject to failure, grade retention, and self-esteem issues related to academic failure.

Second, in order to determine if underachievement is due to limited prior knowledge and other risk characteristics that can be remediated or supported in the general education classroom or due to an underlying disability, it is critical to first use systematic assessments and supports for individualized instruction. Only after these assessments and supports have been tried should children be referred for an evaluation. Thus, contributing child and environmental factors for underachievement should be identified to individualize curriculum and instruction before more intrusive strategies are recommended.

Conditions Associated with Risk: Family Characteristics

Many family characteristics have been associated with children's vulnerability for problems in school. The correlates are presented to help professionals understand characteristics that may create challenges for children and their families. This information should be used to help support families and increase their resources, not to label families or to direct blame. As stated by Turnbull and Turnbull (2001), "Blaming can create a barrier to collaboration between you and the family; and without collaboration you will be less effective in supporting the family, and the family will derive less benefit from you" (p. 5).

Family Adversity and Negative Interaction Patterns

Family characteristics that appear to be linked to children's academic and social problems include marital conflict, maternal depression, family stress, parenting stress, drug and alcohol abuse, low maternal educational level, teenage mothers, single parents, and limited amounts of social support (Campbell, 1998; Correa, Jones, Thomas, & Morsink, 2005; Horning & Rouse, 2002; Kauffman, 2005; Stormont, 1998, 2001b; Stormont-Spurgin & Zentall, 1995; Walker et al., 2004). Some family stressors are ongoing and others are transient. For example, the birth of a baby or moving may cause temporary stress in families. Family stressors alone may not create vulnerability in children (Campbell, 1998). Rather it is the combination of multiple stressors and the lack of resources to manage daily parenting stress that create vulnerability for most children. The most important family characteristics to consider for children who are vulnerable are the interactions among family members.

Children learn a great deal through watching others. If family members use aggression to manage conflict, then children are more likely to learn and to use such behavior in the school setting (Herring & Wahler, 2003; Kauffman, 2005). Furthermore, children are vulnerable for social problems if their parents manage their behavior in inconsistent, punitive, and controlling ways (Walker et al., 2004). Parental negativity and responsiveness to children in the home setting clearly influences children's interactions in the school setting (Herring & Wahler, 2003). Specifically, children will enter elementary school with a lot of knowledge of what "not to do" as a result of all the "don'ts" and "nos" they have heard, but may possess very little knowledge of what *to do* to get their needs met.

Thus, educators need to understand that some behavioral problems may be due to limited support at home for appropriate behavior. Further, professionals should try to collaborate with families as much as possible to help them increase their resources to manage stress and to use effective and supportive parenting strategies. Information on collaborating with families will be provided in Chapter 8.

Poverty

The potential influence of poverty on children's learning is great. It is important to note before a discussion of characteristics associated with poverty that not all children living in poverty will have these characteristics. Some parents who have limited economic resources "do without" so their children can have what they need and do support their children's education. Professionals need to be sensitive to the following possible characteristics, the potential impact that poverty can have on academic and social success, and possible resource needs.

Children who are living in poverty are more likely to have parents who have to move to meet their families' needs and who may not have the time, the energy, or

Many children live in impoverished conditions.

the resources to take their children to plays, museums, or libraries (Espinosa, 2005; Hodgkinson, 2003). Children from low income families tend to watch more television than their peers and have parents who read to them less often than parents from more affluent backgrounds (Espinosa, 2005; Hodgkinson, 2003). Perhaps as a result of the lack of early literacy experiences, children from lower-income families are less likely to possess some of the early skills needed for learning how to read. For example, they may not know the direction to read in English (from left to right), know how to tell where a story concludes, or be able to identify letters (Bowman, Donovan, & Burns, as cited in Espinosa, 2005).

Research has also found that young children who were at-risk due to poverty had self-regulation problems when compared to their same-age peers who were not at-risk (Howse, Lange, Farran, & Boyles, 2003). Furthermore, these self-regulation abilities were predictive of achievement. Overall, children living in poverty are more likely to enter elementary school with different academic and social skills than their peers and are more likely to be low achievers in the primary grades.

Children who are living in poverty often have resource problems, ranging from being able to access materials and equipment needed for projects to having a snack for school. They may also be supervised less after school, which may mean that they don't complete homework and/or don't have an enforced bedtime. Even though many children living in poverty have families who support early learning opportunities and meet their developmental needs, poverty, overall, does create risk for many children and has an influence on children's development and the availability of resources in their environments to meet their needs.

Further compounding the challenges related to meeting children's needs, families who are living in poverty are also more likely to be experiencing other types of adversity, including having teenage and single mothers as the heads of the family. Specifically, "eighty-five percent of all unmarried teen pregnancies occur in families whose income is 200% below the poverty line, and 66% of families headed by a single parent are living in poverty" (Haley & Sherwood-Hawes, 2004, p. 216).

Further, families who are living in poverty are also at risk for becoming homeless. Families with young children represent approximately 40% of the homeless population. Homelessness is increasing every year and affects children from different ethnic backgrounds and geographical areas (Stormont, 2004). Children are the fastest-growing group of individuals who are homeless (Shane, 1996; Stormont, 2004). Children who are homeless are at risk for having the following characteristics (Bass, Brennan, Mehta, & Kodzis, 1990; Burg, 1994; Gonzalez, 1990; National Coalition for the Homeless, 1999; Shane, 1996; Wood, Valdez, Hayashi, & Shen, 1990):

- Incomplete immunizations
- Chronic health problems, including asthma
- Inadequate health care
- Problems securing needed resources for school
- Frequent absences from school

- Significant daily care needs (food, showers, clean or appropriate clothing, hair care products, home dental care)
- Extensive emotional problems, including worrying about family members

Parents who are homeless spend extensive amounts of time trying to secure the needed resources of food, shelter, employment, and education for their children (Stormont, 2004). Most families spend the equivalent hours of a full-time job trying to secure their families' basic needs. Further compounding problems associated with the physical state of homelessness, mothers who are homeless are often fleeing domestic abuse, and many return to their abusive partners to escape the conditions of homelessness (Stormont, 2004). Mothers may become homeless due to a lack of social support. In one study, 22% of mothers who were homeless could not name one person who had recently supported them (Bassuk & Rosenberg, 1988). Single mothers who are homeless often experience multiple challenges. The following quote describes their challenges:

> It is obvious that these mothers are extraordinarily stressed and are facing almost insurmountable problems of single parenting under the difficult circumstances of poverty, lack of extended family support, lack of affordable child care available to them if they could work, and are without a home. In reality, any smaller combination of these circumstances could render almost anyone immobilized, and it is highly unlikely that any improvement can occur without ongoing social assistance and interpersonal support. (Dail, 1993, p. 59)

The importance of schools and communities being prepared to assist in such support efforts cannot be overstated.

Conditions Associated with Risk: School Factors

Schools contribute to vulnerability in students by failing to create conditions that are supportive of children's needs. Researchers have outlined multiple ways that schools, and teachers in particular, contribute to behavioral and academic vulnerability in children (Espinosa & Laffey, 2003; Gunter & Coutinho, 1997; Johnson & Pugach, 1990; Kauffman, 2005; Kokkinos, Panayiotou, & Davazoglou, 2005; Lehr & Christenson, 2002; Maag, 2001; Van Acker et al., 1996; Walker et al., 2004; Zentall & Stormont-Spurgin, 1995). Teacher practices that impact vulnerability in children include using poor instructional practices, having inappropriate or low expectations for children, using inappropriate behavior management practices, and having a classroom environment that is not culturally responsive.

Poor Instructional Practices

Educators need to be prepared for a multitude of different needs in their classrooms. Many children need differentiated or individualized instruction (Kauffman, 2005; Meese, 2001; Mercer & Mercer, 2005; Tomlinson, 2001). This does not imply that teachers need to teach children individually; rather, it means that teachers need to be prepared to alter the curriculum, instruction, assignments, and classroom management practices to be more supportive of different children's needs. If teachers adopt a "one-size-fits-all" approach to curriculum and instruction, then many children who are vulnerable for failure will fail (Kauffman, 2005). Teachers also contribute to risk if they use practices that are not supported by research or that have been documented to be ineffective (Meese, 2001).

Schools in urban areas often face many challenges that directly impact the provision of consistent effective learning conditions and instructional practices for children. Specifically, children in urban settings are at greater risk for having transient administrators (Resnick & Glennan, 2002). Almost half of superintendents in urban areas have been in their districts for less than 5 years. Recruiting and retaining high-quality teachers is another challenge in urban areas. As a result, children in urban areas often do not receive effective instructional practices, which creates or exacerbates their risk for failure. "The issue today is not whether it is possible for urban students to learn well, but rather how good teaching and, therefore, learning can become the norm rather than the exception in urban educational settings" (Resnick & Glennan, 2002, p. 2).

More than 10 years ago, Kozol (1991) illustrated his experiences in an urban classroom in Chicago, which still ring true today:

> The room is sparse: a large and clean but rather cheerless place. There are few of those manipulable objects and bright colored shelves and boxes that adorn suburban kindergarten classrooms. The only decorations on the walls are posters supplied by companies that market school materials. . . . Nothing the children or the teacher made themselves. . . . In a somewhat mechanical way, the teacher lifts a picture book of Mother Goose and flips the pages as the children sit before her on the rug. "Mary had a little lamb, its fleece was white as snow. . . . Old Mother Hubbard went to the cupboard to fetch her poor dog a bone . . . Jack and Jill went up the hill. . . . This little piggy went to market. . . . " The children recite the verses with her as she turns the pages of the book. She is not very warm or animated as she does it, but the children are obedient and seem to like the fun of showing that they know the words. The book looks worn and old, as if the teacher's used it many, many years, and it shows no signs of adaptation to the race of the black children in the school. (p. 45)

Research has documented school conditions that lead to higher achievement and social competence in children in all types of school settings, including urban settings (Resnick & Glennan, 2002). These characteristics will be presented throughout this text.

Inappropriate or Low Expectations

It is important that the culture of the school and/or classroom does not communicate inappropriate or low expectations for children (Lehr & Christenson, 2002). Regarding inappropriate behavioral expectations, from the research it is clear that many children will experience discrepancies between what they can do and what they are expected to do as early as kindergarten. That is, teachers expect children to enter kindergarten with certain social skills and self-regulatory behaviors already intact (Stormont, Beckner, Mitchell, & Richter, 2005). Research, including the perceptions of 3,000 kindergarten teachers, has revealed specific skills that teachers rated as critical to success in kindergarten (Lin, Lawrence, & Gorrell, 2003). Behaviors that kindergarten teachers rated as "very important" or "essential" included:

- tells needs/thoughts
- is not disruptive
- follows directions
- takes turns/shares
- sensitive to others
- sits still and alert
- finishes tasks

Teachers rated children's English proficiency and their academic skills as secondary to these social skills. As mentioned earlier, many children who are vulnerable have not learned or do not consistently use these skills. Teachers should not expect children to demonstrate behaviors that they have not learned and/or are not motivated to use. Furthermore, it is inappropriate for teachers to judge children and prematurely lower their expectations (Kauffman, 2005; Kokkinos et al., 2005; Lehr & Christenson, 2002). Teachers need to have high expectations for all children, especially those who are vulnerable for failure, and should clearly communicate these expectations to their children. At the same time, teachers should adapt instruction and make accommodations to foster success (Kauffman, 2005; Tomlinson, 2001). Successful teachers also consistently and proactively manage behavior.

Inappropriate Guidance Strategies

Many teachers inadvertently create environments that foster rather than prevent problem behavior (Horner et al., 2005; Johnson & Pugach, 1990; Maag, 2001; Stormont et al., 2003; Van Acker et al., 1996; Walker et al., 2004). Inconsistent management creates conditions where children do not know what is expected of them and do not have clear structures to support them a behavior is a problem. Furthermore, some teachers may believe that a reactionary approach to discipline is the *only* approach to discipline. However, it is clear that reactionary discipline in the absence of teaching and supporting appropriate behaviors (proactive discipline) is not effective (Horner et al., 2005; Kauffman, 2005; Lewis, 2005; Mercer & Mercer, 2005; Raymond, 2004; Walker et al., 2004). If children receive attention (even if it is negative) or assistance when they are engaging in problem behavior, then this attention or assistance may increase their use of this problem behavior in the future (Gunter & Coutinho, 1997; Maag, 2001; Walker et al., 2004).

If attention or assistance is what a child is trying to obtain with a specific behavior, then teachers are supporting the continuation of the problem behavior (Alberto & Troutman, 2003).

Teachers also contribute to problem behavior when children use a behavior to escape an unwanted task or activity (Alberto & Troutman, 2003; Gunter & Coutinho, 1997). If a child would rather go to the principal's office than read in front of a group, then they may use certain behaviors (yelling, throwing something, hitting a peer, leaving the room, etc.) to try to make this happen. If teachers allow children to use such behaviors to escape unwanted tasks and activities, then they are inadvertently creating an environment that fosters this type of behavior (also known as negative reinforcement of behavior).

Finally, school professionals and peers within schools serve as powerful models of both positive and negative behavior. Children learn about desired social and academic behavior and ways to treat each other from watching these models:

> Exemplary behavior on the part of the teacher encourages like conduct in
> pupils. Maltreatment by the teacher of any student in the class is very likely to
> encourage students to treat each other with hostility and disrespect. (Kauffman,
> 2005, p. 227)

Cultural Conflict Between Home and School Contexts

Educational professionals need to be aware of the fact that many children enter school with different belief systems from the mainstream culture that is often emphasized in schools. According to Espinosa (2005),

> It is important to remember that young children have formed culturally shaped
> expectations and attitudes for when they are supposed to talk, to whom they should
> talk and what type of language is appropriate in different contexts. . . . When the
> cultural expectations of the home and school vary markedly, the child may initially feel
> some discomfort and anxiety in the school setting. (p. 839)

Teachers can make a large impact on how smooth the transition process is for children from diverse backgrounds by understanding their home cultures and by using culturally responsive practices (Espinosa, 2005; Turnbull & Turnbull, 2001). In a letter to his son's kindergarten teacher, a father describes the cultural alienation his son was experiencing in school. He writes,

> My son, Wind-Wolf, is not an empty glass coming into your class to be filled. He is a
> full basket coming into a different environment and society with something special to
> share. Please let him share his knowledge, heritage, and culture with you and his
> peers. (Lake, 1990, p. 48)

Chapters 3 and 8 will include specific ways to foster culturally responsive classroom practices and curricula and establish meaningful relationships with families. Clearly the need for culturally competent educators cannot be overstated for many reasons including the increase in children from diverse backgrounds and decrease in children representative of one "majority" culture.

Interactions and Outcomes

As stated earlier, risk for failure often increases dramatically when children have multiple risk factors (Campbell, 1998; Kaiser, Hancock, Cai, Foster, & Hester, 2000; Kauffman, 2005; Walker et al., 2004). Overall, child and environmental characteristics interact to compound problems and to create multiple needs for support. The within-child characteristics and environmental characteristics discussed in this text were illustrated in Figure 1-1. From the figure, you can deduce that teachers are needed to teach and support appropriate behavior for children with challenging behavior who have families with limited resources to meet their needs or families who use ineffective child-management strategies.

Alternatively, let's look at Minn, a child with limited English. Minn has a family with extensive resources and supportive parenting practices. However, when Minn enters school, she is met with inappropriate expectations and limited support for her needs. She begins to feel alienated culturally from the rest of the class. Minn starts to develop behavior and academic problems as a result of the interactions between her within-child characteristics (limited English proficiency) and the characteristics of the school environment. In a more supportive school environment, Minn's vulnerability for failure would be reduced dramatically.

Figure 1-2 describes the outcomes often experienced by children who are vulnerable for failure in school. Children are at risk for experiencing many types of negative stressors in their futures, including teenage pregnancy, dropping out of school, antisocial behavior as teenagers and, as adults, incarceration, substance abuse, and unemployment (Kauffman, 2005; Olympia et al., 2004; Walker et al., 2004; Zentall, 2006).

However, other children who are vulnerable for failure have protective factors within themselves (autonomy, social skills, goals for future) or their environments (positive relationships with family and/or teachers). These protective factors interact with risk characteristics and alleviate or greatly reduce their risk (Juntunen & Atkinson, 2002; Rutter, 2000; Shonkoff & Meisels, 2000). Thus it is clear that interactions among within-child factors and environmental characteristics influence children in idiosyncratic ways (Capuzzi & Gross, 2004; Kauffman, 2005; Pianta, 1999; Pianta & Walsh, 1998; Werner, 1990).

The remaining chapters in this book will illustrate characteristics and supports teachers can use with children who are vulnerable for failure in school to lessen their risks and support their resiliency. Teachers should use the information presented in this chapter to gain an understanding about factors that contribute to vulnerability in children. Teachers can make a difference in the lives of children by

According to Research on Within-Child Characteristics:

- Most 11-year-olds with ADHD are years behind in at least one academic area (Barkley, 1998; McKinley, 2003; Zentall, 1993).
- Up to 35% of children with ADHD drop out of school (Barkley, 1998).
- By the end of the third or fourth grade, the stability of serious problem behavior is equivalent to the stability of intelligence (Walker et al., 2004).
- By the fourth or fifth grade, children with antisocial behavior problems are at risk for developing friendships with other antisocial youth; 70% of these youth will be arrested two years after such relationships are formed (Walker et al., 2004).
- After dropping out of school, the majority of children with antisocial behavior problems will be arrested within a matter of years (Walker et al., 2004). In fact, "80% of all crimes are committed by high school dropouts" (Walker et al., 2004, p. 32).
- Children who are limited in their English proficiency are over-referred for evaluations for special education and related services, and many are inappropriately identified as having of specific learning disabilities and speech and language impairments (National Center on Accessing the General Curriculum, 2004).
- Children who are not academically successful in school are at risk for repeating a grade in school; this retention is highly predictive of dropping out of school (Kauffman, 2005).

According to Research on Environmental Characteristics:

- Children who live in impoverished conditions are at greater risk for teenage pregnancies, dropping out of school, unemployment, and incarceration (Kauffman, 2005).
- Homeless adolescents are at risk for leaving school, drug and alcohol abuse, psychological problems, and continuing the cycle of homelessness by having children while they are still homeless (Stormont, 2004).

According to Research on Interactive Influences:

- As the number of risk factors increases, so does the likelihood children will have significantly negative academic and social outcomes (Arnold, 1997; Campbell, 1995; Stormont, 1998, Walker et al., 2004).

Figure 1-2
Outcomes for Children Who Are Vulnerable

creating classroom settings where children's characteristics are understood and strategies are implemented to reduce vulnerability for failure. Let's return to David, from the beginning of this chapter:

Later that week, Mrs. Williams met with the school psychologist to figure out ways to approach David's challenging behavior. This meeting gave Mrs. Thompson a plan that she implemented at the beginning of the second week of school. From the many options she had discussed with the school psychologist, she decided on a few strategies. First, she kept David close to her (proximity control) and observed his behavior. She had a two-column chart on a clipboard at her desk to collect running records of his behavior. She jotted down when his behavior was challenging and when he was very successful. She also used two simple behavior management strategies that day: she provided prompts and cues for appropriate behavior, and she praised him often (her target goal was every five minutes) when he was participating with the group or working on independent assignments at his desk. When the second week was over, Mrs. Williams was exhausted but felt more empowered than the week before. She reviewed her notes regarding situations that were problematic for David and situations where he was successful. She determined that David had problems in the following contexts:

- When he had to work on one activity for more than ten minutes
- When the task was not structured
- When he had to wait to move or talk
- When he had to listen to peers sharing for more than five minutes
- When the task had more than one step
- When he had to use a skill that they had gone over the day before (it seemed as if he completely forgot what they had done the day before).

She determined that David was most successful in the following contexts:

- When he was allowed to help the teacher
- When he was working with one other peer
- In the morning versus the afternoon
- When he was near the teacher

At the end of the first month, Mrs. Thompson met with the school psychologist and a special education teacher to determine specific supports for David in the classroom. They also set goals for assessment, interventions, and collaboration with David's family and determined resources in the school and community that could be accessed to support David.

2

Characteristics That Contribute to Vulnerability for Failure

Yesterday, Mr. Jackson spent two hours after school preparing a science lesson for his third-grade students. As he begins today's lesson, he notices four children are not paying attention. Jon is dozing off in the back. Susan is looking out the window at the first graders who are at recess. Juan is looking right at Mr. Jackson and smiling but has not gotten the materials out for the lesson. Tony is sharpening his pencil, again, and hits Jon on the head as he returns to his seat. Mr. Jackson wonders how the lesson is going to go.

Each risk factor presented in Chapter 1 has unique implications for children's possible problems and potential needs for support. However, many children who are vulnerable for failure share certain educational and social characteristics. For example, all four children in Mr. Jackson's class were not attending to the beginning of his lesson. This chapter will present these characteristics and provide examples of the specific implications such characteristics can have on children's educational and social success. While implementing a characteristic approach to working with children, teachers understand common problems that children who are vulnerable for failure share. Because of this understanding, teachers can be better prepared to differentiate instruction in a way that is beneficial to more learners. The research used to generate the content of this chapter was taken from literature on children with challenging behavior, ADHD, limited English proficiency, underachievement, and family adversity (American Psychological Association, 2000; Barkley, 1998; Belsito, Ryan, & Brophy, 2005; Espinosa, 2005; Espinosa & Laffey, 2003; Gagnon & Nagle, 2004; Kauffman, 2005; Kim & Kaiser, 2000; Lerner et al., 1995; Lewis & Sugai, 1999; Mastropieri & Scruggs, 2004; McKinley, 2003; Meese, 2001; Mercer &

Mercer, 2005; Raymond, 2004; Stormont, 2001a, 2001b, 2002; Stormont et al., 2003; Stormont-Spurgin, 1997; Walker et al., 1995; Walker, Ramsey, & Gresham, 2004; Zentall, 1993, 2005, 2006). Information from other sources will be cited accordingly. This content will serve as the foundation for specific supports and accommodations presented in Chapters 6 and 7.

Attention Problems

Coming to Attention

Coming to attention involves being ready to attend to any communication in the classroom. The importance of this characteristic in the learning process cannot be overstated. If children do not orient their attention to important communications and task instructions from teachers, over time this will greatly affect what they know and what they can do. As illustrated in the case example at the beginning of this chapter, children who are vulnerable are at risk for having difficulty in this area due to many factors. Specifically, whether children are able to quickly and successfully come to attention is greatly influenced by factors such as their

- Physical well-being (tired, hungry)
- Ability to understand directions
- Classroom environment including the
  - Temperature
  - Noise level
  - Seating arrangements
  - Number of children

Teachers need to understand both the importance of securing attention and the difficulty many children will have trying to come to attention.

Selective Attention

Selective attention involves the ability to direct attention to specific information in the environment (after coming to attention). To be successful in a class activity or during a transition, children need to selectively attend to what they are supposed to do. Sometimes, task instructions appear to be clearly provided for most children and they get started on their work without problems, whereas children who did not attend to all or part of the instructions are typically lost.

In the early primary grades, children are required to selectively attend to large amounts of verbal information as they cannot be expected to process significant amounts of written material. If children are not able to direct their attention to teachers' oral communications or to visual cues that help illustrate routines, tasks, or directions, then they will be at a great disadvantage. Further, without specific direction, children may not use the existing cues in the environment to help guide their attention. For example, a teacher could have components of the current activity illustrated with words or pictures on a large whiteboard, which are to be spontaneously followed by children; however, children with selective attention problems will need to be told explicitly to look at the board and use the information to direct their attention.

As children get older, they need to be able to direct more attention to written forms. When children are required to read instructions, children with limited English proficiency and those who are behind in reading will have problems getting started because they may not know what to do.

Sustained Attention

For many children who are vulnerable, sustaining their attention in academic tasks is a significant problem. Sustaining attention to one task may be particularly difficult if the task is boring. For other children, sustained-attention problems may be due to

- The difficulty level of the task (too easy or difficult)
- Interest in the content
- The way the information is communicated to them (oral instructions, multiple steps)
- The requirements of the task (writing, oral retelling)
- The time of day (later in the day is more difficult)

Often problems sustaining attention are due to a poor match between children's characteristics and certain classroom settings. For example, if the task is language based and long, then children who have limited English proficiency may have great difficulty staying on task. If the task is a rote one and involves attention to detail and repetitive steps, then children with ADHD will probably have difficulty staying on task. If children with challenging behavior do not like a specific content area or activity, then they may have trouble staying on task. Children may also have difficulty staying interested in a task due to fatigue, hunger, anxiety about family issues, and/or other factors in their school environment. Classroom activities typically require all three types of attention—coming to attention, selective attention, and sustained attention—to some degree.

Problems Learning Content

Given that attention to the learning task or activity is the first part of the learning process, it is not surprising that children who are vulnerable subsequently have problems learning information. Children may have difficulty learning information because they are required to process, or encode, too much information at one time. For example, if children are inundated with facts from a language that they are not proficient in, they will often have to process information multiple times and may miss some important information.

Other problems are related to failing to work with information long enough for its retention to occur. If a child is worrying about where his homeless parents are or where he is going to sleep that night, rehearsing math facts or even reading or listening to the most interesting story may be impossible. Children's attention may quickly switch from academic tasks to their concerns for their families' physical well-being, and they may not be able to work with information long enough to move it into their long-term memory.

Children who are vulnerable are also likely to have problems retrieving information from their long-term memory. If such information was not learned to a level of fluency (knowledge that is accurate and/also retrieved quickly), then this will affect how or whether a child applies this knowledge. For example, if a child remembers only the first two steps of a process or procedure and not the last two, this will affect the child's performance on that task.

Perhaps the most important academic implication for children who are vulnerable is that they may not have the same prerequisite knowledge that their peers possess. This prerequisite knowledge can be about how to complete a particular process or routine (procedural knowledge) or can be factual knowledge of specific content (declarative knowledge; Raymond, 2004). As a result, teachers cannot assume that children would have learned certain skills simply because they were part of the curriculum the previous year or because they were part of a lesson last week. Children who are vulnerable for failure tend to have gaps in their knowledge.

Maintaining and Applying Knowledge

For children to maintain their knowledge, practice is important. To generalize knowledge, application and practice in multiple settings are important. However, children who are vulnerable face many obstacles while trying to generalize knowledge. The first challenge is to actually learn information thoroughly (or to fluency). As previously explained, prerequisite knowledge is often completely or partially absent for many children who are vulnerable. Because of this, they may not have completely learned a skill and therefore cannot maintain their knowledge about it. In these cases, teachers have to reteach the basics before they expect children to generalize their knowledge to new tasks and settings.

For knowledge to be maintained over time it needs to be reviewed often. And for it to be applied in other settings, children need to be active learners in the application process. That is, children will need to engage in their own learning to apply their knowledge in school and home settings. For reasons that have been previously discussed (attention problems, memory problems), children who are vulnerable may have great difficulty applying their knowledge to new settings. Therefore, teachers need to provide support for children to be more active learners.

Excessive Activity

Activity levels vary, depending on the individual and also the age. Therefore, some young children are significantly more active than others, and young children typically are more active than older children. Children with high levels of activity are often moving, talking, or moving and talking more than others. Children with significant activity needs find it very difficult to change their levels of activity to match the demands of the setting. For example, most young children are typically more active at recess but are also able to change their activity levels to reflect other setting requirements; however, children with higher levels of activity have difficulty in less-active settings and, therefore, they tend to stand out in these settings.

Especially for young children, teachers need to be prepared to incorporate solutions to children's needs for active responding, both verbally and physically, in curriculum and instruction. Children who are excessively active by nature have a very difficult time sitting and listening without moving or talking, especially later in the day. To meet their physical activity needs, they lean back or squirm around in their chairs, tap objects on their desks, and frequently ask to go to the bathroom, sharpen their pencils, and/or throw something away. To meet verbal activity needs, children may interrupt the teacher often, sing or hum, dominate conversations, and talk excessively to anyone who will listen.

Impulsivity

Many children with impulsivity are also very active and have attention challenges. Limited experiences with structured settings and turn-taking also contribute to impulsive behavior. Some children may seem impulsive if they have aggressive styles and are easy to anger. Impulsivity can be defined as acting before thinking of the consequences. If children act before thinking, the implications for academic tasks are clear. It leads to frequent mistakes in mathematical operations. Children may also make frequent errors when reading due to responding quickly and not checking for comprehension. Children who are impulsive have great difficulty waiting to respond, especially in the primary grades. Children who have trouble waiting may

- Blurt out answers frequently during teacher-led discussions
- Interrupt others' activities

- Need excessive teacher assistance
- Rush through work as quickly as possible
- Have problems working alone
- Have great difficulty waiting for reinforcement

Children who are impulsive also violate many social rules while playing and getting along with others. Children who do not ask to join groups, who cannot take turns, who have problems expressing themselves appropriately, and who yell or hit someone in anger (before thinking of the consequences) are likely to be rejected by their peers.

Motivation Problems

Children who are vulnerable may develop motivation problems in their primary years. If children have intrinsic motivation to learn, then they have an interest in learning for the sake of learning (Byrnes, 1996). Being motivated to learn in school may be difficult for some children due to inappropriate or inadequate instruction, language barriers, attention problems, and skill deficits. For many children who are vulnerable, motivation to achieve in school may also be inhibited by different expectations in the home setting, and limited opportunities to understand that effort is connected to positive outcomes.

Further, for some children, their effort is not connected to positive outcomes due to their within-child problems. This may be the case for children with ADHD and children with limited English proficiency. In these cases it is even more vital that teachers are prepared to help children set high goals and to develop supports to enable children to meet their individual goals. Many children who do not feel successful in their efforts will develop learned helplessness and believe that success in school is not related to anything they have control over. Children who are vulnerable need teachers who are prepared to foster their motivation to learn by providing supports, addressed in Chapters 3 and 6.

Organization Problems

Children in the primary grades are typically expected to develop organizational skills. Organization can be defined as a construct that includes the ability to plan, keep track of time, and organize objects (Zentall, Harper, & Stormont-Spurgin, 1993). Each type of organization requires children to

- Attend to details
- Remember to follow certain steps when planning and completing projects

- Have object placement routines to retrieve assignments and materials rapidly
- Have routines at home
- Have routines in school

Children who are vulnerable often have characteristics within them and within their environments that make organization difficult. In a study with children with ADHD, children reported having the following problems more than their same-age peers (Zentall et al., 1993):

- "I have trouble finding my school supplies when I need them."
- "I (do not) put my books in the same place when I come home from school."
- "I do my homework but can't find it when it's due."
- "I lose things at school."
- "I start projects but have a hard time finishing them."
- "I often act or say things before I think."
- "My clothes are crumpled and messy." (p. 116)

When children enter later elementary grades, teachers expect greater organizational and self-regulatory skills. These skills become the study skills that are required for children to be successful as they transition into secondary settings.

Language Differences

Social and academic achievement in the primary grades is moderated by children's language development. Children enter elementary school with a wide range of language skills. Their language development in preschool is influenced by their environments. Were their environments rich with language and early literacy support? Did children participate in social settings with other children where they had to learn how to use language to negotiate their needs in prosocial ways? Children may also receive conflicting messages about how language is used after they enter school. Their past experiences related to how language is used in their home environments may differ from the way it is used in the school environment. Some children may not have the same early literacy skills as their peers have but may have other strengths and experiences that were supported in their preschool environments.

Children with limited English proficiency, also known as English language learners, also have language differences. Chapter 4 will discuss the additional supports that teachers can provide to help children continue to learn in their primary language while they build English skills. Teachers need to understand the factors that can affect children's language development, be prepared to provide support, and meet children where they are and begin instruction there.

Academic Skill Differences

Overall, for a number of reasons, children enter school with different abilities and characteristics. Children who are vulnerable for failure are more likely than their same-age peers to enter school with fewer academic skills and to have lower achievement as they proceed through the primary grades. If their differences are recognized early and teachers' instruction is individualized, then such children are more likely to be successful.

However, if children with limited reading, writing, or math skills do not receive appropriate instruction, they will be at great risk for future failure after leaving the primary grades. This is especially true for reading. After the third grade, children are no longer "learning to read" but rather they are "reading to learn."

One very significant barrier to success for many children who are vulnerable for school failure is a lack of feedback to monitor learning. This lack of feedback is due, in part, to the fact that children may not complete many activities or assignments (see Figure 2-1). Children need to be engaged in learning, receive feedback on their progress, and have adjustments made to instruction based on this feedback. If children who are vulnerable continue through the curriculum without having mastery of prerequisite skills, they will continue to be low achievers. Further, if instruction is not individualized, children will be more likely to struggle and will fall farther behind as they leave each primary grade.

Attention Problems	Difficulty getting started on an assignment, may not know where to begin (step one)
	Poor attention to task requirements, may start on the wrong assignment
	Poor attention to rote or repetitive tasks, may choose not to begin these assignments
	Difficulty maintaining attention due to desire to do something else or due to task difficulty level (too easy or too difficult)
Problems Learning Information	Trouble remembering the directions
	Problems remembering important steps for problem or task completion
	Difficulty handling multiple steps at one time
	Difficulty due to lack of prerequisite knowledge

Figure 2-1
How Educational Characteristics Impact Assignment Completion

Difficulty Applying Knowlege	Difficulty due to lack of learning information to a level of mastery
	Frequent errors due to weak foundational knowledge or lack of practice
	Lack of understanding of when and where to use knowledge
	Lack of engagement in academic settings
	Limited use of self-questioning to support application of knowledge (what am I supposed to do?)
Excessive Activity	Problems regulating movement needs to be able to work on projects (especially pronounced later in the day)
	Problems refraining from talking to others during work time
	Frequent movement to support activity needs such as excessive pencil sharpening, walking around the room, requesting bathroom breaks
Impulsivity	Difficulty waiting for preferred activities
	May rush through work and make many errors
	Problems double checking work or checking whether all components needed for a finished product are present
Motivation	Problems when importance of task is not clear
	Difficulty being interested in a task or activity when no external reinforcement for working is present
Organization Problems	Difficulty planning an approach to a task
	Difficulty organizing needed information for a task
	Difficulty keeping needed materials
	Difficulty securing things needed from home
	Difficulty following through on assignment components at home and at school
	Difficulty getting homework to and from home
Language Difference	Difficulty due to language processing demands
	Difficulty when homework requires parental assistance and family does not speak English
	Difficulty if tasks are not anchored to other interests and learning preferences
	Difficulty if visual supports are not included

Figure 2-1
Continued

Social Problems

Many of the social characteristics of children who are vulnerable are the result of the challenges underlying their academic problems. For example, children's problems related to selective attention, impulsivity, and remembering information will greatly affect their social behavior (see Figure 2-2). Their social behavior will have a profound influence on their relationships with teachers and peers. Many social skills curricula have been published that address the social needs of

Attention Problems	Difficulty learning social skills just by being in an environment with socially competent peers
	Poor attention to nonverbal (gestures and facial expressions) and verbal social information
	Difficulty picking up cues and prompts to support certain social behavior
	Difficulty playing long games
	Difficulty focusing on one activity for a period of time
	Problems changing social behavior based on person interacting with (adult or peer)
Problems Learning Information	Trouble remembering important social information (names, play dates, birthday parties)
	Problems recalling rules for games and activities
Applying Knowledge	Difficulty due to lack of learning social skills to a level of mastery
	Frequent errors due to weak foundational knowledge
	Problems applying new social skills to different people and places
Excessive Activity	Problems playing games where movement is not a main part
	Dominates conversations
	Problems accepting they are "out" and leaving active games (e.g., four square)
Impulsivity	Problems letting others take their turn in games or activities
	Difficulty waiting to calm down before acting
	Difficulty screening thoughts for what is appropriate to say to teachers or peers

Figure 2-2
The Influence of Children's Characteristics on Social Behavior

Motivation	Problems understanding the importance of selecting appropriate behavior alternatives when inappropriate behavior gets them what they want
	Difficulty when no external reinforcement for trying new social skills is present
	Difficulty when using appropriate behavior but peers still respond negatively
Organization Problems	Problems remembering to bring things
	Problems related to time passage (e.g., I will play with you in 10 minutes)
	Problems following through on promises to peers
	May be disorganized when speaking
	Problems creating and/or following rules for play
Language Difference	Difficulty due to language processing demands in social settings
	Difficulty if community is not supported and diversity is not celebrated

Figure 2-2
Continued

children and youth. However, teachers need to understand how individual children's underlying characteristics are interfering with their social success. Specifically, teachers need to address the types of social problems children are having (skill versus production), determine each child's social status with peers, and assess their own relationships with children.

Social Skills

Children's social problems can be grouped into two main categories: skill deficits and production deficits (Lewis & Sugai, 1999). If children have social skill deficits then they have not learned one or more social skills. For example, a teacher could observe that a kindergartner never asks another child for a toy or materials but always grabs the object right out of the other child's hands. The teacher could then speculate that this child needs to learn this social skill. The teacher would then need to teach the skill "Politely asking a peer for something."

However, if children have learned specific social skills but do not use them consistently, then it can be considered a production deficit. For example, a teacher may observe a child using a social behavior in some settings and with some people but not with others.

In addition to determining desired social skills through observation, teachers can also use research to determine skills that peers view as important at different ages.

For example, second graders from a Midwestern town, their parents, and their teachers were interviewed regarding their perceptions of important social behaviors. They believed the following eight social behaviors were important (Warnes, Sheridan, Geske, & Warnes, 2005):

1. Being able to compromise (avoids being bossy or always having to do things his or her way)
2. Being empathetic (helps others when they are upset)
3. Being respectful of peers and adults and their property
4. Being helpful
5. Avoiding using words that are hurtful to others
6. Being happy and positive
7. Being loyal to friends and reliable
8. Being friendly and initiating social interactions with ease

Similarly, teachers need to be sensitive to what the social expectations are in their schools and be prepared to support the development of these skills. For many reasons, children who are vulnerable may struggle with social behaviors that are desired by their peers and teachers in school. The importance of learning appropriate social behavior is also clear when reviewing the kindergarten readiness literature mentioned in Chapter 1. Kindergarten teachers believe that specific social behaviors are more important to success in kindergarten than early academic skills and English language proficiency.

Social Biases

Research has found that children who have challenging behavior problems also have aggressive biases toward resolving conflict. If children have such a bias then they are more likely to use aggressive means for resolving conflict and may not be familiar with prosocial behaviors they could use instead. Further, children with aggressive behavior patterns may interpret neutral situations in a hostile way and may think others are out to get them.

As described in Chapter 1, the media clearly contributes to children's aggressive orientations and behavior patterns. Children who are exposed frequently to aggression in the media, their communities, their schools, and/or their families, are at risk for sustaining aggressive behavior. It will be a challenge for teachers to teach and support prosocial alternatives to children who are flooded with aggressive methods for resolving conflicts.

Peer Rejection

Children who are vulnerable for failure are also at risk for having negative relationships with peers. Children may blatantly reject them ("I don't want to play with him!") or just ignore them. Peer problems may be the result of aggressive or immature behavior, language barriers, or prejudice against particular children.

Teachers can have a great impact on peer acceptance by supporting positive relationships and a positive school climate. These topics are discussed in great depth in Chapters 3 and 6.

Summary

Children bring to school a wide array of skills and abilities in both social and academic domains. Specific educational and social characteristics interact with school environments to greatly increase or decrease children's risk for failure in school. If children have attention and memory problems that go unnoticed or ignored, then they will not be successful in school. If children have aggressive styles of interacting and have not learned prosocial alternatives to get what they need, they will continue to use what they know and will not be successful in school. However, if teachers understand children's characteristics and are prepared to provide accommodations and interventions for their needs, then children who are vulnerable for failure will have the opportunity to experience more success in school.

CHAPTER

3

Foundational Supports

Mrs. Walker thought the school year with her second graders was off to a great start. In fact, she believed her children were transitioning so well that she didn't use as many community-building activities as she usually did. "If I use my time in the beginning of the year more efficiently," she thought, "then I can meet more of the children's educational needs." However, during the fourth week of class, things started to get very tense in her classroom. Children were fighting with each other during peer collaboration activities. She also noticed that two children who were limited in their English proficiency spent a great deal of time alone in class, at lunch, and during recess. Another child with ADHD had already been rejected by his classmates. When Mrs. Walker overheard two children making fun of another child because she wore the same clothes as the day before, she knew things were out of hand in her classroom. In addition, she felt completely responsible for what was happening. The next day she entered the classroom and stated, "Today we are going to start to become a community. Let me tell you a little about myself. . . ."

The first step toward meeting the needs of diverse learners is to reflect on teaching practices that are fundamental for all learners. The following issues (Bredekamp & Copple, 1997; Fox, Dunlap, Hemmeter, Joseph, & Strain, 2003; Kauffman, 2005), for example, need to be considered: Does the teacher positively interact with all of the children or only with some? Are children respectful of one another? Do certain children appear alienated? Does the teacher use appropriate guidance strategies and teaching practices to support the academic and social growth of children? Does the teacher use developmentally appropriate practices and consider the following (Bredekamp & Copple, 1997):

- Child development and learning while choosing activities, experiences, interactions, and material for certain age groups;
- Individual children's needs, strengths, and interests to be able to be responsive to their needs;
- Children's cultural and social backgrounds and experiences to create responsive and meaningful curriculum and instruction?

This chapter presents information on important foundational classroom practices that need to be in place prior to the use of specific assessments and supports for children who are vulnerable for failure. More individualized supports will not be effective if the foundational teaching practices are not present. For example, if a child has challenging behavior and the teacher has a negative relationship with the child, then the supports the teacher uses to work with the child's behavior will probably not be effective. If a child is made fun of for being behind in reading, then that child will be less likely to take risks and read in class.

This chapter begins with information on building classroom community by supporting positive teacher–child relationships and relationships among children. Next, effective guidance strategies and teaching practices are presented, including the development of classroom guidelines, social goals, and intrinsic motivation, and the use of culturally appropriate teaching practices.

Building Positive Teacher–Student Relationships

A positive classroom community is one where the teacher and the children interact in a manner that reflects caring about one another and taking responsibility for the classroom (Jones & Jones, 2001; Lehr & Christenson, 2002; Watson & Ecken, 2003). Some children are harder to establish relationships with than others. Watson (2003) has stressed the importance of teachers finding ways to "both like the child and to let the child know that he or she is liked" (p. 16). Some children are ready to learn and work diligently from the minute they enter the school setting, whereas other children struggle as they try to navigate the social and academic demands of the school setting. Children tend to be more responsive to teachers if they have a supportive and caring relationship with them (Fox et al., 2003; Jones & Jones, 2001; Weinstein & Mignano, 2003). There are many ways that teachers can build such relationships.

Know Each Student

Teachers should get to know each child personally (Weinstein & Mignano, 2003). Perhaps it is obvious that teachers should learn all of the children's names as quickly as possible. Teachers should strive to learn the preferred nickname and correct pronunciation and spelling of each name. Next, it is vital that teachers understand children's support needs. Watson and Ecken (2003) encourage teachers to read all available information on every child they teach in order to understand the type of supports the child may need in the classroom.

Dalton and Watson (1997) present information on one master teacher, who takes a lot of time and care in the beginning of every school year to establish a supportive community. The teacher described the following process as she reflected on the activities she used to prepare herself for the first day of school: "I sat in the seats of the children who seemed to have had a difficult time last year in kindergarten, and I thought about them and how I could make it a good year for them. I do this at particular times with all of my children over the year, and I try to think about how they see the world—their perspective on things" (p. 15).

In *Learning to Trust,* Watson and Ecken (2003) describe another teacher's perspective regarding a commitment to building relationships:

> Unless our beliefs about individual children are working models, subject
> to constant revision, and unless we consciously strive to understand the unique
> qualities of each student, we are likely to resent children who are troublesome.
> Because some children thrive in our classroom, we are likely to conclude that
> those who do not thrive must have something wrong with them. (p. 37)

Another way teachers can get to know children is to spend time with them outside of the classroom setting (Watson & Ecken, 2003). Learning about children by interacting with them during lunch, recess, or an after-school activity can help teachers work more effectively with them in classroom settings. Teachers can also learn a great deal about children by building relationships with their families. Children may have special challenges at home, and teachers can better support those children in the classroom with the knowledge and understanding of such issues. Teachers can also serve as a source of support by linking families with resources that can assist families in meeting their basic needs. To do this, schools need to build the capacity to assist families through collaboration (Turnbull & Turnbull, 2001; Watson & Ecken, 2003). Chapter 8 presents more information on this topic.

Communicate Caring and Model Kindness

In addition to spending time with children outside of the classroom setting, teachers should communicate to children that they care about them in other ways. Teachers can use simple strategies such as saying "Good morning" to each student when they call roll or when children enter the classroom (Dalton & Watson, 1997) and give them the choice of a hug, a handshake, or a high five at the end of the day (Watson & Ecken, 2003). Teachers should also try to understand and honor children's preferences regarding classroom routines such as seating arrangements; children can list three people they would like to sit by and teachers can then try to honor one of their choices (Weinstein & Mignano, 2003).

Developing classroom routines and activities that children view as special, which are not reliant on good behavior, is another way to communicate caring.

Some acts as simple as letting children get an extra drink every day are seen by young children as acts of kindness on the part of the teacher. Being sensitive to the developmental perspectives of young children is another way teachers can demonstrate that they care about their children. For example, using name sticks to facilitate fairness in turn-taking has been described as an essential strategy for young children because they have a strong orientation toward fairness (McClurg, 1998).

Children also notice when teachers ensure that no one is left out (Watson & Ecken, 2003). Teachers should make sure, whenever possible, that all children participate in activities and that all children have what they need in the classroom, from school supplies to snacks. Overall, teachers who are models of kindness create the context for a classroom of kindness where children share positively and solve conflicts constructively. This also helps children to support the use of such strategies by peers in the classroom.

Share Personally

Positive relationships are also fostered by sharing appropriate personal information with children (Watson & Ecken, 2003; Weinstein & Mignano, 2003). Teachers can utilize different methods to achieve this personalization, including serving as a model in classroom community activities, discussed in the next section. For example, if the teacher chooses to display information about each class member on the bulletin board, the teacher could model the format and go first (Dalton & Watson, 1997). Perhaps class members could interview their teacher regarding interests and likes and dislikes. Results of surveys could be placed on the board each day (e.g., Miss Lin likes roller coasters and Mickey Mouse). By going first, the teacher helps children understand the activities.

Children can participate in activities where they also share personal information about a specific topic (Dalton & Watson, 1997; Jones & Jones, 2001; Watson & Ecken, 2003). For example, within the context of literacy activities, teachers can personally respond to children's journal entries. Teachers can also have children write them a letter every Monday regarding what they did over the weekend and/or every Friday on what they did that week that they enjoyed. This activity can also be implemented among peers. For example, children could have a pen pal each week and share this type of information with them. In the following section, more specific examples of building friendships and community are provided.

Building a Community of Friends

Get-to-Know-You Activities

For children to feel a sense of community, a sense of shared interests, expectations, and values needs to be established (Dalton & Watson, 1997; Jones & Jones, 2001; Lehr & Christenson, 2002; Logan, 1998; Watson & Ecken, 2003). Classroom community activities and friendship activities can help support this type of atmosphere. These activities include having children create

- Drawings that represent friendship activities, with captions describing the activity.
- Class bulletin boards and posters that include information on children's ideas, self-portraits, interest areas, or other pieces of information.
- Class quilts, with each student creating a personal square.

Teachers can also foster a sense of community and build friendships by introducing community-building activities that the class participates in as a group or that pairs of children participate in and then share with the group. Dalton and Watson (1997) provide multiple examples, including

- Using a class-web activity. The class sits or stands in a circle and individual children hold a ball of yarn, state something about himself or herself, and then roll the ball to another classmate in the circle. This process continues until everyone has contributed.
- Giving class members the opportunity to choose a class name. Teachers could then link important information about class values and expectations to the class name later.
- Developing a class history book that records special occasions.

Teachers can also support peer relationships in the classroom by having children get to know each other more personally through the following activities (Jones & Jones, 2001; Watson & Ecken, 2003; Weinstein & Mignano, 2003):

- *Guess who?* Children can write brief statements about themselves, including their hobbies, favorite foods, and families and then teachers can read the descriptions and have children guess who wrote the descriptions. For younger children, pictures and oral dictation to the teacher can be used. Or, teachers can read aloud statements that have blanks at the end for children to complete with a picture or words. For example, a statement for the "Guess Who?" activity could be "In my free time at home my favorite thing to do is ____."
- *Facts and fiction.* Children can write down or draw three statements—two that are true and one that is false. Classmates guess which is false. Children can choose what to report about themselves.
- *Unique facts about me.* Older children can write down or draw specific facts about themselves that they do not think other children know. For example, if a child's birthday is the same as that of the child's mother, that may be something unique that the child would want to share. The teacher or children can read each fact and then try to guess the author.

All of the above activities can be performed in small groups or with pairs of children. Additional activities that can be performed in peer dyads include the following (Jones & Jones, 2001; Watson & Ecken, 2003; Weinstein & Mignano, 2003):

- *Student interviews on topics.* Children can interview each other on assigned topics. At the beginning of the year, children can get to know each other's likes and dislikes and then contribute their pair's information to a class diagram or visual chart. Peers could also share, in pairs, what they found out about each other during their interviews. Teachers can allow children to choose a person they do not know to interview or can purposefully pair children. Jones and Jones (2001) provide some sample questions that nine-year-olds may ask their classmates to get to know them better, including:
  1. What is your favorite color?
  2. What is your favorite sport to play? To watch?
  3. What are you proudest of?
  4. Do you have any pets? If so, what are their names?
  5. What is your favorite professional team in football? basketball? and baseball?
  6. What kinds of foods do you like to eat?
  7. If you could go anywhere on a vacation, where would you go? Why?
  8. Do you take lessons? If so, what kind?
  9. Do you like your first name? If not, what would you change it to?
  10. Do you have any hobbies? If so, what are they?

- *Peer share.* Another suggestion for a peer activity is to have children bring an item that represents something special to them. Children can then share this item with a peer. The peer can then ask questions regarding why the item is special, etc. (Dalton & Watson, 1997).

- *Student matching.* Children can be assigned topics and asked to find class-mates with similar characteristics related to the topic (family characteristics, birthday month, etc.).

- *Venn diagrams.* The ways in which pairs of classmates are alike and differ-ent can be displayed in Venn diagrams by the children.

As the year progresses, personal student information may be shared in the con-text of academic activities. For example, children can share personal information about themselves in their writing assignments and through their reading responses (Watson & Ecken, 2003).

Class Meetings

Class meetings can be used both to create and maintain a sense of community in the classroom and to solve problems that arise in the classroom in a collaborative manner. For community building, a morning meeting can be used in which children and their teacher sit in a circle and use the following *greet-share-game-agenda* format (Weinstein & Mignano, 2003).

Children can greet each other by using a handshake or tossing a ball or stuffed animal to the person they are greeting. After the greeting circle has been completed, other activities can follow such as having a few children share some personal news, while other children listen and comment on the sharing or ask questions. For younger children or children who do not like to talk in front of a group, teachers can develop a sharing box, where children write down or draw a picture of their news, and then facilitate the presentation of this information to the class. Some teachers have the goal to have all of their children present some personal information at least once a week (Weinstein & Mignano, 2003). Class meetings can continue after sharing with a game, song, or activity that children like and then conclude with the agenda for the day.

McClurg (1998) presents another format for class meetings, which are referred to as community meetings. According to McClurg (1998), community meetings should occur at the same time each week, last for at least 30 minutes, and include an agenda that is established by the children. The teacher facilitates the discussion of topics, which are ordered by their importance according to the children and placed on a board.

Class meetings (and community meetings) can also be used for classroom ownership of problems and solutions. During these class meetings, children can listen to multiple points of view regarding a problem and try to reach a solution through collaboration. For this sharing and collaboration to occur, it is important that teachers create a context in which children feel comfortable sharing their ideas and feelings (McClurg, 1998). Class meetings for problem solving can be utilized when the teacher or some of the children feel there is a problem in the classroom (see Figure 3-1).

Dalton and Watson (1997) provide a format for solving problems in class meetings, small groups, or with individual children. These authors stress that it is important for children to understand (a) the steps needed to solve problems and (b) that problems are often not solved quickly or the first time a solution is implemented. The steps they provide include

- *Problem definition* (the core of the problem-solving process—helping children see a problem as a behavior or set of circumstances that can be solved and not as a person).
- *Generate solutions through brainstorming* (no evaluations occur during this step).
- *Evaluate solutions and select the best solution* (the teacher can facilitate this process by making sure children are considering all of the information, and letting children know the teacher is available to help them if needed).
- *Plan implementation* (teacher should discretely monitor and help if the solution is not successful).
- *Assessment* (teacher can ask children how well they think their solution addressed the problem, and the teacher's perspective can also be shared).

Figure 3-1
Class Problem-Solving Format

Of course, teachers need to individualize all of the supports and strategies suggested for their children. Some children may not be able to participate in a problem-solving format such as the one suggested in Figure 3-1 without extensive teacher assistance. Teachers should always start from where their children are, both individually and as a group, to determine what support children need to begin to make appropriate decisions regarding themselves and in relation to their peers.

Effective Guidance Strategies and Teaching Practices

Establishing relationships in the classroom and implementing orderly routines are interrelated practices. According to Weinstein and Mignano (2003) "When classrooms are orderly, organized environments, caring relationships can flourish . . . At the same time, one of the ways teachers create an orderly, productive environment is through acts of caring" (p. 8).

Classroom norms, standards, or rules should be generated while teachers are in the process of building caring and supportive classroom environments. According to Jones and Jones (2001), "Unfortunately, students are sometimes expected to behave in compliance with rules and procedures even though the learning environment does not respond sensitively to their needs and interests . . . The educational exchange must function effectively in both directions. Children can be expected to support rules and procedures that enhance learning only if the learning process shows respect for children and their needs" (p. 249).

There are a number of textbooks written on the topic of guidance strategies. For the purposes of this chapter, the guidance strategies and effective teaching supports that are the most critical prerequisites for working with vulnerable learners will be presented.

Establish, Teach, and Support Classroom Guidelines

A major task at the beginning of the school year consists of getting children accustomed to the procedures of the classroom and the school. Research has supported the need to establish procedures and expectations for behavior that are clearly communicated at the beginning of the school year (Horner, Sugai, & Vincent, 2005; Jones & Jones, 2001; Mercer & Mercer, 2005). Furthermore, many young children have significant concerns in the beginning of the school year regarding expectations and routines (Dalton & Watson, 1997). As part of the community-building process, teachers can help children feel more comfortable about their new school year by reassuring them that all of the procedures will be taught. For example, teachers can let children know on the first day of school that they will be helping them access the lunch line, learn how to check out books, find the restrooms, get to their bus line, etc.

Teachers need to specifically teach routines and behavior expectations.

The number of different classroom and school routines can be daunting. There are administrative routines such as taking attendance, calculating the number of children buying lunch, and handing out announcements (Weinstein & Mignano, 2003). Routines for how children move in and out of the classroom also vary from class to class and include routines for entering the classroom for the day, leaving the classroom for the day, going to the bathroom, leaving to go to lunch, and moving within the classroom for different reasons (e.g., sharpen pencils). Additional routines include those surrounding class jobs, and other housekeeping types of tasks (Weinstein & Mignano, 2003). The amount of time spent on routines in primary-grade classrooms can be extensive.

To limit the amount of time children are engaged in noninstructional activities, it is important to make sure that children understand and are able to follow routines. Teachers should model all routines and provide step-by-step instructions for children (Dalton & Watson, 1997). However, the level of teaching needs to be determined by the children. For some classes, extensive teacher support and practice may be needed to learn routines whereas other classes may get the routine on the first day and repeated instructions or modeling further is unnecessary. Teachers can gauge what routines their classes are struggling with at the beginning of each year by having a discussion at the end of the day regarding children's concerns (Dalton & Watson, 1997). In this respect, the procedures that need to be addressed further can be discussed in a community-building type of activity in the form of a class meeting. For example, several children may have the same concerns regarding something that is confusing, such as the routine that children are asked to follow to dispose of their lunch trays. Through this open conversation, children may feel that they have similar concerns and that their teacher cares about them. Teachers should support individual children who need additional assistance in learning specific routines and can also reteach procedures periodically or when many children begin to make mistakes.

Establish, Teach, and Support Classroom Expectations

In addition to establishing, teaching, and supporting procedures, teachers also need to support the development of classroom norms or rules at the beginning of the year. Teachers can either develop rules by themselves and present them to the class or develop the rules along with the class. Some teachers prefer to develop, along with their children, general guides for behavior. They may ask their children how they want to be treated in the classroom and then the teacher can discuss exemplars or ask the children to bring up examples of behaviors that represent this norm. For example, if children state that they want classmates to "be nice," a teacher can post this on a bulletin board and ask children to give examples of what children do that is "nice" and meets this expectation (Logan, 1998). Pictures and notes of "nice behavior" can be posted or discussed in class meetings or during a greeting time the next day to remind children of behavior expectations.

When classes have more specific rules for expected classroom behavior, it is important that teachers reflect on what rules are important, why the rules are important, and that they secure a commitment from children to follow the rules (Levin & Nolan, 2004). If the class develops the rules, then they need to establish rules that they believe are important and provide a rationale for each. Rules should be few in number, clearly defined, taught, and supported in the classroom (Jones & Jones, 2001; Meese, 2001; Mercer & Mercer, 2005).

Regardless of whether teachers develop or facilitate the development of general class norms or specific class rules, children need to be supported in learning specific behaviors that match these expectations. For example, teachers could encourage sharing behavior by making statements such as "I see you are sharing with Jerome." Teachers can also have peers observe their classmates and report children who are demonstrating desired classroom behaviors (being nice, respectful, responsible, etc.).

Establish Classroom Guidelines for Specific Contexts

Teachers need to develop and communicate classroom expectations for specific types of lessons and activities. For example, talking levels will be different in different settings, such as teacher providing instructions, teacher questioning individual children, independent work, center time, peer conferences, cooperative groups, free time, transitions, and announcements over the intercom (Weinstein & Mignano, 2003). Teachers need to communicate their expectations to children. For example, a teacher may say, "Class, I am now providing instruction for your small group work. What level of student talking is appropriate? (after children's reply) That is correct, no talking is acceptable right now because I need everyone's attention."

Teachers will need to review expectations before new activities and settings. For example, if two third-grade classrooms meet to complete an activity or to share an already completed project, then the teachers should discuss expectations for movement, talking, getting the teachers' attention, etc. For other more frequent contexts, multiple rules need to be established to support learners. For example, rules for working in pairs could be developed (Watson & Ecken, 2003). Sometimes such rules or norms could be presented and discussed in terms of social goals. To this end, teachers can openly discuss social goals for the class overall (e.g., being respectful) and for specific contexts (e.g., being respectful during class meetings).

Develop Social Goals

Teachers need to teach social skills to young children. Whenever academic tasks include children working together, it is important for social goals to be developed. Children can help develop the social goals to be achieved while working with each other, and these can be posted on the wall to be used again. Children can also be asked to report on how well they met their social goals during their group work. One example of this process was presented by Dalton and Watson (1997). To support the use of social goals, a teacher handed out index cards with the children's social goals written on them, and children were asked to report on specific behaviors in their groups that matched each social goal. For example, for the goal "We shared work evenly," children wrote "We all thought of words," "We took turns," and "We shared ideas" (p. 44).

As new social goals are created, it is imperative that teachers identify the behaviors that children need to demonstrate to meet these goals. This process is similar to teaching academic content. To this end, children need to receive instruction in social areas, have many opportunities to practice these behaviors, and receive feedback from their teacher and peers regarding their progress toward meeting their goals.

Foster Motivation to Learn and Participate

For children to be successful in school, they need to be motivated to participate in social and academic school activities. Children can be motivated to work toward a particular goal by extrinsic factors, intrinsic factors, or a combination of both (Alberto & Troutman, 2003; Byrnes, 2001; Jones & Jones, 2001). Children who are extrinsically motivated complete tasks or engage in specific behaviors because they want to earn external rewards or privileges (e.g., grades, stickers, candy, special activities). Children who are intrinsically motivated complete tasks or engage in specific behaviors because they are curious, they want to learn, and/or they value the task itself. Teachers should support all children in developing intrinsic motivation for participating in school activities (Levin & Nolan, 2004; Weinstein & Mignano, 2003).

Especially for younger learners, who typically have an intrinsic desire or orientation to learning (Byrnes, 2001), it is important that teachers use the following teaching practices prior to using external motivators. For children who have more intense needs for support in school and who do not demonstrate an intrinsic orientation to learning, external supports should be considered, which are discussed in Chapter 6. To foster intrinsic motivation in children, teachers can

Building on children's interests and using creative teaching strategies helps foster motivation.

(Lehr & Christenson, 2002; Levin & Nolan, 2004; Meese, 2001; Mercer & Mercer, 2005; Raymond, 2004; Weinstein & Mignano, 2003):

- Provide children with feedback regarding their performance and help them link effort to performance.
- Have children develop goals for academic and social behavior. Children can monitor their progress toward achieving specific goals.
- Recognize and support effort.
- Communicate high expectations for children.
- Help children attribute being successful on tasks to factors they can control (e.g., working harder, studying longer, paying attention to tasks at hand).
- Relate content to the real world (see Figure 3-2 for an example).
- Relate content to children's interests. For example, a teacher could say, "I noticed from your diagrams about books that many of you like books about dinosaurs so today I am going to read you a book about dinosaurs."
- Use games, technology, choices, and group work to increase children's interest in lessons and activities when dealing with content that cannot be related to an area of interest or a real-world application.
- Be enthusiastic about the content and use novelty and variety.
- Ensure instructions appropriate to the task are given for children to be successful. In addition:
  - Make sure the task is not too easy or too difficult.
  - Make sure the procedures to complete the task are clear.

Dalton and Watson (1997) describe a "what we learned" and "what I will be able to do" format. A third-grade teacher used this strategy to help children (a) determine what they thought they had learned during the process of conducting research on a country and (b) evaluate how they would be able to use these skills again in the future.

- First, children stated that they felt they had learned many things including, for example, things related to the country they were researching, the process of researching, how to work together, how to organize, and how to revise reports.
- Second, the teacher placed these ideas and others on an overhead transparency labeled "we learned."
- Third, the teacher asked children to work with their partners and discuss why these things were important and how they will help them (as learners) in the future.
- Fourth, the children again shared their ideas with large group, and the teacher recorded their responses on another overhead labeled "what I will be able to do." Children shared many things that they felt they would be able to do in the future as a result of their research project, such as "write stories," "know more things," and "work as a team" (Dalton & Watson, 1997, p. 69).

Figure 3-2
What We Learned and What We Can Do

By increasing children's motivation to attend to and/or to complete different activities, teachers are also addressing one of the most essential practices for student learning, which is to increase children's time engaged in learning (Levin & Nolan, 2004). Understandably, increasing children's time engaged in appropriate activities is also an important guidance strategy. Many of the guidance strategies already discussed can be used to increase children's time on task. Children are more likely to be on task if children are interested in the topic, the activity is appropriate for the children's individual levels, novelty and variety are used in teaching activities and seatwork, and when the activity and the expectations are clearly defined.

The use of these guidance strategies is important for working with all children. In the case of children who are vulnerable, before teachers conclude that behavior problems "reside in the child," they need to evaluate what they are doing to establish community, teach and support appropriate behavior, and motivate children to try to be successful in the classroom.

Culturally Responsive Practices

Even though the number of children who enter kindergarten from diverse backgrounds is growing, the number of professionals who feel "culturally competent" and able to establish culturally sensitive instruction is not. In fact, most teachers leaving their undergraduate programs are not prepared to meet the needs of children who are culturally diverse (Kea, Campbell-Whatley, & Richards, 2004). This lack of preparation is unfortunate. Research has found that education and experience do make a difference in how teachers perceive both their ability to teach more diverse learners and their success in creating more responsive instruction (Kea et al., 2004). The following sections present the areas across the curriculum that preservice teacher education programs should emphasize to support the establishment of culturally responsive pedagogy (Kea et al., 2004). For practicing teachers, this content could be addressed in professional development strands across the school year (Richards, Brown, & Forde, 2004).

Increase Self-Awareness

Teachers can begin their journey toward cultural responsiveness by affirming that everyone is culturally diverse. Each person's "way of thinking, behaving, and being" is influenced by the person's cultural background (Kea et al., 2004; Richards et al., 2004; Turnbull & Turnbull, 2001). One important reason for teachers to develop cultural competence is that they are role models for their children (Stone, 2003; Weinstein & Mignano, 2003). "If we want students to accept and appreciate diversity—ethnic, racial, gender, class, ability/disability—we must model that behavior" (Weinstein & Mignano, 2003, p. 86).

To support different perspectives, teachers need to increase their own understanding of cultural influences and the implications of these influences for classroom practices (Derman-Sparks, 2003a; Derman-Sparks & the A.B.C. Task Force, 2003; Marshall, 2003; Okagaki & Diamond, 2003; Tabors, 2003). As a first step in this process, teachers need to explore their own cultural self and understand that their values, preferences, and ways of viewing the world are unique and not representative of those of all or may be even some of their children (Derman-Sparks, 2003b; Marshall, 2003; Tabors, 2003; Turnbull & Turnbull, 2001). Ramsey (2003) also stressed this need for self-exploration, stating that "As practicing teachers we must constantly examine our own backgrounds and perspectives and be aware of how they influence our assumptions about society and about individual children and families" (p. 26).

In addition to race and ethnicity, educators need to understand other key cultural influences, including geographical location, gender, socioeconomic status, disability status, sexual orientation, and religion (Turnbull & Turnbull, 2001). Teachers need to spend time reflecting on how their cultures influence their perceptions. In this process, it is important that teachers affirm that their perceptions are not the "right way" but just "one way" of perceiving the world (Turnbull & Turnbull, 2001).

Too often children and teachers from the "majority" culture do not have the opportunity to explore their own backgrounds and see themselves as culturally diverse (Turnbull & Turnbull, 2001). Many activities can support cultural self-awareness. In a course or in professional development workshops, teachers can create spatial organizers, poems, songs, or other visual representations of their sub-cultures to present to others. For example, a spatial organizer could have a person's name in the center of a web and then the web could include outer circles representing subcultures, such as ethnicity, geographic location, gender, and religion (Turnbull & Turnbull, 2001). An instructor or professional development facilitator could then lead a discussion regarding which subcultures have been the most influential in their lives.

Learn About Other Cultures

Professionals also need to learn more specific information about other cultures (Marshall, 2003). Teachers can begin this process by focusing, at least initially, on the beliefs, customs, traditions, and values of cultures that are common in their communities (Turnbull & Turnbull, 2001). For example, if a teacher will be teaching in a rural area with high poverty rates and strong Baptist religious preferences, then the teacher should learn more about these cultural influences. Other teachers may teach in schools with high percentages of English language learners from multiple ethnic backgrounds with a variety of socioeconomic and religious backgrounds. Teachers who teach near Indian reservations need to develop a knowledge base of cultural preferences for Native Americans in general and then learn specific cultural nuances of the tribes that reside in their area (Marshall, 2003; Turnbull & Turnbull, 2001). Teachers also need to understand the implications of different religious beliefs for classroom celebrations and be sensitive to religious practices that are followed throughout the year.

Overall, teachers need to understand the day-to-day lives of children from all cultural backgrounds in their communities (Marshall, 2003). Teachers who are more educated and more sensitive to cultural influences can more readily detect children who are feeling marginalized due to their cultural backgrounds and children who have formed rigid stereotypes of specific cultural groups (Marshall, 2003; Ramsey, 2003). Once such marginalization or rigid stereotyping is recognized, teachers can be sensitive to the need for a class meeting or a lesson on the topic (Gartrell, 2003).

Understand Broad Cultural Preferences

Children from various cultural backgrounds may have similar beliefs, orientations, and values that are not embraced in the "majority culture" of their schools. Mercer and Mercer (2005) described the values that are typically dominant in schools in the United States and then compared common values of many children from culturally and linguistically diverse backgrounds. For example, some common values emphasized in schools include competition, individualization (autonomy), timeliness, high academic achievement, and atmospheres that promote interactions with teachers if assistance is needed (Mercer & Mercer, 2005). In contrast, many children from culturally and linguistically diverse backgrounds value cooperation, have collective (family, group) orientations, view time as secondary to other factors (e.g., producing high-quality work, relationships), believe affective growth as an individual is as important as academic achievement, respect authority figures, and obtain information through listening (Mercer & Mercer, 2005; Turnbull & Turnbull, 2001).

Be Sensitive but Not Stereotypic

Developing cultural sensitivity without being stereotypic should a goal for professionals (Espinosa, 2005; Turnbull & Turnbull, 2001). Teachers need to use their knowledge of specific and general cultural preferences to understand values, customs, and beliefs that children from those cultures *may* possess to help inform curriculum and instruction. For example, information from research sources about children who are English language learners or children who are African American should help inform teachers of individual support needs and/or styles of interacting that children from these cultures *may* possess. However, each student should be viewed as a unique child who may or may not represent the research on larger groups of children.

Build and Maintain Positive Relationships

Perhaps the best way to create culturally responsive classrooms is to get to know children and their families (Espinosa, 2005; Turnbull & Turnbull, 2001). Establishing meaningful relationships with families will help teachers understand more about specific and general cultural influences and will also support being sensitive to children's needs without being stereotypic. According to Marshall (2003), teachers could start conversations with families by stating that they would like to know more about their particular values and beliefs as they relate to their children's education.

Include Culture in the Curriculum

Teachers can also promote culturally sensitive classrooms by addressing issues related to cultural perspectives and representation in planned and spontaneous ways (Ramsey, 2003). According to Derman-Sparks and the A.B.C. Task Force (2003), teachers should create a classroom ". . . that is rich in possibilities for exploring gender, race/ethnicity, and different-abledness . . . " (p. 45). The images that children see in their classrooms should reflect the following (Derman-Sparks, 2003a; Derman-Sparks & the A.B.C. Task Force, 2003; Favazza, 2001; Logan, 1998; Marshall, 2003):

- People of various ethnic groups that are prevalent in U.S. society and in the local community.
- A balance of men and women participating in different jobs both inside and outside the home. Both genders should be represented in different types of work (e.g., factory work, sales, lawyer, doctor, teacher).

- Persons with disabilities from a variety of backgrounds participating in work, recreational, and familial types of activities. Adults and children with disabilities should be portrayed in a variety of roles, including leadership roles (as opposed to being portrayed as passive and dependent).

- Different types of family compositions, including, for example, single parents, families with a grandparent serving as the parent, adoptive families, foster families, multiethnic families, and families including a person with a disability.

- Persons from diverse backgrounds who have advocated in the past or are currently advocating for important social causes.

Markers of multicultural/antibias education include planned and multifaceted approaches to supporting diversity in the classroom. The classroom that embraces such an antibias approach to education is one that is proactive in planning for solving social problems, that incorporates children's languages and daily experiences into the school day, and that includes a focus on learning more about all types of cultures, including Euro-American backgrounds (Derman-Sparks, 2003a, 2003b). Too often, cultural diversity is addressed in schools in an add-on fashion, with special events or days to celebrate a particular ethnic background (Derman-Sparks, 2003a). For more information on developing an antibias curriculum for children see Derman-Sparks (2003a, 2003b).

Use Responsive Instruction

It is also important for teachers to understand the instructional implications of being a culturally sensitive and responsible educator. The National Center for Culturally Responsive Educational Systems (Education Development Center, 2003) provides an instructional framework for conceptualizing how to begin to establish "culturally responsive educational systems." Such systems include a foundational belief that children who are culturally and/or linguistically diverse will be successful academically if their diversity is valued and used to promote development and learning. Furthermore, children from diverse backgrounds need to have access to high-quality professionals, programs, curricula, and other resources to help them excel (Education Development Center, 2003).

However, knowledge related to cultural practices and beliefs is not sufficient for responsive classrooms—teachers must also know and use research—based practices (Garcia & Ortiz, 2004). The following instructional practices can help teachers establish culturally responsive instructional environments (Garcia & Ortiz, 2004; Kea et al., 2004):

- Have high expectations for success for all children, including those from culturally and linguistically diverse backgrounds. Match children's learning styles, needs, and preferences with the classroom environment; a mismatch between home and school cultures often contributes to school failure. "For many students, the kinds of behaviors required in school (e.g., sitting in one's seat and only speaking when called on) and types of discourse (e.g., 'Class, what is the title of this book?') contrast with home cultural and linguistic practices" (Richards et al., 2004).

- Share responsibility for children by using school resources, including personnel from other areas or with other backgrounds, to support the needs of children.

- Understand that practices that are added to promote cultural sensitivity may actually do the opposite. Children need to feel their cultures are valued every day in school.

- Use research-based practices that can foster learning and use instructional methods that are valued by and are familiar to children. For example, for children who have cultural values that are more collective in orientation, teachers can utilize peer collaboration methods. Cooperative learning and peer tutoring are two research-based strategies (e.g., Meese, 2001), that could be used to promote learning and social development by creating a comfortable instructional context for children with collective orientations toward learning. Furthermore, Ramsey (2003) reviewed research that noted the importance of forming culturally diverse collaborative teams in classrooms to work on projects together. When children learn about others' perspectives in an environment that respects their differences and highlights their similarities, then community and friendships are facilitated.

Summary

The purpose of this chapter was to create a context for the use of additional supports for children who are vulnerable. More specifically, the relationship-building activities, guidance strategies, and teaching practices presented in this chapter should be addressed prior to the establishment of more intrusive types of approaches. Once these practices are put in place, children who are vulnerable may need no additional supports, minor additional supports, or extensive additional supports. However, additional supports will not be effective if they are provided in a classroom that has not created a caring community atmosphere, has no clear expectations for appropriate behavior, is disorganized, and/or does not attend to children's motivational and cultural characteristics. Professionals can review their community, guidance, and teaching practices by answering the questions in Table 3-1, which are based on the content of this chapter.

Table 3-1
Community, Classroom, and Teaching Practices That Support Children's Social and Academic Development

To what Extent

- Do children feel a personal connection to their teacher?
- Do children feel safe expressing their opinions in the classroom?
- Do children have friendships and respectful relationships with other members of the class?
- Do children and the teacher work together to solve community problems?
- Do children take ownership in modeling appropriate behavior and supporting other children who need additional help?
- Are classroom routines and procedures clear to children?
- Has the teacher specifically taught all routines?
- Are children who need more practice with routines provided with this extra support?
- Are classroom norms or rules established?
- Are classroom norms or rules specifically taught to children?
- Are expectations for specific settings clear to children?
- Are children provided feedback by the teacher, their peers, and themselves regarding how well they are meeting the classroom behavioral expectations?
- Are social skills taught continuously to support classroom community and the social development of students?
- Are social goals developed for activities that include children working together?
- Is the content taught clearly connected to real-world applications?
- Do children connect what they have learned to specific things they will be able to do in the future?
- Are children interested in what they are learning?
- Has the teacher explored how the cultural beliefs of the teacher influence the teacher's beliefs?
- Is the teacher learning about specific cultures in the teacher's community and the influence of these cultural beliefs on learning preferences?
- Are all children's cultural perspectives and preferences understood and accepted?
- Does the teacher promote classroom, instructional, and curriculum contexts that value all children and their backgrounds?

4

Supporting Learners with Unique Support Needs

"It was 3:00 a.m. At a local gas station, a man was trying to bum $5.00 worth of gas off of the attendant as his family waited, shivering, in their junky car. The attendant obliged the family and called a local homeless shelter asking if they would let the family stay even though their doors were closed for the night. The children arrived at the shelter, hungry and cold. Their parents tucked them in and stayed up for awhile chatting with the volunteers. They were homeless because of one bill they could not pay their electric bill. They tried to survive in their trailer without heat, lights, or hot water but it was too hard on their children. The children woke and ate breakfast. Their clothes were wrinkled. They were dirty and extremely tired. They went to school on less than 3 hours of sleep. What will their teachers think when they fall asleep in class? . . . What can these children talk about with their peers? They have had to grow up too fast. Their worries are not the same as other children's. They are worried about their next meal and where they will seek shelter. However, their needs are the same. They need a home and all of the securities that come with it. They also need an education" (Stormont, 2004, p. 403)

Most learners who are vulnerable will need targeted academic and behavioral supports, such as those discussed in Chapters 6 and 7. However, many young children will face additional challenges in school settings and educational professionals need to be prepared to offset such challenges. The following sections will discuss the potential support needs for children who are living in poverty, homeless, and/or limited in their English proficiency.

Children Living in Poverty

Children who are living in poverty may have problems obtaining the resources they need for school. Often, community agencies raise money and support for specific needs in their communities. However, teachers should not assume that families who are limited in their resources due to poverty are out accessing possible resources themselves. Teachers need to be prepared to access resources for children.

Access Resources

Teachers need to have a plan for how to obtain needed resources for children who may enter school without needed school supplies. First, teachers need to determine the resources children will need in the classroom immediately and throughout the year. Teachers can then implement one or more of the following strategies to secure resources for children:

- Work collaboratively with other teachers, counselors, administrators, and communities to develop ways to meet the needs of children.
- Join forces with parent–teacher organizations to create more resources to meet different student needs in their school.
- Develop community resource lists. An example of a resource list that teachers can develop for their children's needs is provided in Table 4-1.
  - Lists could detail the types of resources different support agencies will provide.
  - Lists of supports that could be made available to families could also be generated. Family support needs will be described in detail in Chapter 8.

Table 4-1
Linking Children with Resources

Resource	Support Provided	Criteria for Qualification
Salvation Army	■ Winter wear ■ School supplies	Teacher or parent-identified need
PTO	■ Shoes ■ Birthday snacks ■ Materials for projects	Teacher or parent-identified need
Local volunteer center	■ Birthday presents ■ Holiday presents	Income guidelines
ABC after-school program	■ Before- and after-school supervision and activities	Income guidelines
Local college	■ Tutoring assistance	Teacher or parent-identified need

Finding and linking children to as many resources as possible within the classroom setting may be the most desirable for many children. For example, having to go to the school's lost-and-found to grab a pair of gloves or a hat may be a hassle and/or embarrassing for a student. Having extra winter wear in a cabinet in the classroom would be better. Some additional ideas for teachers to be prepared to supply needed resources for children in their classroom include the following:

1. Have school supplies in the classroom for children who enter school without needed supplies.

2. Early in the year, have a "snack bank" for children who are not be able to bring snacks from home (or who forget their snack). In a newsletter, ask all families to contribute to the bank.

3. During the community-building activities at the beginning of the year, develop a calendar of children's birthdays. Make sure children who may not be able to afford treats are not left out of a classroom birthday celebration. Also remember that not all children celebrate their birthday and teachers need to honor families' preferences.

4. Create an in-class cubby for children with limited resources to store snacks for the week (from the bank) and extra school supplies. Creating this space may help children feel less singled out.

5. Have a closet with extra supplies needed for completing homework activities throughout the year. Be aware of children who may need materials from the closet.

Teachers should also consider other needs that children may have and try to secure resources for children or link them and their families with resources. For example, teachers can discuss with the school nurse how children with incomplete immunizations can meet health requirements and where they can obtain free immunizations.

Support Homework Completion

In most schools, by the third grade and often before, children have homework in the evenings. In some home environments, children who are poor receive the same encouragement for homework completion as children from more affluent backgrounds. In other cases, parents may be working or absent in the evening and therefore may not be available for homework supervision. To support their families, sometimes children may be required to do many chores and watch their younger siblings when they get home from school. Some ideas teachers can utilize to support children with limited family resources for homework completion include the following:

- *Designate homework buddies.* Elect several homework buddies for peer collaboration. These buddies can be contacted in case there are questions regarding homework and projects. The teacher or the class can nominate buddies, but buddies must agree to participate. They can be contacted by phone at night or on weekends.

- *Peer collaboration on homework.* When children do not have phones to contact buddies, the teacher can make special arrangements and allow some class time to be used for peer collaboration.

- *Allow flexibility.* Children with more limited resources may need teachers to be more flexible regarding the amount of homework given and due dates. Young children with limited home resources should not have to stay in during recess day after day because they do not have their homework completed.

- *Teacher time.* If children struggle to complete homework at home because they need some assistance, teachers can try to spend time during the day with children on their homework. Practice and feedback are such important parts of the learning process (Mercer & Mercer, 2005). Even if a teacher devotes only small periods of time a few days a week, it may make a big difference in a student's achievement.

- *Breakfast with the teacher.* Teachers can allow children who utilize free or reduced breakfast to bring their breakfast into the classroom and complete their homework. During this time, teachers would be available to provide extra support if needed. This may also be a nice time to engage in literacy activities.

- *Allow early classroom time.* For children who do not eat breakfast at school, try to arrange 20 minutes before class starts when children can be allowed to enter the classroom and complete their homework or read. Many children spend this time in a gym, sitting on a bus, or waiting in a hallway before school. This time would be much better spent on academics.

- *Allow early library time.* Allow children who have limited access to resources at home, such as computers, to work on projects before school. Teachers can collaborate with school librarians to see if this is a possibility. To avoid behavior issues, teachers need to make sure children understand specifically what information they need to be accessing and the behavior expectations in the library.

- *After school support.* Many schools have after-school programs with supervised activities, and some children may be eligible to receive tuition waivers. Teachers can collaborate with the after-school staff to ensure that children are supervised in completing their homework in this setting.

- *Utilize preservice teacher support.* In schools located in communities with colleges and universities, there are typically preservice teachers available who need to complete various field activities for their coursework. Their help could be sought to provide extra homework support and/or supervision.

- *Use other resources.* Most schools have the capacity to meet the needs of their children (Mercer & Mercer, 2005). Educational professionals need to be creative in how school resources are used. Perhaps the counselor, principal, assistant principal, librarian, or older children can assist in providing more individual support to children.

Support During Transition

Children who live in poverty may also need support if they have to transition from one school to another. Many children who live in poverty, especially if they are homeless, move quite frequently. Teachers could provide support for such children by creating a "mobile folder" that goes with the student. It is important that at least three sources of information are in a child's folder:

1. *A "MEET Juan/Susie" paper.* This paper could serve as a means for community building in both the sending and receiving classrooms. All children in the student's sending classroom could complete this paper and the teacher can shape it using the activities discussed in Chapter 3. This paper could then be used by the new teacher to introduce the child to his or her new classmates.

2. *Recent assessment data.* Both formal and informal assessment information should be in the child's folder, as well as some of the child's recent work.

3. *Summary of the student's strengths and need areas.* The sending teacher should document, even if the teacher has had the student only for a month, specific characteristics of the student. Information should include the child's interests, leadership skills, learning preferences, family values, and other relevant information. Teachers can also document successful support strategies that have been utilized for homework support or behavior management

Additional Support for Children Who Are Homeless

All of the supports outlined for children living in poverty are also important for children who are homeless. In particular, given the hectic nature of some homeless shelters and of conditions when families are "doubling up" with other families, special arrangements, such as those listed in the previous section, may need to be made regarding homework completion. In addition, teachers or home–school communicators (when available) should also work with officials at homeless shelters to try to secure a quiet place to enable the child to complete homework, at least to a certain extent, in the evenings or on weekends.

Children who are homeless may need some additional support given their lack of a stable physical home environment (Stormont, 2004). Children who are living in transient housing conditions may not always have access to showers, baths, and clean clothes. Having resources such as soap, shampoo, hair products, and some selection of clean undergarments and clothing in school would potentially help children feel better in school and help minimize social isolation. Children could access these resources through a school nurse and use a bathroom that other children don't have access to.

Finally, children who do not have a stable place to put their belongings after school may appreciate having a special place in school, perhaps around their desk, to post pictures and keep special items. For children who have lives after school that change on a daily, weekly, or monthly basis, having some physical space to put possessions that are important to them may help them feel a sense of stability.

Children with Limited English Proficiency

When children with limited English proficiency (LEP, also referred to as English language learners) enter school, many are already behind their English-proficient peers in early language and reading skills (Espinosa, 2005). Many factors contribute to the increased risk that children with LEP will experience failure in school and may be inappropriate referred for an evaluation for special education and related services (National Center on Accessing the General Curriculum, 2004). Teachers need to understand the challenges that children with LEP may face in school and use research-supported practices to meet their educational needs and buffer them from failure.

Research in the area of supporting young children with LEP emphasizes the need to both support children in continuing to develop their language abilities in their primary language and provide planned, authentic, and meaningful experiences in English (Espinosa, 2005; Freund & Rich, 2005; Stormont, et al., 2003). Researchers have provided suggestions for how teachers can support children both in their primary languages and in developing English skills (Espinosa, 2005; Freund & Rich, 2005; Garcia & Ortiz, 2004).

Supporting Children in Their Primary Language

Many experts have underscored the importance of fostering growth in children's primary languages (Espinosa, 2005). Children need to develop higher-level language skills in their primary language to make sense of the world and to build literacy skills in a second language (Freund & Rich, 2005). To support children in the

Growing numbers of children enter school with limited English proficiency.

development of their primary language, teachers can use the following strategies (Espinosa, 2005; Freund & Rich, 2005; Stormont et al., 2003):

- Establish relationships with professionals, older children, family members, and community members from different language backgrounds who can provide support in the classroom.
- Include labels in the classroom in children's primary languages.
- Support early literacy in children's primary languages by adapting books, songs, and other materials.
- Support early literacy home activities with children by sending home stories, songs, and other activities in children's primary languages and by collaborating with families.
- Stress the importance of families using children's home languages during family activities.
- Include children's primary languages in daily routines.
- Learn and pronounce correctly some vocabulary from children's home languages.

Supporting Children in English Language Development

For young children who are immersed in a world that makes little sense linguistically, it is critical that teachers create an environment that is as comfortable and familiar as possible. Teachers can help children with LEP make some sense of this "noise" by using some of the following strategies (Espinosa, 2005; Freund & Rich, 2005; Stormont et al., 2003):

- Create classroom routines that are predictable and familiar to children.
- Create classroom social environments where children with LEP can work formally and informally with children who are fluent in English to build their language skills.
- Build classroom communities where diverse language backgrounds are celebrated and friendships between children from different backgrounds are promoted.
- Encourage vocabulary development by creating a context where words are connected with their meaning through repetition, body movements, and gestures. For example, when talking about a telephone, the teacher could say the word "telephone" and hold a pretend telephone to the ear to communicate the meaning of "telephone" through body language (McCathren, personal communication).
- Make language as concrete as possible, use shorter sentences with clear main ideas, and speak at a steady rate with pauses.
- Use think-alouds to model language for children.

- Use visual representations of concepts as much as possible to support learning.

- Allow children time before they start speaking in English in front of a large group. Children may want to spend a lot of time listening before they begin to speak in English more frequently. Encourage children to volunteer to participate.

- Have peers who are English-speaking serve as supports for learners with limited English. Have children with LEP teach words in their primary languages to children who are English-speaking.

- Check frequently for understanding of language.

- Secure and use experiences and background knowledge in children's primary languages to support instruction in English.

Supporting Children in Reading

Effective reading instruction for students from linguistically diverse backgrounds includes the same components as effective instruction for all learners (Slavin & Cheung, 2003). However, the language in which reading instruction should be grounded has been an area of controversy. In a synthesis of the research in the area of reading with children with LEP, Slavin and Cheung (2003) presented important insights into what the literature to date supports. Overall, as with the development of language, children appear to do better if their primary language can serve as a familiar anchor for developing reading skills. That is, research has found that reading instruction in both the primary language and English, immersion in the primary language first, and then reading in English are more beneficial to learners than an approach that does not incorporate children's primary language. "Rather than confusing children, as some have feared, reading instruction in a familiar language may serve as a bridge to success in English, as decoding, sound blending, and generic comprehension strategies clearly transfer among languages that use phonetic orthographies, such as Spanish, French, and English" (Slavin & Cheung, 2003, p. 20).

Preventing Overreferrals for Special Education Evaluations

Students from linguistically and economically diverse backgrounds are at risk for being overrepresented in referrals for special education and related services. As discussed throughout this text, teachers need to understand the importance of culture in interpreting the behavior of students. Furthermore, Garcia and Ortiz (2004) provide insight into what teachers need to do to support children in the general education classroom before referrals for special education evaluations are made. In addition to creating a responsive school environment where diversity is embraced and celebrated (as discussed in Chapter 3), teachers can use the following supports (Garcia & Ortiz, 2004), which have been or will be presented in detail in the remaining chapters:

1. Intervene early when learners are struggling with academic or behavioral skills.
2. Use assessments and research-based strategies to support struggling learners.
3. Collaborate with families and other professionals to ensure that instructional and curriculum supports have been examined for cultural responsiveness.
4. Access resources to support children.

Summary

In some states, including California, approximately half of all children live in or near poverty—the majority are not White, and one in three are English language learners (Espinosa, 2005). As the composition of the United States changes over the next few decades from having one "majority" culture to having more than half of the population from "minority" cultures, it is even more imperative for schools to reflect this shift (Espinosa, 2005). Schools need to be prepared to address the unique needs of children with limited resources due to poverty and homelessness. Schools also need to be prepared to provide additional support for children with limited English proficiency. When they enter school, children need to feel that it is a safe place for them to learn. For schools to feel like a community for all learners, diversity needs to be respected and valued.

Using Assessment to Inform Instruction

Recall David from Chapter 1. He was a challenging first grader with multiple needs for support. When evaluating his case, questions such as the following might have occurred to you regarding his social behavioral and academic needs:

- What are David's academic performance levels in different subject areas?
- How long can David attend to different tasks and activities?
- What behaviors are preventing David from being more engaged in academic lessons and activities?
- What specific settings or activities are associated with appropriate and inappropriate behavior?
- What activities does David like to do?
- Are there any peers who would work well with David?
- Does David have the social skills needed to engage in successful social interactions with peers?

These questions should guide the selection of assessments to support decision making. For children with multiple risk characteristics, teachers may have to address behavior needs prior to or in conjunction with academic needs. For example, if a child is constantly out of his seat, not attentive to instruction, and one year behind the appropriate grade level in reading, then multiple supports need to be provided for the him to be successful. A teacher can use an effective research-based strategy to address a child's academic needs. However, if the child is not behaviorally ready to receive the instruction (e.g., constantly out of seat, not equipped with materials, unwilling to participate), then the child will not learn.

Chapter 5

Assessment-Driven Instruction

Assessment is defined as "the process of collecting, synthesizing, and interpreting information to aid in decision making" (Airasian, 1996, p. 4). The importance of collecting assessment data for targeting and monitoring instruction cannot be overstated (Alexandrin, 2003; Choate, Enright, Miller, Poteet, & Rakes, 1995; Espinosa, 2005; Mindes, 2003; Salvia & Ysseldyke, 1991; Stecker, Fuchs, & Fuchs, 2005; Ward & Murray-Ward, 1999). Assessment should be part of daily instruction and not used only at the end of specific units or at the end of the year. If teachers do not routinely collect focused assessment information on children, then appropriate instructional decisions cannot be made (Choate et al., 1995; Stecker et al., 2005; Witt, Elliott, Kramer, & Gresham, 1994). Without assessment information, teachers will not be able to determine whether certain children are progressing very slowly, lacking prerequisite skills, or developing more severe behavior problems over time (Alexandrin, 2003). Moreover, "a primary goal of any assessment is to determine what a student can and cannot do and how that student learns best in order that successful interventions can be designed." (Witt et al., 1994, p. 8).

Formative assessments are assessments that teachers can use to provide ongoing feedback regarding children's behavior (Airasian, 1996; Cohen & Spenciner, 2005). *Summative* assessments are less useful for ongoing decision making as they are collected at the end of units, semesters, and school years. When working with academic and social behavior, it is important to have tools available for ongoing monitoring and decision making. Therefore, this chapter focuses on utilizing different types of formative assessments for decision making.

Formative assessments "provide information when it is still possible to influence the everyday processes which are the heart of teaching" (Airasian, 1996, p. 82). Espinosa (2005) further states that informal formative assessments are the most important tools for making appropriate instructional decisions for children who are culturally and linguistically diverse. Thus, for learners who are already vulnerable for failure, it is even more critical that teachers collect formative assessment data to ensure that their instructional strategies are effective.

The following sections will describe the methods available to identify social behavioral and academic problems, determine specifics about child behavior before intervening, and monitor the effectiveness of interventions. Moreover, a section on additional methods for identifying academic problem areas will follow this section. The process for implementing both social behavioral and academic assessment will include the following (Alberto & Troutman, 2003; Choate et al., 1995; Stecker et al., 2005):

- Determining where to begin instruction
- Continuously monitoring instruction
- Using data to inform instruction

Identifying Social Behavioral Problems

Problematic behavior can be identified through informal communication with families and professionals and through more structured interviews. Focused observational time, where behavior is observed for a period of time or captured on an occurrence basis, can also be devoted to specific children. Professionals can use one or more of the methods provided in this section to determine what specific problems children are having and the environmental factors that are associated with appropriate and inappropriate behavior.

Communication and Interviews

Teachers can gather information about children's behavior by interviewing previous teachers and families. During interviews, they can ask questions that are specific to children's current problems. For example, if a child has problems working independently, teachers can ask significant family members and previous teachers whether this has been a problem in the past or if it is a new problem. Collecting this information can help teachers understand any family stressors that may be influencing a child's behavior in school. For example, if a teacher notices that a child has significant problems staying on task during academic instruction and also plays alone much of the time and sits alone at lunch, significant family members should be contacted to discuss this pattern. The teacher can also request family permission to obtain additional information from past teachers. Perhaps, this behavioral pattern is new and has surfaced after the death of a close relative. Possible supports needed for this child may include consultation with the school counselor, assistance in reentering social situations, special time with the teacher, and targeting specific academic skills for instruction. However, without this information, this child may be subjected to more intrusive interventions when she is having a normal and transient reaction to a family stressor. It is therefore important that educators do not make assumptions about children's experiences outside of school.

Families differ widely in their openness and trust of educational professionals (Turnbull, Turnbull, Erwin, & Soodak, 2006). Accordingly, professionals should try to establish trusting and collaborative partnerships with all families (Turnbull et al., 2006). Strategies to facilitate such partnerships are provided in Chapter 8. When communicating with families to obtain information on children's behavior, teachers may want to consider the following prompts to guide the framing of interview questions:

1. What are my main concerns regarding this child?
2. What do I know about this child?
3. What additional information do I need to help support this child?
4. How can I ask family members questions in a way that shows respect and creates an avenue for further conversations in the future?

The following example may provide guidance for teachers on how to start a conversation with families:

> As often as possible I try to learn more about all of my children and their families. I teach these children for only one year, whereas you have raised them and will continue to raise them for several years. I would like your help in getting to know what I can do to teach and support _____ in the best way possible. May I ask you some questions regarding how _____ learns best, what _____ likes and dislikes, _____'s behavior at home, and any possible areas to work on with _____?

Anecdotal Reports

Anecdotal reports can also be used to target specific problem behavior. The information obtained from these data can target main problem areas and generate ideas for intervention supports. When using this assessment, the observer first collects continuous observational data on an individual, without targeting a specific behavior, and then analyzes these records to determine specific problems. Many professionals refer to these reports as "running records" and use this type of assessment to gather information across the school year on each child's academic and social behavior in different contexts (Mindes, 2003; Wortham, 2005).

Collecting this type of data requires the complete attention of the observer. This makes this type of assessment challenging for classroom teachers to use for longer periods of time (20 to 30 minutes) with individual children. Often, another teacher, an instructional aide, paraprofessional, school psychologist, preservice teacher, or counselor can be utilized to collect this data. If other personnel aren't available, then videotaping could be used.

Logistically, when using this assessment technique, it is important to objectively collect extensive amounts of information. Professionals collecting this information should target a specific setting that has been problematic for a child (e.g., morning journal time, independent math work, reading group) and collect notes from the ongoing assessment in that setting. Before initiating the data collection, the observer should note the date, time, details about the setting, and individuals present (Alberto & Troutman, 2003; Wortham, 2005). Next, the observer should write down everything that is happening in the setting including statements and actions of the target child, statements and actions of others toward the group or the target child, and details related to how long certain events, interactions, or responses occur.

Finally, it is vital that the observer is objective in the report and does not include interpretations of behaviors. For example, objective notes would include statements such as, "Shawna was looking out the window for approximately 5 minutes. Then the teacher looked in Shawna's direction, sighed, and asked her a question about what the teacher had just read to the class. Shawna said that the man was sad because his dog died. The teacher did not respond to this answer and asked another student a question . . ."

Subjective notes with interpretations would include statements such as, "Shawna was bored with reading. She did appear to answer a question correctly but the teacher was annoyed and did not acknowledge her answer." With subjective note-taking, the observer takes away the richness of information that could be collected in the report. Objective note-taking allows for the report to be analyzed by more than one person, which then allows for multiple perspectives and interpretations. Alberto and Troutman (2003) provide several questions to direct this analysis:

1. What are the behaviors that can be described as inappropriate? The behavior analyst should be able to justify labeling the behaviors as inappropriate given the setting and the activity taking place.
2. Is this behavior occurring frequently, or has a unique occurrence been identified?
3. Can reinforcement or punishment of the behavior be identified? The reinforcement may be delivered by the teacher, parent, another child, or some naturally occurring environmental consequence.
4. Is there a pattern to these consequences?
5. Can antecedents to the behavior(s) be identified?
6. Is there a pattern that can be identified for certain events or stimuli (antecedents) that consistently precede the behavior's occurrence?
7. Are there recurrent chains of certain antecedents, behaviors, and consequences?
8. Given the identified inappropriate behavior(s) of the student and the patterns of antecedents and consequences, what behavior really needs to be modified, and who is engaging in the behavior . . . (pp. 97–99)

Anecdotal reports can be collected at one time or across several days. To help determine potential interventions, anecdotal reports can also be collected in settings in which the target child does particularly well. For example, data collected across several days may indicate that a student is not successful in a setting where peer or teacher attention and feedback is not available; however, data may also reveal that this child is successful when working with one other peer and when working on the computer. Overall, anecdotal reports can be used to identify specific behavior problems and to provide information for intervention selection.

Anecdotal Incident Records

Teachers can also use incident records to document problem behavior and to identify contexts that may be contributing to the behavior (Meese, 2001). In addition, these records can be used to document children's growth in certain areas and use of specific skills in certain contexts (Eliason & Jenkins, 1999). This assessment tool is different from anecdotal reports because here the documentation is completed *after* behavior occurs and children are not observed continuously (Airasian, 1996; Cohen & Spenciner, 2005; Wortham, 2005). For teachers who are not able to find support for collecting continuous data on a child, these types

Child:

Setting information:

  Date:

  Time:

  Activity:

  Peers involved:

Specific behaviors of concern:

Consequence for behavior:

_____ ignored

_____ attention (peer or teacher, positive or negative)

_____ terminated activity

_____ allowed to go to another activity

_____ time-out

_____ other: _____

Figure 5-1
Anecdotal Event Quick Summary Form

of records could provide insight into main problems to target for interventions. For problem behavior, Figure 5-1 is an example of a quick, fill-in-the-blank record of an incident.

Anecdotal records and reports can be summarized in A-B-C formats (i.e., antecedent-behavior-consequence) to try to determine triggers for problem behavior and consequences that may be reinforcing problem behavior (Mastropieri & Scruggs, 2004; Meese, 2001). Teachers can use the template in Figure 5-2 to organize their notes on children and to try to develop ideas related to underlying reasons for behavior to inform instructional supports. If a teacher documents a pattern of

Child: _____	Date: _____	
Antecedent: *"Before" Factors* *Who, when, where,* *and what is happening* *in environment*	**Behavior:** *Specific Details* *Intensity, duration*	**Consequence:** *After* *Positive, negative, and* *neutral responses*

Figure 5-2
A-B-C Observational Assessment Summary

behavior that is linked with predictable consequences, then the teacher can use this information to design an intervention. For example, if Jon's talking out is recorded on three separate instances and followed each time by peer attention, then peer attention may be supporting this behavior. If Jon finds attention to be positively reinforcing, then his teacher needs to plan for him to receive this attention when he participates appropriately in class activities. (See Chapter 6 for more information on working with problem behavior.) Another example would be if Marik's off-task behavior is documented only in settings that require reading; this information would then be useful to inform the teacher of his needs for support in reading (see Chapter 7).

Identifying Target Behavior

With the information collected from communications, anecdotal reports, or anecdotal incident records, various behaviors may be targeted for interventions, including:

- On-task behavior during specific settings
- Talking without permission during specific settings

- Taking supplies before asking
- Getting out of seat or area without permission
- Failure to participate in cooperative learning groups
- Verbal aggression toward peers and/or teachers
- Physical aggression toward peers
- Failure to complete work during specific settings
- Failure to complete homework

Developing Descriptive Definitions

After a specific behavior has been targeted for intervention, it is important to create a very specific definition of the behavior to allow for accurate data collection. Definitions should include detailed descriptions of observable behavior (Lewis, Powers, Kelk, & Newcomer, 2002; Stormont, Smith, & Lewis, 2006; Witt et al., 1994). If two people can use the definition and collect virtually the same data at the same time, then the definition is strong. If two people interpret examples of the behavior differently, then the definition is weak.

For example, consider the following definition for on-task behavior: "Child is engaged in appropriate tasks." The definition is not specific and involves subjective interpretations; it depends on what the *teacher* perceives as "engaged" and "appropriate." A better definition for on-task behavior would be "Child is following behavioral expectations specifically described by the teacher for the setting, including reading, writing, creating assigned products (models, maps, posters), working with peers, asking questions related to assignment, staying in appropriate areas of the class, and collecting information from classroom materials."

When teachers create specific definitions of what they want children to do during different settings, they need to make sure to teach these behaviors to children, which is a foundational support described in Chapter 3. Teachers will also want to revise their definitions as new considerations emerge.

Assessment of Specific Behaviors

Once a behavior is targeted, teachers need to collect information that more specifically describes the behavior. These data serve to paint the current picture of behavior, which can then be compared to data collected after interventions are initiated. The first factor to consider in this process is the specific type of behavior to be observed. That is, is the behavior a continuous behavior or a discrete behavior? *Continuous behaviors* include those that occur for periods of time and typically cannot be counted with accuracy because they do not have a clear beginning and end (Alberto & Troutman, 2003). For continuous behaviors, teachers may want to capture the percentage of time they occur during specific settings. For example, a child may appear to be "never on task during reading." However, data collection may indicate that the child is on task 50% of the time during reading and is on task more in the beginning and middle of reading time.

Conversely, a *discrete behavior* is one that can be counted because it has a clear beginning and a clear ending (Alberto & Troutman, 2003). Examples of discrete behavior include verbal outbursts, throwing objects, aggressive acts, and leaving an area without permission.

There are many observational methods that can be used to assess both types of behavior. The methods that are perhaps most feasible for teachers include those that can be utilized while teachers are engaged in other activities. Event recording and time sampling are two teacher-friendly methods for collecting information on different types of behavior.

Event Recording–Discrete Behavior

When using event recording, observers count the number of times a behavior occurs in a given time frame (Alberto & Troutman, 2003; Witt et al., 1994). Teachers can count the number of times a child demonstrates any type of discrete behavior, including:

- Raising hand
- Answering a question
- Talking out of turn
- Bringing needed materials
- Turning in homework
- Yelling
- Hitting
- Running in classroom

To prepare for event recording, a professional needs to select a child, a setting, and the amount of time for the observation. The professional then counts the number of times the behavior occurs and records this information in some format (e.g., tallies on an index card, check marks on a paper fastened to a clipboard). When collecting this data over several days, teachers can determine the frequency of the behavior. This type of data is very useful for creating goals for improvement, progress monitoring, and reporting behavioral support needs to families and other professionals. The extent of a problem behavior is much clearer when stated objectively with data. Consider the following statements: "Juan is always out of his seat in class" versus "Over the past week during journal time, Juan got up and wandered around the classroom an average of 5 times in 30 minutes." "Natasha never does her homework" versus "Over the past week, Natasha turned in 2 of her 10 homework assignments."

Time Sampling–Continuous Behavior

When using momentary time sampling, the observer takes a specific time period, divides it into equal intervals, and then observes the child or several children at the end of that interval only (Meese, 2001). When using time sampling, the goal is to try to determine the frequency of a continuous behavior without having to observe the entire period. The specific steps for time sampling include the following (Alberto & Troutman, 2003; Mastropieri & Scruggs, 2004):

- Select the time period to observe the behavior in a specific setting.
- Divide this time period into equal intervals (e.g., 30 minutes divided into six 5-minute intervals, 60 minutes into six 10-minute intervals, etc.).
- Have a sheet with the specific behavior listed on it, the times for observation, and the coding scheme (e.g., X for on task, – for not on task).
- Determine what cue will be needed for observation. Teachers can use a headset connected to a tape or CD with prerecorded beep tones to indicate when a certain period of time has elapsed. Teachers can also rely on a stopwatch, clock, or their watches.

Alberto and Troutman (2003) provide an example of a form for time sampling data collection (see Figure 5-3). Figure 5-4 is another example of a time sampling record for task completion behavior at 5-minute intervals (Wortham, 2005). This format allows for observers to take descriptive notes rather than coding whether a behavior occurred in a specific interval. This example also includes a variation of time sampling where the data collection began at the onset of the time period of sampling and proceeded at 5-minute intervals thus allowing for four pieces of time data to be collected rather than three.

Additional Methods

Some behaviors may require alternate observational methods. Some additional methods that can be used to assess the amount of time that specific continuous behaviors occur include *duration recording* and *latency recording* (Alberto & Troutman, 2003; Cohen & Spenciner, 2005; Meese, 2001). These methods require ongoing observation of a child, which make them less feasible for teachers to utilize without additional resources. When using duration recording, an observer starts recording a behavior when it begins and stops recording when it ends. If a teacher wants to document how long a child is engaged in a behavior, then a simple stopwatch or a timer on a watch is all the teacher needs.

Often, this type of data helps illustrate the extent of specific problems. When communicating with a school psychologist or a family member about a specific behavioral issue, it is beneficial to have this information. For example, rather than saying, "Dequan seems to leave his work area and wander around the classroom for long periods of time," a teacher could say, "I have collected information on how long Dequan is out of his work area during our morning literacy time and, over the past two days, he has spent 90 minutes wandering around the classroom."

Student: _____

Behavior: _____

_____

Date:_____   Time start: _____

                                 Time end: _____

                                 Total time period:_____

Observer:_____

CODE: X=occurrence   O=nonoccurrence   (note at the end of each interval)

15	30	45	00
15	30	45	00
15	30	45	00

Data Summary

Number of intervals of occurrence:
Percent of intervals of occurrence:
Number of intervals of nonoccurrence:
Percent of intervals of nonoccurrence:

Figure 5-3
Time Sampling Data for a 3-Hour Observation Period, with 15-Minute Intervals

Source: From *Applied Behavior Analysis for Teachers*, 6th Edition (p. 121), by Paul A. Alberto and Anne C. Troutman, 2003, Upper Saddle River, NJ: Pearson Education. Copyright © 2003 by Pearson Education, Inc. Reprinted by permission.

Similarly, latency recording helps document how long it takes children to engage in something after directions to do it are given (Cohen & Spenciner, 2005). Children with compliance issues may refuse (outright or passively) to get started and it may take three prompts for them to begin working.

Again, when designing an intervention, it is vital to have the information on the extent of the problem before strategies are put in place. For example, before intervention, the record could say, "Suzette required four prompts to initiate tasks or follow instructions and complied after three to four minutes had elapsed." After supportive interventions are put in place (see Chapter 6), it could say, "Suzette typically complies after one prompt and within 20 to 30 seconds."

Child Name(s): <u>Joanie</u>
Age: <u>5</u>
Location:<u> Rosewood School Kindergarten</u>
Date and Time: <u>May 17, 10:45–11:00</u>
Observer: <u>Susanna</u>
Type of Development Observed: <u>Joanie Has Difficulty Completing Tasks</u>

Event	Time	Notes or Comments
Art Center—leaves coloring activity on table unfinished	10:45	Some of Joanie's behaviors seem to be resulting from failure to follow procedures for use of materials.
Library—looks at book, returns it to shelf.	10:50	
Manipulative Center—gets frustrated with puzzle, piles pieces in center—leaves on table. Pulls out Lego blocks, starts to play.	10:55	Behavior with the puzzles may come from frustration.
When teacher signals to put toys away, Joanie leaves Lego blocks on table and joins other children.	11:00	Joanie may need help in putting away with verbal rewards for finishing a task and putting materials away. Encourage Joanie to get help with materials that are too hard.

Figure 5-4
Example of Time Sampling

Source: From *Assessment in Early Childhood Education*, 4th Edition (p. 102), by Sue C. Wortham, 2005, Upper Saddle River, NJ: Pearson Education. Copyright © 2005 by Pearson Education, Inc. Reprinted by permission.

The amount of time children who are vulnerable for failure spend disengaged from academic instruction is extensive (Kauffman, 2005; Lee, Belfiore, Scheeler, Hua, & Smith, 2004). When teachers utilize systematic methods for targeting and intervening with behavior that is interfering with engagement in learning, children's academic learning time will most likely increase (Lee et al., 2004; Mastropieri & Scruggs, 2004).

Monitoring Social Behavioral Progress

After specific behaviors have been targeted and interventions have been put in place, teachers can use the same types of data collection methods described in the previous sections to monitor children's progress. For example, if a teacher selects frequency recording to record a child's participation behaviors in a specific setting, then the teacher can continue to use it to record the instances of this behavior after beginning an intervention. This allows teachers to judge the general effectiveness of their interventions. Teachers can plot this data after the baseline (before intervention) behavior data on the same graph to more closely inspect progress. Questions to guide interpretations of behavioral data include:

- Is behavior changing in a positive direction?
- Is behavior changing in a negative direction?
- Is there no change in behavior?

It is important for teachers to collect data on behavior over time to ascertain children's needs. A child may quickly respond to an intervention but then revert back to previous behavioral patterns a few weeks later. Teachers need to make instructional decisions based on children's ongoing needs for support. Some may respond very positively to a simple intervention and that may be all they need, while some others may need additional supports along with the intervention. For example, Juan may respond very positively to an intervention to increase participation but he still needs additional language supports to be able to participate more fully in class. Chapters 6 and 7 will provide examples of supports and interventions.

Determining Where to Begin Academic Instruction

There are multiple ways that teachers can identify academic areas of concern. Teachers may monitor children's progress on specific skills throughout the year and provide families with mid-quarter and quarter or mid-trimester and trimester reports. Thus, in many schools, teachers are providing information on children's progress on specific academic behaviors 6 to 8 times a year depending on whether they divide the school year into trimesters or quarters. Although teachers provide this type of *summative* assessment information on children's progress, it is not always clear what *formative* assessment data they are using to link children's performance with instruction.

Teachers are responsible for helping children learn the school curriculum, which is typically driven by state and national standards (Mindes, 2003; Raymond, 2004). However, children may enter the third grade, for example, without mastering the second-grade curriculum in some areas. For many children, school records and past portfolios are available that summarize their growth across the previous year and performance in all areas at the end of the year. However, for some children such records are not available. For others, especially children at risk for failure in school, significant regression of skills and knowledge may occur during the summer and teachers cannot assume they have the same skills they had at the end of the previous year.

Therefore, teachers need to have quick, objective ways to determine where to begin instruction with children (Cohen & Spenciner, 2005; Mindes, 2003). Teachers have many choices of assessment techniques to assist them in this process. Teachers in the primary grades should typically allow themselves some time to establish the academic performance levels of all children in the class. However, for children who are vulnerable for failure, it is important that teachers secure this information immediately.

Whenever possible, it is important that teachers try to meet with children, before or shortly after school begins, to obtain quick assessments of their current levels of learning and development in specific areas. Teachers can use assessment systems, criterion-referenced measurement, and assessments of prior knowledge to determine instructional levels and supports needed for children to be successful.

Developing Assessment Systems

Different national associations and research panels have published standards for primary grade children in different areas. For example, the National Council of Teachers of Mathematics has published content and process standards to guide curriculum development (National Council of Teachers of Mathematics, 2005). Many states align their standards to these national standards and articulate more specific skills, processes, and behaviors that meet different standards. For example, for the national content standard "Numbers and Operations," the state of Missouri has different levels of learning, including "Describe or represent mental strategies." Specific behaviors listed under this category include "recognize numerals up to 31" for kindergarten and "describe or represent the mental strategy used to compute addition problems" for first graders (Missouri Department of Elementary and Secondary Education, 2004). School districts typically develop their curriculum around state standards, which are also linked to summative assessments at specific grade levels. Curriculum outcomes are often listed on children's grade level report cards.

To inform both where to begin instruction and how children are progressing in the curriculum, teachers can align their curriculum, instruction, and assessment by developing an assessment system based on their district's grade-level-targeted curriculum outcomes. This involves a systematic analysis of the curriculum to determine the specific skills children need to have to master the curriculum (Choate et al., 1995). Assessment systems can include skills articulated on checklists to determine whether children have mastered or have fully or partially acquired specific skills on lists (Mindes, 2003). In addition to the district curriculum, teachers can consult scope and skills sequences for specific skills within curriculum areas as described in textbooks and published curricula. An example of a checklist for first-level math skills is presented in Figure 5-5.

After teachers develop specifics related to the behaviors to be assessed, there are several ways they can collect information for assessment, including, for example, observing children interacting with peers or materials, prompting children for skills in natural settings, using technology to surface specific skills, and working one on one with a student and explicitly requesting that they demonstrate specific skills. Teachers can use these same methods to monitor children's progress. Figure 5-6 is an example of a checklist a teacher could use to target and monitor specific pragmatic language behaviors over time.

Criterion-Referenced Tests

Criterion-referenced tests can also be utilized to determine children's academic performance in specific areas. These assessments provide a better picture than broader formal achievement tests of children's performance levels in specific areas. Whereas achievement measures can inform teachers of how children perform

```
                          CHECKLIST
                          LEVEL 1
    Name_____          Date_____
    Age _____        Math Teacher_____  Unit _____
                                                   Advisor _____

    Dates
    I    M      NUMERATION
    _____ 0. Knows vocabulary:
                   __same __ different __ more __ less __ before __ after
    _____ 1. Rote counts:
                   __1 __2 __3 __4 __5 __6 __7 __8 __9 __10
    _____ 2. Counts objects:
                   __1 __2 __3 __4 __5 __6 __7 __8 __9 __10
    _____ 3. Matches equivalent sets with concrete objects.
    _____ 4. Reproduces equivalent sets with concrete objects.
    _____ 5. Matches like pairs
    _____ 6. Matches unlike pairs
    _____ 7. Compares nonequivalent sets with concrete objects
    _____ 8. Reproduces nonequivalent sets with concrete objects
    _____ 9. Sorts objects using more than one classifying characteristic
    _____ 10. Matches numerals:
                    __1 __2 __3 __4 __5 __6 __7 __8 __9 __10
    _____ 11. Identifies numerals:
                    __1 __2 __3 __4 __5 __6 __7 __8 __9 __10
    _____ 12. Constructs sets for numerals:
                    __1 __2 __3 __4 __5
    _____ 13. Names numerals:
                    __1 __2 __3 __4 __5

                MEASUREMENT
                A. Linear
    _____    1. Matches objects
                      __size __length __width __height
    _____    2. Compares objects
                      __size __length __width __height
    _____    3. Seriates objects
                      __size __length __width __height
                B. Weight
    _____    1. Classifies objects according to weight
                      __heavy __light
    _____    2. Compares objects according to weight
                      __heavy __light
    _____    3. Demonstrates use of balance
    _____    4. Identifies instruments for measuring weight
```

Figure 5-5
Mathematics Checklist: Level 1

Source: From *Assessment in Early Childhood Education,* 4th Edition (p. 123), by Sue C. Wortham, 2005, Upper Saddle River, NJ: Pearson Education. Copyright © 2005 by Pearson Education, Inc. Reprinted by permission.

Child: _____Katelyn_____		Observer/Teacher: _____Sarah_____	
Language Behavior	Date #1:	Date #2:	Date #3:
1. Responds to verbal greeting and departure routines	✓	✓	✓
Appropriate facial expression		✓	✓
Appropriate verbal response		✓	✓
2. Responds to story questions	✓	✓	✓
Detailed or inferential responses			✓
3. Expresses needs/wants		✓	✓

Figure 5-6
Longitudinal Checklist of an Individual Child's Pragmatic Language Behaviors

Source: From *Language Development in Early Childhood,* 2nd Edition (p. 313), by Beverly White Otto, 2006, Upper Saddle River, NJ: Pearson Education. Copyright © 2005 by Pearson Education, Inc. Reprinted by permission.

in comparison with same-age peers, criterion-referenced tests can tell teachers whether children have mastered certain skills. This information can then be used to determine where to begin instruction in specific content areas (Olson & Platt, 2004). However, oftentimes teachers can obtain this information through systematic use of their own informal assessment systems that are already linked to district standards. Therefore, rather than arbitrarily using criterion-referenced tests to determine children's performance levels, it is important to have a purpose for using such assessments. Questions to guide this process include:

- What skills does the test measure?
- How do these skills align with the curriculum my school uses?
- Are these skills prerequisite for understanding main ideas in the current curriculum?
- Can these skills be assessed in the context of classroom activities?
- Do certain children show very significant deficits in an area that requires detailed assessment information to design remedial instructional supports?

Determining Prerequisite Skills Needed for Success

The previous sections described how teachers can use standards and scope and skill sequences to assess knowledge and development in specific areas. This section describes how teachers can determine instructional needs by evaluating the curriculum and the prerequisite knowledge and skills children will need to be successful. Teachers can use this information to develop children's prerequisite knowledge and to provide supports for children to be more successful (see Chapter 7).

Children in any elementary grade will have a wide range of academic skills. In a first-grade classroom, some children may be able to read at the third-grade level while some others may not yet know all of the letters in the alphabet. Since children learn best when teachers are able to tap into what they already know, teachers can use pretests or pre-assessments to understand the prior knowledge that children have obtained in all subject areas.

Prior knowledge assessments for younger children could include an assessment of whether children know the meaning of certain vocabulary words, whether they understand prerequisite math concepts, and whether they have the social behaviors needed to be successful. To guide the construction of these assessments, teachers can use the following prompts:

- What vocabulary words need to be understood to be successful in this unit?
- What social behaviors are needed?
- What concepts will children have to understand in order to participate in this unit?
- How will past experiences of some children influence their success in this unit?

Monitoring Academic Progress

Once specific areas have been targeted for academic instruction, it is important that teachers systematically monitor children's growth. As stated in the previous sections, many assessment systems are used to assess current performance and monitor growth in specific areas. Common everyday *informal assessments* need to be linked with the overall assessment system that teachers are using or to areas targeted through criterion-referenced assessments. Especially for learners who are already behind in one or more areas, teachers need a framework for closely examining progress. Therefore, progress monitoring should include the following:

- Targeted goals for growth
- Precisely defined skills within each goal area
- Teacher assessments of progress
- Child assessments of progress
- Adjustments when progress is slow, including determining supports needed to be more successful

Teachers can use many types of informal assessments to measure children's learning and development, including *product assessments, performance assessments, portfolio assessments* and *curriculum-based measurement* (Choate et al., 1995; Freund & Rich, 2005; Stecker et al., 2005).

Product Assessments

Product assessments measure children's knowledge of specific content in the form of tests, quizzes, and by evaluating other types of work such as graphs and posters (Cohen & Spenciner, 2005). Such assessments also include probes, which are quick assessments of specific skills. Probes for young children may include an assessment of letter sounds, shapes, one-to-one correspondence, ability to hear specific sounds in spoken words, and understanding key elements of a story.

For older primary grade children, assessments of both children's ability to read certain curricular materials aloud and their comprehension of the content can also be done. Teachers can obtain product assessments from commercial materials, websites, or create them independently. Math probe sheets are very common and offer detailed information about children's current level of performance (Meese, 2001; Mercer & Mercer, 2005). In any content area, well-constructed assessments should inform instruction (Cohen & Spenciner, 2005). Often, teachers need to conduct an error analysis of probes to determine where to begin instruction.

Error Analysis

To ensure that instructional time is maximized, it is important for teachers to analyze children's error patterns (Olson & Platt, 2004). Miscue analysis is a common type of error analysis in reading (Cohen & Spenciner, 2005). Error analysis can be used to analyze errors on written probes or in naturalistic problem-solving contexts (e.g., using manipulatives to solve problems). Using a math quiz as an example, Olson and Platt (2004) provide a series of steps to use to analyze student errors:

1. After scoring the items, list the student errors (e.g., on the addition fact worksheet, Jan is missing $9 + 8$, $7 + 8$, and $6 + 8$).

2. Make a hypothesis as to the error pattern (e.g., computational error, basic addition facts, especially the 8 facts).

3. Test the hypothesis by examining the correct problems to see if any have the same pattern (e.g., Jan calculated $6 + 4$, $5 + 6$, and $9 + 2$ correctly, so none of the correct ones involved the basic addition facts of 8).

4. If not correct, redo the hypothesis (e.g., steps 1–3 again).

5. Teach the correction of the error (e.g., Jan needs to be retaught the basic addition facts of 8). (p. 67)

The use of error analysis is critical with children who are vulnerable given the number of reasons they could be making errors. Children may have knowledge gaps, language barriers, or attention problems that are affecting their performance. Consider the following example:

A second-grade child who is underachieving takes a weekly written probe on basic addition facts. Every week he gets only 40 to 50% correct. The teacher has him study the same facts on flashcards with a peer or on the computer the next week. This continues for two more weeks until the teacher makes two observations. First, when being drilled by a peer or on the computer, the student gets 100% of the answers correct. Second, the teacher scrutinizes the written probe and notices that he has missed all the questions in the last two rows. The last three answers are illegible. She then gives him different probes with 10 problems each on three different days. He scores 100%, 90%, and 100% on these three shorter assessments. Without conducting an error analysis, the teacher would not have known that the child's problem was not necessarily linked to the content but rather with the other requirements for sustained attention and fine motor responses.

Performance- and Production-Based Assessments

Performance-based assessments assess children's abilities to demonstrate their knowledge of specific behaviors, skills, and abilities by actually doing something (Ward & Murray-Ward, 1999). Production tasks focus on children's creation of a product (Ward & Murray-Ward, 1999). To support children's ability to be successful in such assessments, teachers may provide them with specific examples of other children's work to serve as benchmarks (Airasian, 1996; Cohen & Spenciner, 2005). Children and teachers can determine the format in which students will demonstrate growth in a specific area. Possible formats include (Cohen & Spenciner, 2005; Freund & Rich, 2005):

- Constructing a written product such as a cartoon, a book, or another type of illustration
- Demonstrating knowledge through a song, story, or play
- Creating a game
- Building a model
- Conducting a simple experiment

Children must understand the specific requirements of the performance or product (Ward & Murray-Ward, 1999). In addition to providing benchmarks that include exemplary past work, teachers should provide checklists that represent all the components that will be assessed and assessment lists. Assessment lists should include points or descriptors next to specific components of the task, to help children understand what will be assessed and to allow teachers to make more precise interpretations of children's performance. As with portfolio rubrics, teachers must strive to make the task assessment criteria clear enough that several teachers evaluating a child's performance would come up with the same results (Ward & Murray-Ward, 1999). Airasian (1996) provides the following guidelines for establishing performance and product criteria:

1. Select the performance or product you will be assessing and perform the activity or create the product yourself. Take detailed notes of the steps involved.

2. Create a list of the most important components of the product or performance. Use this list to have an idea of the main instructions that can be given to help children.

3. When observing a performance, keep the number of criteria for observation to a minimum. Focus on the big picture ideas and not on the less important details.

4. Team with other professionals to develop criteria. Establishing common criteria benefits both teachers and children.

5. Create criteria that can be easily observed or objectively measured (if product).

6. Avoid vague terms and words in criteria. Teachers should state criteria in observable terms to avoid subjective interpretation.

7. Create the list of criteria in the likely order of observation.

8. Don't reinvent the wheel. Check to see if other professionals (in your building or in the professional literature) have created criteria for the performance or product you are assessing before you make your own.

Portfolio Assessment

Portfolios are often used to document children's growth over the year in specific areas. For the purpose of monitoring growth, a process portfolio would be the most appropriate (Cohen & Spenciner, 2005). A *process portfolio* includes artifacts of children's work that represent their performance at different times across the school year. Portfolios should include children's work aligned to the curriculum standards (Cohen & Spenciner, 2005). When selecting artifacts to include, both children and teachers should be involved. Teachers can assess growth as represented in artifacts by constructing simple checklists of features that need to be present, or they can carefully design more detailed assessments, such as rubrics.

Rubrics should have three main features, including *performance criteria, performance levels*, and *performance indicators* (Olson & Platt, 2004). The criteria include specific qualities that represent mastery of knowledge in specific areas. Criteria in different areas could include, for example, use of capitalization in writing or

Portfolios should be used to help children monitor their own growth and set goals for improvement over time.

demonstration of understanding a math concept by using illustrations. The performance levels indicate how the student performed in relation to the criteria. Levels are usually illustrated with descriptors representing mastery, emerging mastery, or no mastery. Goodrich provides level descriptors of "Yes, Yes but, No but, and No," which would be easily understood by children in the primary grades (Olson & Platt, 2004).

Performance indicators integrate the criteria and the level of performance to represent where a student is currently in specific areas. In other words, the indicator would describe criteria across the performance levels. The indicators are basically just the specific definitions of what work would receive a "yes but. . . or a yes," by determining features that are present and features that are missing from students' work.

Monitoring growth requires precision in assessment. It is important that teachers use objective and clear wording in rubrics so that they can have consistency across children and over time. To determine if there is some level of precision and sensitivity to growth, a teacher could solicit another teacher to evaluate a few children's work using the criteria or rubric. If the teachers' evaluation of the artifacts using the rubric yields similar results then teachers can have more confidence in the rubrics they develop.

Children need to engage in self-reflection regarding their artifacts. Therefore, it is important to develop clear criteria to assess growth in artifacts to support children in self-evaluation. Especially with younger children, it is important to provide guidance in what they should be looking for in their own artifacts. Children can reflect on their work using the following prompts (Olson & Platt, 2004):

- What am I learning that this work represents?
- When looking at my old work, what am I doing better?
- What do I need to work on?

This is also a good time for teachers and children to determine areas they need to continue to work on and if children need any supports or need instruction presented in a different way to allow them to be more successful. Mindes (2003) provides an example of a class presentation rubric, which could be used to monitor performance and to target areas for future improvement (see Figure 5-7). Other examples of rubrics for evaluating drawings, class discussions, and book reports are included in Figures 5-8, 5-9, and 5-10.

Observation

The most common assessment used by primary grade teachers is observation (Freund & Rich, 2005; Mindes, 2003), and teachers tend to informally note information obtained from observations (Ward & Murray-Ward, 1999). That is, especially with younger children, teachers often make mental notes of what they observe children doing in the classroom. Mindes (2003) provides examples of how teachers use observations to assess what children are learning and resources teachers can use for informal assessment in specific content areas (see Figure 5-11).

While observations are powerful and informative for general instructional purposes, more systematic observations are needed to guide instructional decision

Class Presentation Rubric for Third Grade					
	Yes	No	Superb	OK	Needs some improvement . . .
■ I made a graphic organizer to show the main points. 　■ The organizer is neat. 　■ Spelling is final draft accurate. 　■ There are details to support the main idea. ■ I made pictures to illustrate my topic. 　■ The pictures are neat. 　■ They are related to the topic. ■ I thought about questions that my classmates might ask. ■ I practiced my presentation. ■ I am ready for my classmates to judge my work.					

Figure 5-7
Example of a Class Presentation Rubric for Third Grade

Source: From *Assessing Young Children,* 2nd Edition (p. 139), by Gayle Mindes, 2003, Upper Saddle River, NJ: Pearson Education. Copyright © 2003 by Pearson Education, Inc. Reprinted by permission.

making especially for children who are already behind. This does not mean that assessment needs to occur in contrived formal settings. Rather, systematic direct observations for instructional decision making need to be framed to include the skills teachers are targeting for different children (Otto, 2006; Ward & Murray-Ward, 1999).

Science Drawing Rubric for Kindergarten		
	Yes	No
■ I drew the picture to represent the item viewed (e.g., leaf, rock, bug). ■ I used realistic colors for the drawing. ■ I labeled the drawing.		

Figure 5-8
Example of a Science Drawing Rubric for Kindergarten

Source: From *Assessing Young Children,* 2nd Edition (p. 139), by Gayle Mindes, 2003, Upper Saddle River, NJ: Pearson Education. Copyright © 2003 by Pearson Education, Inc. Reprinted by permission.

Class Discussion Rubric for First Grade			
	Very well	Most of the time	Need to work on this
■ I can sit and listen to my classmates. ■ I can wait for my turn when I am eager to add a comment. ■ I can say something related to the topic. ■ I can speak up loud enough to be heard by everyone. ■ I can appreciate the comments of my classmates even when I think that they are silly or not related to the topic.			

Figure 5-9
Example of a Class Discussion Rubric for First Grade

Source: From *Assessing Young Children,* 2nd Edition (p. 138), by Gayle Mindes, 2003, Upper Saddle River, NJ: Pearson Education. Copyright © 2003 by Pearson Education, Inc. Reprinted by permission.

Book Report Rubric for Second Grade		
	Yes	No

■ I read the whole book.
■ The report tells:
  ■ Title of the book.
  ■ Author of the book.
■ I wrote two or three paragraphs about the book.
■ The paragraphs tell:
  ■ What the book is about.
  ■ Who the main characters are.
  ■ What I like about the book.
■ I checked the writing according to the class editing guidelines.		

Figure 5-10
Example of a Book Report Rubric for Second Grade

Source: From *Assessing Young Children,* 2nd Edition (p. 138), by Gayle Mindes, 2003, Upper Saddle River, NJ: Pearson Education. Copyright © 2003 by Pearson Education, Inc. Reprinted by permission.

Thus, for running records, teachers should identify key skills they are working on with children and analyze errors and measure growth in these areas. In addition, teachers can develop lists of skills they are targeting for anecdotal observations and document when skills are observed (or not). Skills targeted for observation with individual children could include (Freund & Rich, 2005):

- Showing independent work habits in specific settings
- Words read correctly while reading aloud
- Questions answered correctly during reading comprehension activities
- Retelling a main event from a story

Otto (2006) provides examples of focused checklists designed to measure oral language behaviors in context (see Figures 5-6 and 5-12). When observations are more systematic, teachers can obtain valuable information on children's performance. "Systematic observation focuses on particular behaviors, allowing the observer to gather information that might otherwise be overlooked" (Freund & Rich, 2005, p. 156).

Curriculum-Based Measurement

One assessment strategy with extensive research support for children vulnerable for failure is curriculum-based measurement (CBM). When using CBM, teachers select an intervention area for target children, determine a specific goal or outcome for children, and continually assess children to determine if they are making adequate progress. This method was originally developed by Deno and his colleagues to provide teachers in special education with a technique to monitor students' growth over time (Deno, 1985). In an extensive review of the literature to date, Stecker et al. (2005) describe key features of curriculum-based measurement and factors related to successful outcomes with CBM. Key features of CBM include:

- *Determination of a desired outcome* and of measures needed to monitor progress toward outcome over time. The measures used to monitor growth are short and taken from a variety of sources, which all reflect the same targeted outcome.
- *Frequent data collection graphed* to show visual growth patterns. Teachers collect data on children's growth and plot this on a graph. The assessments are conducted at least once a week, and children's growth toward the curricular goal is visually inspected to determine if current instructional strategies are meeting children's needs.
- *Specific procedures are followed to promote success* for both teachers and children. Research has supported specific procedures that increase the effectiveness of CBM.
- *Extensive support is available* to bridge the research to practice gap for teachers. Several sources are available on the web to support the implementation of CBM in elementary classroom settings (www.interventioncentral.org; www.studentprogress.org).

Math Assessment

Teachers watch children perform classroom activities to see/assess what they are learning.

Activities to observe children performing include:

- Group games involving logico-mathematical thinking (Kamii, 1985, 1989b, 2000). An example is the game "Always 12" consisting of 72 round cards bearing the numbers 0 through 6. The object of play is to make a total of 12 with 4 cards. Two to four children can play. The winner is the child with the most cards (Kamii, 1989b).
- Using computers to record data; calculators to add, subtract, multiply, divide.
- Counting and using numbers as names.
- Activities involving the demonstration of number facts, properties, procedures, algorithms, and skills (Schultz, Colarusso, & Strawderman, 1989).
- Geometric analysis of characteristics and properties of 2- and 3-dimensional geometric shapes, including recognizing, naming, building, drawing, comparing and sorting shapes; investigating and predicting results of putting together and taking apart geometric shapes (NCTM, 2000).
- Measurement activities including recognizing attributes of length, volume, weight, area, and time; comparing and ordering objects; using standard and non-standard measures as tools (NCTM, 2000).

Examples of specific informal tasks that can be used follow:

M&M® Task for Pre-K to Second Grade

Materials

Small bags of M&M's®, napkins, paper, crayons, markers, or other recording materials.

The Task

Conduct this task in small groups or with individual children. Give each child a bag of M&M's®. Ask each child to show the color distribution in the bag. Explain that each bag will have a different amount of candy of each color, so that there is not one right answer, but multiple answers to this problem.

Allow children to express their answers in diverse ways. Children may draw circles to represent the numbers of red, green, yellow, and so on. They may summarize their count—2 green, 3 red, and so on. They may prepare a graph.

The teacher's role in this task is to observe. Ask the children to give a product showing their work. When finished, children may eat the M&M's®.

(Continued)

Figure 5-11

An Example of Informal Assessment and Resources for Teacher Use in a Specific Content Area

Source: From *Assessing Young Children,* 2nd Edition (pp. 273–274), by Gayle Mindes, 2003, Upper Saddle River, NJ: Pearson Education. Copyright © 2003 by Pearson Education, Inc. Reprinted by permission.

Scoring the Task

- 0 = unable
- 1 = can sort by color, but cannot illustrate the solution
- 2 = can identify same, more, less
- 3 = illustrates task
- 4 = makes a pictorial graph
- 5 = makes a numerical or tabular graph

Pizza Party for Second Grade

Materials

A large cardboard circle, resembling a pizza.

The Task

Conduct this task in small groups or with individual children. Show the cardboard pizza form to the children. Tell the children to pretend that they have two pizzas that size. The two pizzas are for a party. Seven boys and five girls will attend the party. Then say, "We want to give everyone a piece the same size. How can we do that?" Ask children to illustrate the answer to this question. Explain that each child may answer this question in different ways.

Supply paper, crayons, markers, pencils, or other recording materials and scissors for children to show their work. Allow children to express their answers in diverse ways. Children may draw circles and divide the pizza; they may cut out paper to represent pieces and children; they may illustrate the answer with fractions, and so on.

The teacher's role in this task is to observe and ask the children to give a product showing their work.

Scoring of the Task

- 0 = no idea
- 1 = drawing stick children (or hatch marks) to decide the number of pieces needed
- 2 = cutting up paper to show the answer
- 3 = drawing fractional representations of circles
- 4 = showing the answer arithmetically with numbers

Figure 5-11
Continued

Although CBM was originally developed to support children with disabilities, it is important to underscore the need to use this systematic technique with children who are achieving below expectations and therefore have a need for close monitoring (Belfiore, Auld, & Lee, 2005; Stecker et al., 2005). Research has found that CBM is very effective in improving achievement for children who were "low achieving" (Fuchs & Deno, 1994; Stecker et al., 2005). However, teachers need support in utilizing features of CBM and need assistance in using the data to inform instructional changes. That is, teachers may be able to systematically collect and graph data but not know how to adapt their instruction based on slow student growth.

Child's Name: ___Sarah T.___	Date Observed: ___2/15/02___	
Oral Language Characteristic	Characteristic Present	Characteristic Not Present
Speaks confidently in group settings	✓	
Speaks distinctly enough for adults to understand	✓	
Speaks in expanded sentences		✓

Figure 5-12
A Checklist Designed to Measure an Oral Language Behavior

Source: From *Language Development in Early Childhood,* 2nd Edition (p. 312), by Beverly White Otto, 2005, Upper Saddle River, NJ: Pearson Education. Copyright © 2005 by Pearson Education, Inc. Reprinted by permission.

Accordingly, if several teachers in a school want to begin to use CBM, then professional development opportunities could be provided by a school assessment specialist (e.g., school psychologist), who could also serve as an ongoing consultant for teachers to assist in the data analysis.

Summary

If teachers have a greater understanding of how to determine and monitor children's instructional needs, they will be more likely to effectively teach children who are vulnerable for failure (Alexandrin, 2003; Belfiore et al., 2005; Espinosa, 2005; Stecker et al., 2005). Unfortunately, children who are vulnerable for failure are also vulnerable for having assessment information used in ways that are not developmentally appropriate or ethical (Mindes, 2003; Turnbull et al., 2006). This chapter focused on formative assessments. Formative assessments help inform teachers in their day-to-day work and have been cited as being more appropriate for learners who are vulnerable for failure (e.g., Espinosa, 2005). As one teacher stated in a recent article, "It is too late if you wait to see if students have mastered skills on formal assessments only" (Alexandrin, 2003, p. 54).

Further, the No Child Left Behind Act calls for teachers to use research-based practices in their instruction (Turnbull et al., 2006; Yell & Drasgow, 2005), and using assessment information to guide instruction is a research-based practice (Alexandrin, 2003; Belfiore et al., 2005; Meese, 2001; Stecker et al., 2005). Other research-based practices are presented in the remaining chapters to support appropriate behavior, academic growth, and collaborative partnerships.

Supporting Appropriate Behavior

Marcus

Marcus, a first grader, is playing alone on the playground. He is tossing a playground ball in the air and appears to be in his own little world. A little girl approaches him and asks him if she can play with him. "No. It's my ball!" he says. She leaves and another boy comes by and catches the ball after Marcus tosses it in the air. Marcus screams so loudly that almost everyone on the playground turns and looks at him, and the boy returns the ball to Marcus. The playground supervisor tells Marcus to put the ball up. Marcus refuses and keeps tossing the ball as if he can't hear her. She asks again. He refuses.

Lilly

"What a soft name for such an aggressive girl," says Lilly's new third-grade teacher, Mrs. Jackson, to her second-grade teacher, Ms. Espinosa. Mrs. Jackson says she is scared of Lilly and is seeking advice from Ms. Espinosa. Mrs. Jackson has had a rough month with Lilly and things seem to be escalating. Mrs. Jackson admits that she avoids Lilly and tries to keep her busy. She doesn't know much about her. What scares her the most is Lilly's aggressive behavior toward the other students. The most extreme example was when Lilly threw a table over and it landed on another student, who was slightly hurt but really shaken up. She will frequently pinch, kick, hit, and verbally taunt her classmates. Not surprisingly, Lilly always plays and works alone.

Marshall

"Marshall is such a sweet little boy but he doesn't seem to have much control over his behavior," his mother tells his kindergarten teacher, Mrs. Chen.

His biggest challenges are in walking inside, keeping an inside tone of voice, and waiting for very desired activities. Marshall was not in a preschool program. His kindergarten teacher reassures his mother that she is prepared for these types of behaviors and will help him learn how to adjust. However, by midyear, Mrs. Chen has run out of options to help Marshall and does not feel he has learned any social behavioral skills since he has been in kindergarten.

Social behavioral problems like these are common in the primary grades. Unfortunately, working effectively with such problems is not as common. Too often, teachers feel unprepared to take a systematic approach to working with behavioral issues and may rely on reactive rather than proactive approaches (Gunter & Coutinho, 1997; Kauffman, 2005; Maag, 2001; Meese, 2001; Walker et al., 2004). As discussed in Chapter 1, children have different preschool experiences and many enter elementary school without the social skills needed to be successful in the school setting. Typically, children learn and maintain behaviors that have been successful in their preschool environments. For example, if a child screams or cries at home and a sibling gives in because of this behavior, then this behavior (screaming) may also be used in the school setting. If a parent tends to give in to a child when the child whines, then the child may view this as an effective social skill. Children may also have challenging behavior due to their within child characteristics (e.g. ADHD). Thus, children enter school with some skills that need to be replaced with other skills that are more socially desirable.

Research-Based Practices for Supporting Appropriate Behavior

In addition to using systematic data collection to determine the types of problems children have, teachers need to use proactive research-based interventions (Kartub, Taylor-Greene, March, & Horner, 2000; Lewis et al., 2002; Taylor-Greene et al., 1997). Using a proactive approach emphasizes the teaching involved in working with social behavior. It is especially critical for young children to have time to learn and practice appropriate social behavior rather than being punished for using the only skills they have mastered. Teachers teach academic behavior very differently than they teach social behavior. Academic errors are used to inform instruction whereas social errors are often met with serious consequences and no instruction (Lewis & Sugai, 1999; Maag, 2001; Walker et al., 2004). This orientation needs to change for more children to be successful.

As discussed in Chapter 5, to work effectively with social behavior, teachers need to use objective assessments to guide instructional decisions. Human beings are subjective by nature and when children have challenging (and often annoy-ing) behaviors, teachers need to rely on objective measures of behavior. For example, a teacher may be under the impression that a child is sustaining challenging behaviors. However, when data are reviewed, it is clear that the child has gone from running in the hallway 5 times a day to 5 times a week. That is a behavioral change. Perhaps the child needs a little more support to reduce this behavior even more. Monitoring progress also allows teachers to see if an intervention is not working and the behavior is not changing at all or getting worse.

Overall, research has clearly provided a framework for working with social behavior problems. Using systematic data collection for targeting behavior problems and monitoring progress is a research-based practice (Alberto & Troutman, 2003; Sugai et al., 2000; Taylor-Greene et al., 1997). Research has also supported the use of specific interventions for all children, small groups of children, and individual children. A review of these interventions follows.

Positive Behavioral Support

School-wide positive behavioral support (PBS) is a systematic approach to sup-porting appropriate social behavior in all children (Sugai et al., 2000). School-wide PBS has been effective in improving social behavior and increasing time engaged in academics for elementary school children (Nakasato, 2000; Scott, 2001; Sugai, Horner, Lewis, & Cheney, 2002), and support for incorporating fea-tures of PBS in preschool settings is emerging (Stormont, Lewis, & Beckner, 2005; Stormont, Covington, & Lewis, 2006). When schools use systems of PBS, they choose to adopt a system-wide approach for teaching and supporting appropri-ate behavior that is driven by data collected by school teams. Schools have teams that personalize the features of PBS for their school settings and who coordinate data collection and system reform. If a school or a school district wants to begin to use school-wide PBS, they can go to the Center for Positive Behavioral Interventions website (pbis.org). This website can provide professionals with resources, access to national, regional, and state conferences, and any training that is available in their area.

School-wide PBS is grounded in an extensive research base that supports the use of positive reinforcement, cuing and prompting, direct instruction, and using data for decision making (Colvin, Kameenui, & Sugai, 1994; Horner, Sugai, & Vincent, 2005; Kartub et al., 2000; Lewis et al., 2002; Taylor-Greene et al., 1997). School-wide PBS has been used in schools with high percentages of vulnerable learners and has decreased the number of problem behaviors and increased the amount of time devoted to instruction (Eber, Sugai, Smith, & Scott, 2002; Lewis, Powers, & Newcomer, 2001; Stormont et al., 2006; Taylor-Greene et al., 1997). The key features of school-wide PBS are used to clearly establish specific behaviors that should be taught and supported in school settings (Horner et al., 2005;

Stormont et al., 2005). The overall process for implementing school-wide PBS includes

- Forming a representative team of school staff to drive and monitor the process
- Choosing approximately five expectations to guide rule generation
- Determining specific behaviors that fall under each expectation for classroom and nonclassroom settings (playground, lunchroom, bus, etc.)
- Teaching each expectation
- Providing support (cues and positive reinforcement) for choosing appropriate behavior
- Defining consequences for behaviors
- Choosing a data collection system to monitor progress (e.g., office referral system)
- Aligning professional development and school improvement with PBS implementation

The behavioral expectations and specific behavior exemplars that match these expectations are often arranged in the form of a matrix. The expectations are listed horizontally in the first column and the specific settings are listed vertically on the first row. The specific behaviors that match what the expectation would "look like" in specific settings are listed in the corresponding columns. A sample matrix that would be appropriate for children in the primary grades is provided in Figure 6-1. A more elaborate matrix, which was developed and used by an elementary school using school-wide PBS, is presented in Figure 6-2. The behaviors on the matrix represent what professionals want children to do instead of problem behavior. For example, if children argue with adults when asked to do something in several school settings, one of the behaviors listed under "Be Responsible" could be "Follow directions the first time asked." Another example representing what professionals want children to do instead of their problem behavior (pushing, pulling hair, etc.) is "Keep hands and feet to yourself."

After a school develops a matrix, it is used by all professionals in the school. Classroom teachers can form their own rules for their classroom but the playground, hallway, cafeteria, and bus rules would be the same for everyone. This supports the use of similar words across settings and people. Everyone in schools using PBS should learn "the language." If children are running in the hall, a custodian may say, "Be safe and use your walking feet." Teachers are responsible for teaching each skill using an explicit instruction format. Figure 6-3 provides an example of a lesson that a kindergarten teacher could use for teaching the behavior "walk instead of running" for the expectation "Be safe" for all school settings, except recess and physical education.

Once these school-wide classroom and nonclassroom expectations have been established, taught, and supported, some children will need additional support in learning and using appropriate behavior (see Figure 6-4). The triangle in Figure 6-4 illustrates the continuum of supports that is built within a school-wide PBS system.

Expectation	Classroom	Hallway	Cafeteria	Playground
Be Kind	■ Share materials ■ Help friends ■ Use gentle words when upset	■ Use kind words ■ Keep some distance between you and peers	■ Clean up messes ■ Be a helper if asked ■ Say "please" and "thank-you"	■ Use kind words ■ Follow game rules ■ Share
Be Safe	■ Use materials correctly ■ Return from errands quickly ■ Walk	■ Walk ■ Keep hands and feet to self ■ Inside voices or voices off	■ Walk ■ Keep hands and feet to self ■ Inside voices	■ Stay in area ■ Use equipment correctly
Be Responsible	■ Follow teacher instructions ■ Use inside voices	■ Listen to adults ■ Be where you should be ■ Form lines when asked	■ Listen to adults ■ Quickly follow directions ■ Stack chairs before leaving	■ Listen to adults ■ Line up first time ■ Help your friends

Figure 6-1
Matrix of Behavior Expectations at Taylor Elementary School

The bottom level represents the percentage of children who will be successful when the universal supports are established (i.e., teaching and supporting of behavioral expectations, clear consequences, and monitoring of systems through ongoing data collection). Small group supports and individualized supports are utilized for the 15 to 20% of children who need more support (Sugai et al., 2000). Small group supports may involve forming a social skills group made up of children with frequent office referrals that would meet once or twice a week. Individualized support may include conducting a functional behavioral assessment and developing a positive behavior intervention plan to support a child's individual needs (Lewis & Sugai, 1999).

As school-wide PBS initially requires systems change and extensive work, it typically takes 3 to 5 years before schools have all systems in place (Lewis & Sugai, 1999).

Parkade Pride Expectations			
I am . . .	All/Classroom	Hallways	Assemblies
Kind	■ Include others ■ Use polite words ■ Keep hands to self ■ Help others ■ Be a friend	■ Keep hands and feet to self ■ Allow others to work as you enter the room	■ Listen to the presenter ■ Clap only when finished
Safe	■ Keep hands and feet to self ■ Walk in building ■ Use materials and equipment appropriately	■ Walk ■ Follow walk zones ■ Know where you are at in the hallway	■ Enter and exit the gym in an orderly manner
Cooperative	■ Follow directions the first time ■ Take turns ■ Share with others ■ Problem solve ■ Be a team player	■ Wait for directions before leaving ■ Follow rules without reminders ■ Follow transition routines	■ Take turns asking or answering questions ■ Follow directions
Respectful	■ Be a good listener ■ Treat others the way you want to be treated ■ Allow others to be different ■ Acknowledge other's ideas	■ Walk quietly so others can continue learning ■ Use polite language ■ Follow directions	■ Keep hands and feet to self ■ Stay seated flat on bottom in designated area
Peaceful	■ Use a calm voice ■ Walk quietly so others can learn ■ Keep body peaceful ■ Follow transition procedures	■ Walk quietly ■ Enter and exit classrooms quietly	■ Show appreciation by applause only
Responsible	■ Take care of self ■ Do your job ■ Accept outcomes of behavior ■ Make good choices ■ Be honest	■ Take care of self ■ Allow others to resolve their own problems ■ Be honest	■ Take care of self ■ Do your job ■ Accept outcomes of your behavior ■ Be honest

Figure 6-2

Matrix for Parkade Elementary

Source: Courtesy of Parkade Elementary School, Columbia, Missouri.

I am . . .	Bathroom	Playground
Kind	■ Give turns ■ Allow for privacy	■ Invite others to join in ■ Include all who want to play ■ Accept skill differences
Safe	■ Report any problems ■ Wash hands with soap and water	■ Use equipment appropriately ■ Stay in designated areas ■ "Green to go"
Cooperative	■ Give turns ■ Follow bathroom procedures	■ Agree on rules before starting ■ Follow game rules ■ Be a team player
Respectful	■ Respect privacy of others ■ Clean up after self	■ Keep the rules the same during the game ■ Use appropriate language (no put-downs) ■ Line up when the whistle blows
Peaceful	■ Use a quiet voice ■ Enter and exit the bathroom quietly	■ Problem solve conflicts ■ Return from the playground quietly
Responsible	■ Flush ■ Clean up after self ■ Return to class ■ promptly	■ Take care of self ■ Allow others to resolve their own conflicts ■ Do your job ■ Accept outcome of behaviors

Figure 6-2
Continued

However, research has found that once systems have been established and teams are functioning efficiently, the impact on social behavior and academic achievement is significant (Eber et al., 2002; Lewis et al., 2001).

Social Skills Instruction

If teachers teach in schools that aren't using systems of school-wide PBS, then they can still use some of the features. Teachers can use the matrices from a school-wide PBS approach to design social expectations for their classrooms and teach them in the same way. Using school-wide PBS systems would strengthen the effectiveness of social skills instruction because consistent support for appropriate

Target Skill: Walk Instead of Running

Instruction:

- Discuss why walking in the classroom is important. Talk about safety concerns versus adult-imposed consequences for running.
- Discuss when walking is needed and when running is OK. Talk about when children have had to walk outside of school. Talk about any accidents that students have had when running inside.
- Describe what walking looks like (skill steps):
  - Go slowly
  - Feet stay close to ground
  - Feet are calm
- Teacher *models* walking and has a few students model.
- Teacher (and only teacher) *models* crazy running feet and trips over something or knocks something over.
- Have students practice walking in a circle going very slowly.
- Have students trace others' feet on construction paper and place feet in classroom in an area (row or circle) where students who need to practice more can practice.
- Have children draw a picture of why it is important to walk.
- Homework 1: Ask students to walk to the dining table to have dinner.
- Homework 2: Talk to parents about walking. Have children cut out a small paper foot or use a premade paper foot and have parents sign the foot to indicate that they talked about it with their children.
- Maintenance Support: Have children walk every day for a few minutes (can also have them practice to a song).
- Individual Support: Use proximity, prompts, and extra practice with children who need more support.

Figure 6-3
Social Skill Lesson Plan

behavior is present across settings. If children have very challenging behavior and the school is not using school-wide PBS, often teachers will need to follow children into other settings (recess, lunchroom) and teach and support desired behavior in those settings.

Teachers will want to support the entire class in learning their overall classroom rules and routines (refer to Chapter 3); however, some children will need more explicit instruction on additional social skills. Prior to implementing research-based practices for individual children, it is important that teachers first select a system for targeting and monitoring behavior change. Data collection can help

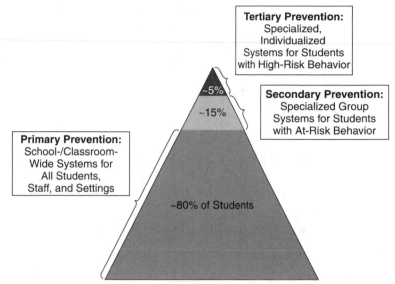

Figure 6-4
Continuum of School-Wide Instructional and Positive Behavioral Support

teachers determine if children have a *social skill deficit or social skill production problem* (Lewis & Sugai, 1999). If children have a skill problem, then they need instruction on the specific skill and its components. If children have a production problem, then they have the skill in their repertoire of social behaviors, but they just do not consistently use it. For example, consider a child who had a skill deficit for the behavior "walking inside" at the beginning of the year. By February, she has learned how to walk inside but she is still running several times a day. She now has a production problem.

Thus, teachers need to determine if social skills instruction is needed or if children need to be reminded to use skills they already have. When working with social skills deficits, teachers need to use data to determine the skills that are most important for children to learn to be successful in their school environment. According to the research presented in Chapter 1, many kindergarten teachers expect children to be able to self-regulate and control their emotions (Stormont et al., 2005). Therefore, some teachers may choose to work on building social skills such as:

- Asking for help when upset (rather than crying or screaming)
- Talking calmly with friends (rather than yelling)
- Keeping hands to self (rather than hitting, grabbing, etc.)
- Finding something to do when finished working

There are also many published curricula that teachers can reference to determine skills that one or more children need to learn. *Skillstreaming the Elementary School Child* provides 60 different social skills organized in five different categories (McGinnis & Goldstein, 1997). The categories and one sample skill for each include:

- Classroom survival skills
  - Asking for help
- Friendship-making skills
  - Joining in
- Skills for dealing with feelings
  - Knowing your feelings
- Skill alternatives to aggression
  - Responding to teasing
- Skills for dealing with stress
  - Dealing with being left out

When using published curricula, teachers need to modify the curricula to be more sensitive to the specific needs of their children (Sugai & Lewis, 1996). After teachers have chosen the social skills they want to teach, they need to provide explicit or direct instruction on these skills. Such instruction includes analyzing the skill to determine specific components of the skill. This is similar to a task analysis where one would determine the specific steps involved in performing an academic (or any) task successfully. Once the skill components are identified, teachers organize this information for instruction. For example, for the skill "Preparing for recess," a teacher could identify the following skill components:

- Put work away
- Wait at desk until time (teacher signals)
- Walk to door
- Wait in line
- Keep hands to self
- Walk in line
- When on playground, go have fun

The skill components for the skill "Asking for help" could include:

- Decide you need help (you are stuck)
- Decide what you need help on
- Raise hand or walk to teacher's desk
- Wait for teacher
- Ask for help

For children who need a lot of support when working independently, teachers can select and assign peers who can also be solicited for assistance. "Ask a peer" would then be added as a skill component. In many social skills curricula, these skill steps are already provided for teachers (e.g., McGinnis & Goldstein, 1997). During instruction, teachers highlight the importance of the skill and its components, provide models as examples and nonexamples of the skill, have children practice the skill to mastery, and then have children use the skill in different settings to promote generalization (McGinnis & Goldstein, 1997; Sugai & Lewis, 1996; Walker et al., 1995). It is important to stress that the examples modeled for children need to appear realistic to them (Sugai & Lewis, 1996). Figures 6-3 and 6-5 are examples of direct instruction formats with all the key components of effective social skills instruction.

Teachers can support individual children with social skills deficits in the context of more less explicit lessons by making sure they have the same prior knowledge as their peers and by specifically assessing their understanding of the main ideas. For example, a teacher is going to use literature to support the social concept "how and when children need to get help for friends." This concept will then be contrasted with tattling. However, many children with social problems do not master social concepts, like the one just mentioned, through literature and class discussion. The following are some examples of how teachers could add more support for individual children:

- Interview children prior to the lesson to establish their prior knowledge. If a child cannot draw many examples from her past experience related to the concept, then the teacher will need to help her. Support for providing sufficient prior knowledge could include having the child ask three peers questions about their experiences to learn more about the topic.

- Highlight the main idea that is important to focus on in the lesson and provide relevant examples from children's environments. Also provide an outline to help children focus on important main ideas.

- Prepare several specific questions related to the main idea and make sure children with social problems can answer those questions or retell important parts of the lesson or story.

- Pair children with more specific needs with appropriate peers during application and practice activities.

Overall, when social skills lessons involve more constructivist teaching strategies, teachers will often need to provide more direct support (e.g., explicit instruction and assessment) for children with social problems to ensure they are learning the main ideas. Literature can and should also be used within direct instruction formats to help children apply their social knowledge to different contexts. Figure 6-5 is an example of a lesson plan for a social skill that includes literature selections containing authentic examples of the social skill. These have been developed by an elementary PBS team and are titled "Cool Tools."

Skill Name: Be a Friend

Context: All Settings

Teaching Examples

Example: Sally is sad. Jenny puts an arm around her and tells her, "It's okay," and stays with her until she feels better.

Nonexample: In the cafeteria, Tommy trips and spills his food. His friend Gary begins laughing and pointing.

Example: In the cafeteria, Sophie trips and her tray spills onto the floor, several of her friends stop and begin to help her clean it up.

Kid Activity

1. Create a poster or collage showing acts of kindness.
2. Have students discuss or write about what they think it takes to be a good friend or what they look for in people they would like to become friends with.

After the Lesson
(During the Day)

1. Ask students to share examples of how they are kind at home.
2. Talk about situations or emotions which require a friend's understanding.
3. Place a kindness jar for students to write notes about kind acts they see in their rooms or around the building and put them in. Share the kindness comments at the end of the day. Younger students can draw pictures and write names of those observed.

Extension Ideas

Read aloud stories that deal with friendship issues.

Chrysanthemum
Kevin Henkes

Elizabeth and Larry
Marilyn Sadler

Elizabeth, Larry and Ed
Marilyn Sadler

A Friend Like Ed
Karen Wagner

Little Yellow and Little Blue
Leo Lionni

The Sneetches
Dr. Seuss

Chester's Way
Kevin Henkes

Song: Make New Friends
(Best sung in rounds)

Figure 6-5
Cool Tools for the Behavioral Expectation: I Am Kind

Source: University of Missouri Center for School-wide Positive Behavior Support (2001). "Cool tool" social skill lesson plan. Columbia, MO: Author.

Make new friends,

But keep the old.

Some are silver,

And the others gold.

Activity: Rig-a-jig-jig

Half of the class makes an inner circle that faces out while the other half makes an outer circle that faces in. The inner circle moves in the clockwise direction while the outer circle either stands still or moves in the counterclockwise direction. Everyone sings, and when the verse ends everyone freezes. Students greet the friend across from them following teacher example or guidelines and then the song and steps are repeated several more times.

A rig-a-jig-jig and away we go,

Away we go, away we go.

A rig-a-jig-jig and away we go,

Hi ho, Hi ho, Hi ho.

As I was walking down the street,

Down the street, down the street.

A friend of mine I chanced to meet

Hi ho, Hi ho, Hi ho.

(Stop, greet, repeat)

Figure 6-5
Continued

After children have learned social skills, many still need a lot of support using their new skills. Positive reinforcement and precorrection are research-based practices that can be used to support the production of appropriate behavior after skills have been taught and are in children's repertoires. These strategies can help children maintain their appropriate behavior across time and in different settings.

Positive Reinforcement

Positive reinforcement, rewards, and recognition are terms that are often used interchangeably but differ in significant ways. *Positive reinforcement* is a behavioral principle that occurs in every classroom setting throughout the day (Maag, 2001). *Rewards* include tangible items that are given to children based on specific behavior (Alberto & Troutman, 2003). *Recognition* involves a more reflective process where children are supported in evaluating their own behavior and acknowledging their accomplishments (Weinstein & Mignano, 2003).

Recognition is the most widely accepted consequence for behavior in elementary settings. However, many young children who are vulnerable for failure are less intrinsically motivated in school. Thus, using recognition alone may not be enough to motivate children to participate in lessons and activities to promote academic and social behavioral learning. Furthermore, even if teachers believe they are using recognition alone to support positive behavior often they might be inadvertently misusing positive reinforcement.

Many teachers fall into a trap of reinforcing negative behaviors (with attention) and ignoring positive behaviors (Gunter & Coutinho, 1997; Kauffman, 2005; Maag, 2001). When using positive reinforcement strategies, teachers try to pair positive consequences with appropriate behavior to increase the occurrence of the appropriate behavior in the future. For example, a teacher wants Jon to work on his journal writing for 10 minutes. To support his on-task behavior, at the end of every 3 minutes, she goes over and pats him on the back and says quietly, "You are working hard on your journal." If Jon begins to increase his on-task behavior when the teacher is using this systematic behavioral praise, then praise is a positive reinforcer for Jon. If, however, Jon stopped working as soon as she praised him and refused to start again, then perhaps the praise was disruptive and/or punishing for Jon.

Positive reinforcers need to be selected on an individual student basis. What one child finds reinforcing, another may not. Some examples of consequences

Children need feedback when their behavior is appropriate.

that children in the primary grades may desire include teacher attention, getting to do special activities, having extra recess time, and receiving tangible items. An interview or a questionnaire would help teachers figure out what children might desire. Figure 6-6 is an example of interview questions children could complete in pairs as part of a community-building activity in the beginning of the

1. Which are your two top picks?
   - Extra recess
   - Computer time
   - Playing a game (inside)
   - Listening to music
   - Helping the teacher
2. Which is your top pick?
   - No homework night
   - Free time in class
3. Which are your two top picks?
   - Candy
   - Stickers
   - Pencil
   - Marker
   - Eraser
4. If candy was a top pick, which two would you pick?
   - Piece of chocolate
   - Tootsie roll
   - Sucker
   - Jolly rancher
   - Piece of gum
   - Starburst (what is your favorite flavor?)

Peer Interview Steps:

1. Teacher assigns each of a pair of students a number 1 or 2 and writes it on interview sheets. Strong readers are assigned a number 1.
2. Teacher provides overview of why activity is important (e.g., to get to know each other better and for teacher to use later).
3. Teacher reads the questions first for students who may struggle to read independently.
4. Peers interview each other on separate sheets of paper, with number 1 going first.
5. Peers share information with class.
6. Teacher can compile information and develop an appropriate math activity based on information.

Figure 6-6
Interview Questions for Community-Building Activity

year. A picture chart could be used for young children. They could then share their "favorites" with peers in the class. Conversely, teachers can also interview a child to determine the child's desired rewards.

Providing rewards using "if . . . then . . ." statements is another powerful reinforcer for many children; especially when they have choices. This strategy is referred to as the Premack Principle and the dessert principle—if you eat your green beans . . . then you can have a cookie (as cited in Mercer & Mercer, 2005). One first-grade teacher utilized this strategy with a kindergartener who struggled to stay on task. She developed a folder with pictures of what she wanted him to be doing at any given time (e.g., doing work, reading, writing, computer time), and pictures representing things he liked to do, including coloring, games, puzzles, Play doh, and blocks. These pictures were laminated and affixed to a Velcro strip inside the folder. Then on the outside of the folder she had a two-column table with one column labeled *If* and the other *Then* (see Figure 6-7). She used this strategy throughout the day to help the child stay on task. She began with small amounts of time engaged in an activity to earn a reinforcer and then gradually increased the time.

Praise is a simple type of strategy that, when delivered quickly and sincerely, is often a powerful positive reinforcer for individual children and small groups of students (Maag, 2001; Stormont et al., 2006). Specific behavioral praise also sets the occasion for teaching to occur. Teachers need to always underscore what a child is doing that is being acknowledged or praised. This type of praise becomes *constructive feedback* for children (Alberto & Troutman, 2003). For children with less structured early school experiences, this type of support is warranted and often makes the difference between participating in class all day and spending excessive amounts of time in the principal's office.

Figure 6-7(a)
Teacher and Student Choices presented in an *If* (Schoolwork) and *Then* (Reward) Format
Source: Courtesy of Jessica Bach, Parkade Elementary School, Columbia, Missouri.

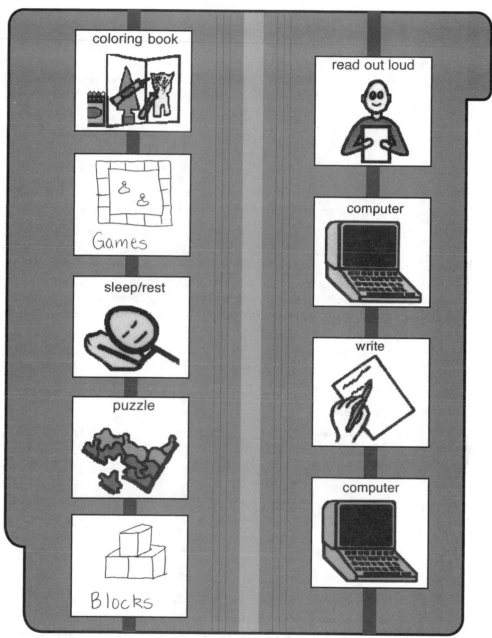

Figure 6-7(b)
Alternate Activities for *If* (Schoolwork) and *Then* (Reward)
Source: Courtesy of Jessica Bach, Parkade Elementary School, Columbia, Missouri.

Although the use of verbal praise as a reinforcer has been linked to increases in intrinsic reinforcement, widespread use of other types of potential positive reinforcers is less accepted in the field of elementary education (Weinstein & Mignano, 2003). However, the use of extrinsic reinforcers has been validated as a way to reengage children who are vulnerable for failure in school (Kauffman, 2005; Weinstein & Mignano, 2003). If children are participating in academic tasks, then they are more likely to see the value in such tasks. Teachers should always combine individualized strategies to support greater interest and involvement in learning with extrinsic reinforcement for children who need a little extra incentive to try tasks that they have not historically liked or succeeded in.

Weinstein and Mignano (2003) provide helpful tips for teachers when considering the types of "rewards" to give to children in their classrooms:

1. Consider ways to recognize children's accomplishments (including academic and behavioral) without using rewards. Such recognition could include having a class meeting at the end of every day where accomplishments are shared. (Even if some children who are vulnerable for failure receive extrinsic rewards, they could still participate with their peers in this activity. Eventually the extrinsic reward could be faded and replaced with this type of acknowledgment.)

2. Use specific, sincere, and immediate verbal praise for behavior. This may increase children's motivation to learn. However, it is important to consider whether public praise is reinforcing and culturally appropriate for individual children.

3. Do not use tangible reinforcers if children enjoy the activities. Such rewards should only be used when the task is something children do not enjoy.

4. When using tangible rewards, make sure to link the receipt of the reward to participation and performance.

5. Select rewards on an individual basis and keep the system as simple as possible.

Precorrection

Precorrection is an effective, proactive way to teach and remind students of appropriate behavior before they have a chance to make mistakes (Lampi, Fenty, & Beaunae, 2005; Walker et al., 2004). If children have a tendency to engage in problem behaviors due to impulsive decision making, attention problems, or for any other reason, precorrective statements can help them focus on what they are supposed to do (Walker et al., 1995). Precorrection comprises the following steps (Lampi et al., 2005; Mercer & Mercer, 2005; Walker et al., 1995):

1. Determine the setting and circumstances surrounding the problem behavior (lunchroom, recess, hallway, during small group work).

2. Identify the expected behavior for the setting.

3. Teach children who are having problems the specific behavior that is desired in the target setting.

4. Practice the specific behavior with children.

5. Cue children for the desired behavior immediately before that setting.

6. Modify the environment, if needed, to help children be more successful.

7. Acknowledge improvement in behavior.

The following is an example of how a teacher could apply the information obtained from behavioral assessment, discussed in Chapter 5, and utilize the pre-correction strategy.

Mr. Lin's Class Learns Lunch Rules

Several of the children in Mr. Lin's first-grade class have difficulty following the lunchroom procedures. Event recording assessments indicate that on 4 out of 5 days, more than one of his children had a negative report filed by the lunch staff. Mr. Lin observes the setting to determine more specifics about the problem. His students walk in the lunchroom, quietly pick up their trays, sit in their assigned seats, and talk in an acceptable manner while eating. However, upon dismissal from lunch, at least five of Mr. Lin's students do not follow the expected procedures.

Accordingly, Mr. Lin teaches his students the expected behavior in the lunchroom when no other students are present. Mr. Lin modifies the context by asking the lunch supervisor to provide a prompt for expected behavior immediately before dismissal. Mr. Lin also uses behavioral rehearsal with his students when he asks them to state the expected lunch behavior immediately before that setting. Mr. Lin provides 5 minutes of free time for students when they are successful at lunch that day.

For the first week of intervention, Mr. Lin enters the lunchroom 5 minutes before dismissal and provides a prompt for appropriate behavior. During the first week, Mr. Lin observes students and records success/failure as a group. Over time, he fades his assistance and asks the lunch supervisor to collect this data. After breaks and long weekends, Mr. Lin plans to review the routine with students.

Cues

Similar to precorrection, providing cues is another way to proactively support appropriate behavior. Briefly stating the three appropriate steps children need to follow to get ready for lunch will help some children who may impulsively rush to the door without their lunch and without putting away their materials. Cues, gestures, and clear instructions stated in similar ways are also effective supports for children who are still learning the English language.

Visual cues are also important for directing attention to appropriate behavior choices. Children can be provided with specific behaviors or steps listed on cards that are laminated to their desks. These can then serve as cues and help support children in monitoring their own behavior. Two first-grade teachers created checklists to serve as cues for their children (see Figures 6-8 and 6-9). The checklists include activities that children can do when they have finished their work at their seats or when they have finished all three center activities.

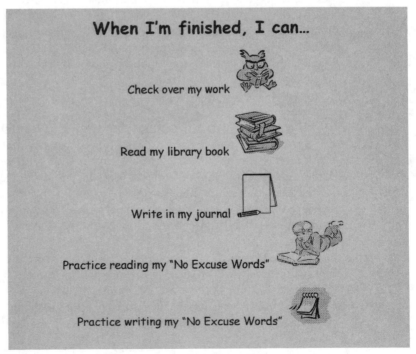

Figure 6-8
Self-Monitoring Checklist Used When Children Finish an Activity
Source: Courtesy of Deanna Bickel, Parkade Elementary School, Columbia, Missouri.

If you finish all 3 center activities you can...

1. Go to the library

2. Read books

3. Do extra work in your folder

Figure 6-9
Self-Monitoring Checklist Used When Children Finish Center Activities
Source: Courtesy of Jessica Bach, Parkade Elementary School, Columbia, Missouri.

Consequences

In addition to proactively working to prevent problem behavior and to support the use of appropriate behavior (using precorrection, social skills instruction, positive reinforcement, etc.), teachers also need to think about consequences for specific behaviors. At the beginning of the year, when rules are being developed, teachers need to make sure children understand the consequences for breaking different rules. Teachers also need to be very consistent in their enforcement of the rules. This consistency doesn't mean that teachers can't individualize the rules for children who are vulnerable. For example, if there is a particular consequence for a specific behavior in a teacher's classroom but the teacher can see that a child has had a rough day already, the teacher can say, "Marcus, were you being safe when you _____? I know you have had a rough morning so I am going to give you a warning. What will happen if you _____ again?"

Teachers also need to determine behaviors that can be teacher-managed and those that are more serious and should include a referral to the office. Teachers can collaborate with other teachers, school counselors, school psychologists, or teacher assistance teams to determine behaviors that are more serious and warrant an office referral for children of different ages.

When providing consequences for problem behavior, teachers also need to be mindful of the school factors that contribute to problem behavior, discussed in Chapter 1. Some children want to be removed from the classroom because of certain environmental factors and will actually engage in problem behavior because they have used it to "escape" certain tasks in the past. Teachers need to collect data for certain consequences to see if they are actually reducing or increasing problem behavior. If consequences are decreasing problem behavior, then they are punishing. If they are increasing problem behavior, then they are reinforcing behavior. Consider the following example.

Sally hates reading out loud. When it is her turn to read she gets out of her chair and wanders around the classroom. The teacher redirects her back to her group. She returns to her seat for less than 5 minutes and begins to wander again. The teacher redirects her again. This time she refuses to return to her group and goes to her desk. The teacher, busy listening to other groups, ignores her. The next day, Sally does the same thing.

In this example, Sally is probably wandering around to avoid reading. Redirection and ignoring are not changing her behavior. As a result, Sally will probably continue to wander during reading time. Some ideas for Sally from discussions in this chapter and Chapter 5 include the following:

- Determine if Sally is able to read at the level of her group.
- Observe Sally's behavior while in the group and collect information regarding when she leaves the group (e.g., is it when it is her turn to read?).
- If Sally gets tired or wants to leave the reading group, give her an acceptable way to do so (have her raise hand and ask teacher for a break).
- Determine positive reinforcers to use to increase Sally's on-task behavior if she is able to read at the level of the group.
- Provide additional supports, discussed in Chapter 7.

The following section also includes strategies that Sally could use to monitor her own behavior in her reading group.

Self-Management

Because of their unique characteristics (e.g., attention, memory, impulsivity, social skills problems), children who are vulnerable will most likely need assistance regulating their own behavior (Hall, 2005; Mercer & Mercer, 2005; Vanderbilt, 2005). Children in early primary grades will need a teacher to monitor their behavior and assist them in developing goals for improvement. Children will also need different levels of support to be able to shift the responsibility for monitoring, evaluating, and managing their behavior from their teacher, to shared responsibility, and then to independent management.

When using self-monitoring and recording with young children, it is important that only a few behaviors are targeted, and that picture prompts are provided to serve as cues regarding appropriate behavior (Vanderbilt, 2005). Self-monitoring cards with checklists or templates with specific steps to use for problem solving or with specific social skills components to refer back to on a daily or hourly basis are helpful for many children. Behaviors targeted for self-recording and self-monitoring may include:

- Asking for help
- Preparing for recess
- Appropriate behaviors for specials, recess, or lunch
- Making good choices when angry
- Making gosod choices when work is finished (refer to Figures 6-8 and 6-9)

Technology support is available to help young children develop more control over their own behavior. *KidTools* is a program available to professionals free of charge at http://kidtools.missouri.edu. KidTools, one of several educational resources available at this website, was developed to support children, ages 7 to 10 years, with challenging behavior. KidTools offers a variety of templates for teachers and children to use collaboratively to support behavioral change. Teachers need to read the descriptions of the program and information related to successfully implementing the tools, both of which are available at the website. Figure 6-10 displays the menu of six templates that children and teachers can select from. The animated children on the screen narrate each step of the process.

KidTools can support children in determining specific behaviors for self-monitoring using countoon templates (see Figure 6-11). When using countoons, children create an individualized self-monitoring card by selecting specific behaviors that they need to demonstrate (e.g., raise your hand) and corresponding pictures for each to refer back to.

KidTools also includes a template of the STAR strategy, which is a problem-solving strategy. Children who are vulnerable can develop their own individualized STAR template and describe how they will **S**top, **T**hink, **A**ct, and the **R**esults of their plan (see Figure 6-12). For any social behavior that young children are working on,

Figure 6-10
KidTools Menu

Source: First Step KidTools: Fitzgerald, G., & Semrau, L. (1999) [Computer Software and CD].
University of Missouri/U.S. Department of Education Grant #H029K70089.

a checklist with the specific skill or another type of visual support can be taped to
their desk or posted in the classroom and reviewed often as an appropriate and
necessary support.

Using Contingency Plans with Children

Teachers can support behavior by developing positive, child-selected consequences for meeting specific behavioral expectations. Such expectations can be
for the entire class or just for one or two individuals. Contingencies can also
be linked with individual children's goals or class goals. Contingencies are
only effective if children have social behavioral skills but are not using them
consistently.

Contracts. Children and teachers can work together to determine behavior
that needs to change (Meese, 2001; Mercer & Mercer, 2005). When creating contracts, teachers need to make sure that children acknowledge the need to change a
specific behavior and are willing to work on making different choices. Figure 6-13
is an example of a template that teachers can use with children. Contracts typically
include a statement of the problem behavior that needs to be worked on, the goal
for behavior change, a specific reward or reward choices for reaching the goal, and

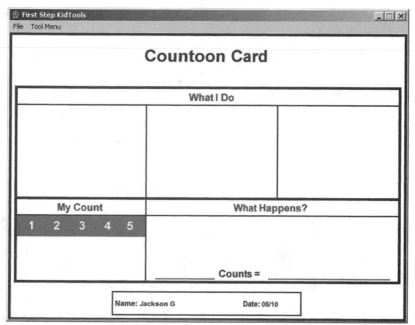

Figure 6-11
KidTools Countoon

Source: First Step KidTools: Fitzgerald, G., & Semrau, L. (1999). [Computer Software and CD]. University of Missouri/U.S. Department of Education Grant #H029K70089.

the signatures of the child and the teacher. Figure 6-14 is an example of a completed contract. KidTools also offers contract templates that teachers and children can complete together (see Figure 6-15).

Class-wide Supports for Appropriate Behavior

Peers can be taught how to support appropriate behavior by teaching them specific words to say to friends when they are making bad choices. Rather than avoiding children, telling on them, or saying "No!," peers can learn what to say and do. Specific peers can be recess and class monitors who help others solve problems. All children should be made to feel included at recess and supported in learning how to get along with their peers (see Chapter 3 for more information on building community).

Children can also choose to work toward earning special privileges as a class. Deanna Bickel and Jessica Bach, two first-grade teachers at Parkade Elementary School in Columbia, Missouri, report that their children typically like to earn the following:

- Popcorn and movie party
- Special theme days (crazy hair day, crazy feet day, pajama day)

First Step KidTools
File   Tool Menu

STAR Card

Title: _____

		Follow STAR?		
		Time	Yes	No
STOP				
THINK				
ACT				
RESULTS				

Name: Jackson G   Date: 05/10

Figure 6-12
KidTools STAR Plan

Source: First Step KidTools: Fitzgerald, G., & Semrau, L. (1999). [Computer Software and CD].
University of Missouri/U.S. Department of Education Grant #H029K70089.

- Cookie party
- Picnic at a park
- Extra free time

Teachers can also support children with challenging behaviors by instituting a positive peer reporting system in their classrooms. Positive peer reporting has been documented to be effective for young children with social problems

Student: _____

My goal is to improve in the area of _____.

If I am able to _____, then I will get to choose either a

_____ or

_____. I agree to work hard on this.

Signed: _____

Optional: Teacher and student graph behavior.

Progress notes or graph:

Figure 6-13
Sample Contingency Contract

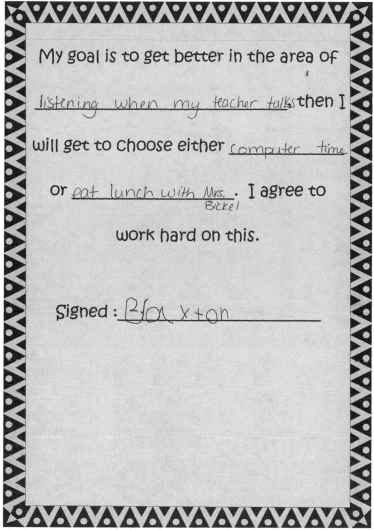

Figure 6-14
Contract with Goal Setting and Rewards to Support Appropriate Behavior
Source: Courtesy of Deanna Bickel, Parkade Elementary School, Columbia, Missouri.

and essentially teaches peers to notice and support their classmates' positive behavior (Skinner, Neddenriep, Robinson, Ervin, & Jones, 2002). This strategy may be effective in changing children's social status with peers because peers are taught to pay attention to all of the appropriate behaviors children with challenging behavior demonstrate across the day. Even children with significant behavior challenges comply with the majority of their teachers' requests

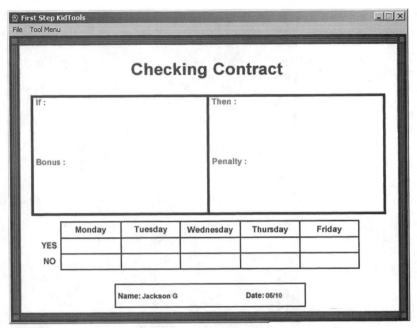

Figure 6-15
KidTools Contract

Source: First Step KidTools: Fitzgerald, G., & Semrau, L. (1999) [Computer Software and CD].
University of Missouri/U.S. Department of Education Grant #H029K70089.

and engage in more appropriate than inappropriate behaviors (Gunter &
Coutinho, 1997). However, the traditional punishment orientation of teachers
and tattling orientation of peers typically leads to greater attention to inappropriate behavior (Maag, 2001; Skinner et al., 2002; Van Acker et al., 1996;
Walker et al., 1995).

Positive peer reporting can also be combined with goal setting for children with
challenging behavior. Utilizing both strategies involves the following steps (Erwin,
Johnston, & Friman, as cited in Skinner et al., 2002):

- Teacher identifies children who are struggling socially in class (e.g., withdrawn,
  rejected by peers, high rates of aggression).
- Teacher meets with children to help them identify goals for behavioral
  improvements.
- Teacher makes sure children agree to be "Stars of the Week" and understand
  that their classmates will be focusing on their social behavior.
- From the group of children with social needs, the teacher randomly selects one
  child for the week.

- The teacher introduces the positive peer reporting process in a class meeting on Monday:
  - Peers are instructed on the child's goals for behavioral improvement (e.g., Jon is working on talking through problems instead of yelling).
  - Peers are told to write down or draw a picture when they see their classmate making good choices in different settings.
  - The teacher provides multiple examples of what children could write or draw. The teacher emphasizes using detailed descriptions (e.g., "Jon was kind in art—he let me use his paints") instead of generic words (e.g., "Jon was nice during art").
  - Teacher chooses and describes the times of day that positive peer reports will be shared with the teacher and the target "Star."
  - Optional: Peers can earn some type of small reward for completing the positive peer report. For example, a kindergarten teacher gave peers who participated in positive peer reporting pretend honey (cotton balls) to fill a honey pot when a behavior was reported. When the honey pot was filled the class got a reward.

Many teachers use variations of positive peer reporting in their classroom. Refer to Figure 6-5 for a description of a kindness jar where students place comments or draw pictures to represent acts of kindness they see throughout the day.

Additional Supports

Just as it is important to differentiate academic instruction for children with diverse learning needs, it is equally as important to differentiate social behavioral instruction. If children need different types of reminders, more practice, or stronger reinforcement to choose to use appropriate behavior, then teachers need to be prepared to accommodate these needs. Some children may benefit from having home–school plans, mentors, leadership opportunities, creative reinforcers, and more tangible or intense positive reinforcers. For example, the home–community–school plan that Rio's first-grade teacher uses includes behaviors associated with a class that the child participates in within the community. His teacher and mother developed a home–school communication sheet that includes teacher ratings each day for specific behaviors that are also emphasized in his extracurricular class (see Figure 6-16).

Dealing with Bullying

Many children know of someone who is a bully or who has been the victim of a bully. Many chapters in this book identify proactive strategies to prevent such aggression from occurring, including setting a school-wide principle that everyone

Rio's P.R.I.D.E. Report
Date 10-13-05
(1= Not at all True...5= Very True)

Perseverance

*Keeps trying when things are difficult.
(writing time, reading new books, math time – asks for help appropriately after he has tried on his own)

1   2   (3)   4   5

Respect

*Keeps hands to self.
(recess time)
*Listens when others talk.
(carpet time and share circle time)

1   2   3   (4)   5

Integrity

*Keeps their word.
(does what he tells Mrs. Bickel he's going to do when he goes to music, art, P.E., counselor, library)

1   2   (3)   4   5

Discipline

*Uses words instead of fists when there is a problem.
(recess)

1   2   3   4   (5)

Enthusiasm

*Expresses appreciation when given something
(tell teachers and students thank you for treats, reward time, etc.)

1   2   3   4   (5)

Renee Maxwell

Figure 6-16
Rio's PRIDE Report: An Example of Teacher–Parent Collaboration

> Renee -
>
> Is it possible to sign + return these daily? Please let me know.
>
> Thanks!
>
> Mrs. Bickel
>
> Yes! That's perfect. That way I can keep track of his improvements.
>
> Thanks :)
>
> Renée

Figure 6-16
Continued

is valued and safe in school. At the classroom level, teachers need to build a sense of community among their students, and teach and support rules to achieve it (refer to Chapter 3). Even with these strategies in place, some children may still use aggressive types of behavior toward specific children. When these types of problems surface in a school, children need to be taught specific skills for dealing with conflict and how to recognize when it is important to let adults know. Adults in schools need to select and consistently implement consequences for bullying behavior. At the same time, teachers also need to support prosocial skill development in children who engage in bullying (Cohen & Spenciner, 2005; Salend & Sylvestre, 2005; Walker et al., 1995). For children with serious behavior problems, teachers should consult with other professionals in the school (e.g., utilizing the expertise of a professional trained in functional behavioral assessment) and try to develop a greater understanding of such children's specific behavior patterns and appropriate, including more intense, interventions (Kauffman, 2005; Lewis, 2005; Walker et al., 1995).

Case Examples Revisited

Information from this chapter and Chapter 5 should support teachers in working more effectively with behavior problems. For any child with challenging behavior, there is a process teachers can apply. Recall the three case examples from the beginning of this chapter. The first step in working with these children is to collect observational data on the children to obtain more information on the problem behavior. The additional information obtained through observation should provide insight into the nature of the problem and the type of social problem or deficit (skill or production). After the type of problem is determined across the period of a week, teachers or aides should observe the child three to five times to obtain a current "picture" of the child's behavior. Once the data are collected, teachers can begin interventions and use the same observational system for monitoring growth. Figures 6-17, 6-18, and 6-19 detail the assessment and intervention strategies that should be utilized for each of the case examples.

Collect observational data on playground using **anecdotal reports**.

Determine main problem for intervention = **Skill deficit**. Skill deficit is not being calm when others interrupt play activity.

Collect data (frequency count) on number of times at recess Marcus yells or screams when another child interrupts his play. Data across three recess periods show an average of three times a period.

Target intervention:
1. Teach the social skill "how to stay calm when others interrupt your play."
   Specific skill steps could include:
   * Calmly say, "Give the ball (or other object) back please."
   * Count to five and ask again—keep your cool.
   * Go and tell the supervisor if it is not given back.
2. Could also use the STAR planning sheet for what Marcus will do when others interrupt.
3. Use prompts and reminders to encourage use of new skill on playground.
4. Provide reinforcement for use of new skill immediately after recess.

Continue data collection to monitor intervention: Week 1 of intervention Marcus screamed or yelled one time during recess. In week 2 it was down to two times for that week (total).

Next step for Marcus: Continue to monitor use of new skill. Try to support Marcus in sometimes playing with others during recess.

Figure 6-17
Behavioral Intervention with Marcus

Collect observational data in classroom with help of school psychologist, aide, paraprofessional, or preservice teacher using **anecdotal reports**.

Determine main problem for intervention = **Skill deficit**. Skill deficit is not asking for help or to do something else when frustrated with class work. (After five anecdotal records it was determined that Lilly's aggression occurs when she is working alone and seems to get stuck or frustrated. She will lash out at nearby students who look at her or walk by her.)

Collect data (frequency count) on number of times in five 30-minute periods of independent work time Lilly is verbally or physically aggressive. Lilly is aggressive, on average, four times (mostly verbal) per observational period.

Target intervention:
1. Teach the social skill "When you want a break from working or need help, come see the teacher."
   Specific skill steps could include:
   * Know when you are stuck or getting tired
   * Get up and walk to teacher's desk
   * Ask for a 5-minute break
   * Draw in journal or other calm activity
   * Get started with peer support (chosen by teacher)
2. Provide support for self-regulation using 2a or 2b:
   2a. Use a checklist with these steps on them or a countoon from KidTools
   2b. Use the STAR planning sheet and/or goal setting with Lilly
3. Use prompts and reminders to encourage Lilly to use new skill during independent work time.
4. Provide reinforcement for use of new skill immediately after she makes the right choice.

Continue data collection to monitor intervention: Week 1 of intervention Lilly was aggressive one time per independent work time. Each time the aggression was verbal. Week 2 Lilly was not aggressive during independent work time.

Next Step for Lilly: Continue to monitor use of new skill in target setting. Work on Lilly's aggressive behavior in lunch and at recess. Work on developing more friendships with other classmates, and consider using positive peer reporting to support positive behavior in classroom and nonclassroom settings.

Figure 6-18
Behavioral Intervention with Lilly

Collect observational data in classroom using **anecdotal reports**.

Determine main problem for intervention = **Production deficit**. Production deficit is not walking.

Collect data (frequency count) on number of times Marshall runs in classroom setting. Across five observation periods of one hour each, Marshall ran an average of four times.

Target intervention:
1. Have Marshall trace his feet on paper, make copies, and place in a row (close together) in the side or back of the classroom. Have Marcus practice using his walking feet several times the first few days of intervention. This is not a punishment or consequence.
2. When transitioning from one activity to another, cue Marshall before he leaves to walk.
3. Acknowledge Marshall's use of walking.
4. Place a paperclip in a cup each time Marshall walks.
5. At end of day count the paperclips with Marshall and write down the number on a small piece of paper shaped like a foot. Staple the foot to his backpack so he can show his family.

Continue data collection to monitor intervention: Week 1 of intervention Marshall ran an average of one time per observation period. Week 2 he ran an average of one time per period.

Intervention change: Even though his behavior is changing, the teacher thought Marshall might need more support so she added another component at the end of week 2. The teacher gave Marshall a paper foot to hold when he transitioned from one activity to another to remind him to walk. In week 3 Marshall ran one time total across five Observational Periods.

Next Step for Marshall: Continue to monitor use of skill. Work on using skill in hallway and lunchroom. When this skill is used consistently, target next behavior (e.g., using inside voice).

Figure 6-19
Behavioral Intervention with Marshall

Supporting Academic Growth

Destiny

The task at hand is simple enough for the other third-grade students. Destiny bites her lip as she tries to read the prompt on her worksheet. She overhears someone at her table say, "What event has been important in your life and why?" Destiny tries to remember this but she quickly forgets several words and she doesn't know what "event" means. She understands that she is supposed to be writing something about her life so she begins jotting down some facts about herself and drawing a picture of her house. Her teacher walks around to see how everyone is doing and tells Destiny to stop playing and get to work on her writing assignment.

The third-grade year is almost over. For Destiny, this year has been worse than the first three. She is beginning to feel dumb. As she gets older, her teachers seem to be more and more frustrated with her. Destiny is clearly bright, very verbal, and artistic. However, she has attention problems, a limited vocabulary, and her reading and writing level is that of a second-grade beginner. She is motivated to learn. She is very popular with her peers; however, she is embarrassed to ask other children for help.

Martin

Martin, a second grader, is practicing his math. He looks at his paper, writes random numbers, and says "1 plus 1 is 2, 2 plus 2 is 4, 2 plus 3 is 5." His teacher directs him to write out answers to written word problems. She reads the problems aloud for children who are struggling with some of the words. Martin is supposed to be solving addition problems such as, "Sally brings two cookies and three brownies for the bake sale. How many treats did she bring?" He is also supposed to draw his strategy for getting his answers. However, Martin continues to write his numbers on his sheet and whisper "his math" (1 plus 1, etc.).

Martin has attention problems, skill deficits, and significant behavior issues, primarily during math. He does not have the foundational math skills needed to understand what he is being asked to do. He doesn't understand the concept of addition and has problems with number sense overall. To him, math is a song you sing. He has learned the math facts he knows from flashcards that his grandmother reviews with him every weekend. He doesn't understand how the word problems relate to what he knows about math.

Jon

Jon rushes into class as the bell rings. His clothes are clean but crumpled and his zipper is unzipped. His first-grade teacher expects students to be in the classroom when the bell rings, so he gets one check for this behavior. When children get three checks they miss recess. After the morning announcements and routines, the teacher asks the class to begin their writing work. A huge prompt on the board says "Writing work = Write about you" and has pictures and topics to help children generate ideas. Jon opens his desk to get out his folder for journal writing. He can't find it. As he removes large chunks of papers from his desk he is oblivious to the noise he is making. When he looks up, his teacher is standing over him with a disappointed look on his face. One more check. Then Jon remembers that his teacher keeps his journal because he keeps losing it. After he gets his journal he looks for something to write with. He can't find anything and begins asking his classmates. Then he stands up and yells, "Hey, does anyone have a pencil?" One more check. He has only been in school for an hour. Unfortunately it is a typical day for Jon.

Destiny, Martin, and Jon need their teachers to help them be more successful in school. Children are expected to master many academic and organizational skills in the primary grades. They are also expected to leave the third grade with a purposeful approach to obtaining and relating information and solving problems. To build these competencies, children need to have the prerequisite skills to work with the new information, be actively involved in their learning, and be able to generate multiple strategies for figuring out how to approach different academic tasks. Unfortunately, many children do not develop these skills in the primary grades and are left behind at this point in their academic lives.

Teachers need to close the gap between what children should know and what they do know during the primary grades. To do this, they need to be prepared to provide supports for learners with diverse learning needs. Further, to optimize learning, teachers need to use research-based practices. Accordingly, this chapter will first present the supports teachers can use to increase children's success in the classroom. The characteristics from Chapter 2 will serve as an organizer for the first part of this chapter. The rest of the chapter deals with other instructional strategies to enhance learning opportunities for children.

Supports for Learners

There are many simple strategies that teachers can utilize to increase children's engagement in learning. The following supports were taken from literature on children at risk for failure in school (Adelman & Taylor, 1993; Espinosa, 2005; Lerner et al., 1995; Mastropieri & Scruggs, 2004; McKinley, 2003; Meese, 2001; Mercer & Mercer, 2005; Raymond, 2004; Smith, Polloway, Patton, & Dowdy, 1995; Stormont-Spurgin, 1997; Zentall, 1993, 2005, 2006; Zentall et al., 1993).

Attention Problems

Coming to Attention

Several strategies can be used to support gaining children's attention to instruction, announcements, or directions during the school day. Teachers can use one of the following "attention signals":

- Clapping a few times and have children clap back
- Singing a part of a song and have children sing the rest
- Saying the first few letters of a word and have children say the rest ("L-I-S" "T-E-N")
- Having a class name as a cue for attention, for example "Mrs. Geneux's second-grade tigers"
- Having an attention signal that is more visual, such as raising one hand and putting the other over the mouth
- Having a "student of the week" use the attention signal
- Turning the lights in the classroom off and on and having another signal when out of the classroom
- Playing soft music for 5 seconds
- Having a "listen" visual cue that the teacher carries at all times (so it would probably be small)

Almost every teacher has some type of attention cue. However, attention cues don't always work. When using attention cues, it is important to teach and practice the cues the first week of school (refer to Chapter 3). Teachers should recognize students who listen to the cue ("I have the attention of Marcus, Lucy, Natalie, etc.") and should practice with students who are struggling. For example, if Keisha is not coming to attention, her teacher can remind her of the cue for coming to attention and practice with her before calling the class to attention. Also, teachers should not begin to speak until every child has come to attention. Children who do not come to attention will typically start asking others partway through the instructions what the teacher has said and then more children are off-task. Teachers can also use physical proximity and stand by children who struggle to come to attention before providing the attention signal and/or have those children help with the attention signal.

Selective Attention

To help children attend to important directions during listening tasks, teachers need to be sure to highlight the most important information and try to limit the amount of detail they provide. Other strategies teachers can use to emphasize important information include:

- Using a special visual cue to signify that what they are about to say to children is very important.
- Changing the tone of their voice or using a funny voice to highlight that something they are saying is important.
- Restating the key parts or main ideas of directions and instructions.

During independent seatwork activities, teachers need to go directly to children with attention problems and ask them to restate what they are to do first, second, and third on specific tasks. If children can't restate these steps, then teachers can write them down and provide visual cues when needed. Such a visual cue can include a list of steps on the board and a sample problem or story starter for children to refer back to as needed. Children can also rewrite directions or draw prompts on an index card and staple this in their journal or work page or tape it to their desks. They can then be taught how to use self-instruction with these cards. This support also helps students with sustained attention problems, impulsivity, and memory problems.

Teachers and children can also work together to highlight or underline the most important information on assignments. Color can be added to highlight a specific part of the instructions that children may overlook, or to highlight math operation signs to limit impulsive errors. The importance of children understanding what to attend to during seatwork and homework assignments is critical. For homework assignments, teachers should use these supports to help children understand the "main ideas" of assignments. Ultimately, as children move out of the primary grades, they will need to use self-management strategies to prompt their attention to specific cues and to get started on assignments.

Teachers can also help children selectively attend to the daily routine and anticipate what is coming up next by having advanced organizers in the classroom. For example, a poster or dry erase board with a picture and/or a description of what children should be doing could be used for different times of the day. Steps can also be listed to direct children to what they should be doing within certain time periods. This strategy is similar to the visual cues and self-monitoring supports discussed in Chapter 6.

- Work in journal
- Read a book to peer buddy
- Study spelling words
- Draw pictures for project

Figure 7-1
My Choices

Sustained Attention

Many of the selective attention supports also help sustain attention. Other supports for sustaining attention include providing many different activities for children to complete during an academic time. Teachers can create a list of four or five different ways students can work on their writing, reading, math, etc. For example, rather than having students write in a journal for 30 minutes, they can select from the choices a teacher has provided and choose to write for 10 minutes, interview a peer on their journal entry, select three new vocabulary words to use next time, and practice handwriting on a prepared worksheet. Children can also prioritize the order in which they want to do their work (see Figure 7-1 for an example).

Teachers should always observe children to ensure that they transition smoothly from one activity to the next. When children are seated together at tables, teachers can use peers to prompt students when they get off-task. Some children may need external reinforcement for staying on task and completing assignments and, in such cases, teachers can use positive reinforcement strategies (refer to Chapter 6) for increasing attention to tasks. Finally, Sydney Zentall (2005), an expert in the area of ADHD, recently conducted a review of research-based practices for selective and sustained attention problems. Figure 7-2 presents some additional examples from her review, which haven't already been discussed.

Problems Learning Information

Attention and memory problems often co-occur as children have to first attend to information before they can learn. In addition to the supports listed in the previous sections, children who struggle to work with information long enough to learn also need appropriate supports. Mastropieri and Scruggs (2004) have underscored the importance of making information more concrete for children who struggle to learn information. Tasks are more concrete for children when they include "external memories," such as lists of steps to follow or visual representations of the activity or steps in graphic organizers. For children who can handle the amount of content but forget or are not able to also process the steps, this support may be enough.

✓ Eliminate conversations during complex or new tasks

✓ Allow children to choose another place in the classroom to work if distracting conversations cannot be avoided

✓ Begin with clearly organized easier tasks that get increasingly more complex after exposure and practice opportunities have been provided

✓ Use goal setting and self-evaluation of performance

✓ Teach self-reinforcement (child provides own reinforcer such as a stamp or sticker) to increase task engagement and persistence (every five problems give yourself a sticker for trying)

✓ Use mirrors to increase attention to task

✓ Shorten instructions for tasks

✓ Use more variety and novelty later in tasks

✓ Use novelty and variety during rote and repetitive tasks

✓ Allow children to move or engage in an additional activity during the end of a task

✓ Include music in the background—especially during math

✓ Provide reinforcement at higher frequencies to support practice opportunities

✓ Provide immediate feedback

Figure 7-2
Supporting Attention to Tasks

Source: Summarized from "Theory- and Evidence-Based Strategies for Children with Attention Problems" by S. S. Zentall, 2005, *Psychology in the Schools, 42,* pp. 821–836.

However, some children may need the lesson to be modified. Teachers can provide children with outlines of the main ideas of lessons and a reduced amount of content to work with at the end of a lesson. Having children work with one paragraph rather than 2 pages, or 3 spelling words rather than 10, can help them work with the content to mastery. For other children, teachers may need to modify the assignment in other ways. For example, rather than filling in blanks, students can circle one of two choices.

For children who have problems securing information from their long-term memory, teachers can help them by providing links between prior knowledge and new information. For example, a teacher can outline what children already know about a particular topic and help them understand how the new information is connected to their prior knowledge. Effective teachers secure prior knowledge and help all children make connections when learning new information. However, for some children, teachers may need to devote more time to surfacing prior knowledge and they may also need to teach or reteach some prerequisite skills.

Essentially, teachers should never assume that children possess the skills needed for any assignment. Teachers need to specifically assess children's skills by asking them questions and observing them while completing practice opportunities. Children may have learned certain skills but they are not fluent (e.g., can answer questions in an area quickly and accurately). If fluency in one area is an expectation for the next unit or lesson, then this needs to be assessed. Additional practice may be needed to build fluency for some children. Maintaining knowledge over time and using knowledge in new settings are also challenging for many children. Additional supports for maintaining and generalizing knowledge are presented later in the chapter in the section on differentiated instruction.

Excessive Activity

Children with high levels of activity need to take more breaks and move more. One support that is appropriate for students with both attention problems and hyperactivity is to have students work on 10-minute tasks during independent seatwork and then have some activity in between tasks. For example, students can conference with their teacher regarding the three things they will be doing during their seatwork. These tasks can be written on index cards. A child can take one index card, complete the task at the child's seat or another appropriate area in the classroom, and then walk to the teacher's desk, turn in that card, and pick up the next card. These small activity breaks help children with activity needs, and the smaller tasks would help children with attention problems. Other supports for students with high levels of activity include the following:

- Give children classroom jobs that allow for movement, including passing out papers, collecting materials, taking notes to other teachers, and delivering the lunch count to the office. If a child is very active and also impulsive and the teacher has concerns about the child's ability to independently walk to the office and back, then allow another (very responsible) child to go as well.
- Allow children to stand at their desk while working on projects.
- Allow children to talk more and move around the classroom more.
- During group sharing time, include a small ongoing job for a child with hyperactivity, such as passing the bear to the next child or having a microphone to introduce the next child who will be sharing.
- Allow children to have quiet toys or objects to manipulate while working and listening. These do not distract children with hyperactivity; they help them meet their activity needs so they can attend to the task at hand.
- Never take away recess from a child with activity needs. To do this is like depriving a child from having lunch. As a last resort, recess may be modified to include children walking around the gym or a track.

Teachers need to be prepared to answer the "fairness" question from parents, children, or perhaps other students. Although children are sensitive to any display of favoritism on the part of the teacher, they also need to understand that everyone is unique and some children have different needs. Watching a teacher make a choice to be supportive of another child rather than punish the child for behaviors they have little control over can be seen by children as an act of kindness on the part of the teacher. Such supports help children appreciate diversity.

Impulsivity

Children are impulsive for different reasons (e.g., due to brain-based differences, limited experience with structured environments, or limited control over emotions). Regardless of why children act without thinking of consequences first, teachers need to teach children how to make more thoughtful choices and to provide children with substitute responses while waiting for assistance. Teachers need to be very proactive with impulsive children, especially when they are young. Once teachers have identified settings that are problematic for children, they can use precorrection (refer to Chapter 6) to highlight appropriate behavior.

Teachers also need to help children fill their downtime by including prompts of things they can do when they complete assigned tasks and activities. During class, these options can be drawn by the children or the teacher, laminated, and taped to children's desks. Two examples of such prompt cards were presented in Chapter 6. Additionally, teachers can provide visual supports for children to guide what they can do when they get stuck on an assignment (see Figure 7-3). Teachers can find an educational task that students like and need more practice doing while they wait for teacher assistance. The key educational support for children who are impulsive is to limit the amount of time they have to wait without having something else to do. Even waiting for 1 minute can be very problematic for children who are impulsive. Reviewing and acting on choices is a good activity even if children spend only 1 minute on the wait-time activity.

Teachers also need to provide supports for children who frequently interrupt the teacher. Sydney Zentall (2006) describes two supports for children with impulsive behavior. The first includes having a picture or drawing of a parking lot displayed in the classroom. When a child interrupts the teacher or wants to discuss something off the current topic, the teacher can put the idea in the parking lot to be shared at another time that day. Another strategy for interrupting in group settings is giving a child a number of objects (tokens, Popsicle sticks) to represent the number of times in a given activity the child is allowed to share "ideas."

✓ Stick a sticky note (where I am)
✓ Raise hand until teacher sees me
✓ Select from choices while waiting card

Choices on Index Card:

■ Ask a peer
■ Work on other problems
■ Draw in journal

Figure 7-3
Steps When I'm Stuck

Another problem time for children who are impulsive is recess. Children need support for coming up with alternative activities when they have to wait in line too long to play four square or tetherball. Children also need support when their play is interrupted (game ends, another person wants to play basketball with them, etc.). Teachers can review good choices with children before recess every day. For children who need a lot of support, a peer buddy can be assigned who reviews and supports good choices at recess.

Overall, the key behavioral supports for impulsivity are to proactively "get ahead" of problem behavior by reviewing expectations and to limit the amount of time children spend waiting.

Organization Problems

Supporting work habits that are more thoughtful and organized is critical for children in primary grades. By the fourth grade, many teachers spend little time teaching organizational skills and just expect children to be organized. However, children with organization problems need more instruction in this area to be successful in school. Supports for organization are divided into supports for object organization and supports for time organization.

Organization Object

For children who frequently lose materials or who leave at home things to be taken to school and vice versa, developing better object organization is essential. One support for object organization involves creating in-class spaces for placement of school materials and homework. Children should be taught rules and routines for material and completed homework placement. Pictures can be used for younger children to indicate where objects should be placed in the classroom. It is also beneficial for children to turn in homework at the very beginning of the school day (so there is less time to lose it).

Teachers also need to allocate time to teach organizational skills in class. Teachers should spend time teaching the steps involved in completing and returning homework. For older primary grade children, steps can include:

- Making a note of the assignment on a homework planning sheet.
- Making a note of additional materials that are needed for the completion of the assignment at the bottom of the planning sheet (e.g., a book, a ruler, a pencil, colored pencils, etc.).
- Making a checklist of things that need to be brought back to school.
- Creating a place for parent signatures on the checklist—one for homework completion and one for checking that needed materials (including homework) are in the backpack to be returned to school. This checklist can be in an assignment folder and include the following steps:
  ✓ Needed materials in backpack.
  ✓ Homework completed.

✓ Homework packed.
✓ Family member has checked the first three: _____
✓ Take backpack to classroom.
✓ Turn in homework.
✓ Have teacher sign: _____

Children can also use two different colors of assignment folders—one containing work to be taken home and another to indicate work to be brought back to school. Similarly, children can have an assignment folder with index cards paper-clipped to both sides of the folder—one with a checklist of things to do at home and the other to remind the student of work that needs to be taken home. Similar types of supports for object organization, which are appropriate for children in kindergarten and first grade, include creating backpacks made of construction paper and laminated with visual prompts representing what needs to go home and what needs to be brought back to school. For example, the backpack can have a picture of a book drawn on it and a note, which indicates that a child needs to take home a book to read for homework and to give a note to the child's family. The other side of the backpack can be a different color and include a picture of a school to indicate what children need to bring back to school. If the following day is pajama day, then a picture of pajamas could be drawn on the backpack. Teachers and children can draw on the laminated backpack together, at least at first, to make sure children understand the process and can decipher what the pictures mean. Variations of this strategy can include using stickers on sheets of paper or index cards to indicate objects that need to go home and those that need to be brought back to school the following day. These homework reminders should be in a prominent place in children's backpacks or pinned to the outside of their backpacks.

By supporting children's understanding of routines to support organization, teachers are laying the groundwork for helping children understand how to use more sophisticated organizational tools in the future. Too often, middle school youth with organization problems carry around their daily planners for an entire year without ever using them.

Other supports for homework include leaving homework assignments on an answering machine on a daily basis so families can call and check. Children can also have homework buddies who are assigned to call and make sure they have homework done and packed to return to school. Teachers can provide reinforcement for improvements in object organization. Teachers can also use contracts (refer to Chapter 6) and collaborate with children to determine goals for greater organization.

Time/Planning

As children move into the third and upper elementary grades, they have homework that is due at different times and larger projects that require planning. Children need to be taught how to plan for completing homework. In addition to planning for what to take home and to bring to school, children also need to be taught how to complete homework in a timely fashion and how to organize their time in school wisely. Teachers need to have a consistent schedule that they visually display and follow to help children understand the daily routine and times for different activities. Children can be taught to make lists of things they need to do in a time frame (hour, morning, afternoon) and cross off activities as they complete them. Children can also be allowed time for planning at the end of class (e.g., to make a list of things they need to do at home or the next day).

Similarly, older primary grade children can be allowed time at the end of class to get started on homework and then be supported in determining how long the homework will take them to complete at home. Children can assign "Times To Do" (TTD) on sticky notes and attach these to their homework assignments. For example, if a child started her math in class and completed half of the problems in 10 minutes, the child could write a TTD of 10 minutes on a sticky note and put it on her sheet. Children in the third grade may not have a clear understanding of time and fractions of assignments so teacher support will be needed in determining TTD (see Figure 7-4). Figure 7-4 includes an example of a planning sheet younger children can complete with different levels of teacher support.

Organizational supports for arranging content in clear visual displays are also beneficial for children with organizational problems. These types of graphic organizers are discussed later in this chapter. Another organizational area that is very important for children as they move through elementary grades is planning for larger projects. Teachers need to conduct task analyses of different projects and include each subtask on a planning sheet for children. Teachers can also conduct these types of analyses with older children to support their development of self-questioning strategies. Each step of the project can be listed on a planning sheet. Then children can be supported

Area	Part completed				Time To Do the Rest			
	All	Most	Some	None	5min	10min	15min	20min
	All	Most	Some	None	5min	10min	15min	20min
	All	Most	Some	None	5min	10min	15min	20min
	All	Most	Some	None	5min	10min	15min	20min

What needs to go home? Any materials needed from school?

■ _____

■ _____

■ _____

Plan, check off when packing backpack, have teacher
sign: _____

Figure 7-4
Homework Planning Sheet: Determining Homework Times To Do (TTD)

Step	Completion Date	Teacher/Student Initials
1.		
2.		
3.		
4.		
5.		

If I have a problem or do not meet my dates, I need to:
- Change my plan
- Meet with teacher
- Ask for help if I am stuck

Figure 7-5
Planning for a Project

in planning for each step of the project, setting dates for completing different tasks, and listing completion dates as they complete each part of the task. Figure 7-5 can be used to support children's planning for project completion.

Skill Deficits

As discussed in Chapter 5, it is very important to identify children's current knowledge in specific areas in order to determine their instructional needs. Teachers need to determine which skills are prerequisites for other skills and ensure children have mastered these skills. Curriculum standards can help teachers determine the prerequisite knowledge needed for different units (refer to Chapter 5).

For example, if children do not have an understanding of a mathematics concept needed for the next unit, then they need to be supported in learning this information. Some children need a little extra practice to strengthen particular skills to move forward in the curriculum. However, in other cases, they may be significantly behind their peers and need teachers to meet them where they are and provide modified assignments for them. Martin, in the case example at the beginning of this chapter, was not ready for the lesson. He needs some instruction and practice opportunities related to developing number sense. This conceptual understanding is the foundation for understanding mathematical operations (Gersten & Chard, 1999). Until he is supported in developing more sophisticated number sense, Martin will not be successful in the math curriculum. Therefore, Martin should be allowed to work on math problems that are at his level. For example, if other children are working on simple addition problems, Martin may be working on counting tangible objects (e.g., plastic cookies) and assigning quantities. In addition to determining appropriate levels for instruction, teachers must also be prepared to use research-based practices to increase children's opportunities to learn (Baxendell, 2003; Hall, 2005; Mercer & Mercer, 2005).

Using Research-Based Instructional Practices

The past four decades have yielded a significant amount of research on effective teaching. Research-based practices can be defined as those practices that enhance children's social and/or academic achievement (Lembke & Stormont, 2005; Meese, 2001). In this section, practices with substantial research support will be presented and include differentiated instruction, direct instruction, graphic organizers, questioning strategies, and student-mediated instruction.

Differentiated Instruction

According to Hall (2005),

> To differentiate instruction is to recognize students varying background knowledge, readiness, language, preferences in learning, interests, and to react responsively. . . . The intent of differentiating instruction is to maximize each student's growth and individual success by meeting each student where he or she is, and assisting in the learning process. (p. 1)

Teachers who differentiate instruction need to carefully plan for what specific children may need before, during, and after instruction to enhance their learning (see Figure 7-6). The characteristics of learners should be considered during differentiation. An example of how teachers can plan for diverse learning needs is presented in Table 7-1.

Differentiating instruction also includes attending to three factors related to teaching:

1. The content teachers will teach.
2. The instructional strategies or the process teachers use to teach the content.
3. The product or the way students demonstrate mastery of content (Hall, 2005; Tomlinson, 1999).

These three components will be addressed in a before-instruction, during-instruction, and after-instruction framework.

Before Instruction

Before instruction, teachers need to conduct a curriculum evaluation and determine how to organize their instruction accordingly. The general education curriculum should be evaluated to determine the specific content covered (Raymond, 2004). Specifically, teachers need to evaluate curricula for different content areas and assess whether the content and overall organization of the curricula are clear and inclusive. When curricula fall short on clarity and/or inclusiveness, teachers need to fill in the gaps. Questions that teachers can raise regarding curricula include the following:

- Are the goals and objectives clear?
- Do the goals and objectives serve as an organizing structure for different units within the curriculum?

Before Instruction:
- Evaluate the curriculum
- Determine support needs
- Determine teacher and student readiness
- Individualize curriculum for children

During Instruction:
- Secure prior knowledge
- Provide experiences to enrich or foster prior knowledge
- Focus on big ideas
- Minimize detail that is not important
- Connect content to real life
- Allow extensive practice
- Use games for rote material
- Use peer tutoring for building skills
- Ask questions to solicit understanding
- Secure understanding of material before children begin independent work

After Instruction:
- Reteach and provide more practice
- Teach strategies to increase active involvement with information
- Assign homework in another setting
- Plan for reviews to strengthen knowledge

Figure 7-6
Planning Sheet for Differentiating Instruction

Source: From Margo A. Mastropieri and Thomas E. Scruggs, *The Inclusive Classroom: Strategies for Effective Instruction,* 2nd Edition, © 2004. Adapted by permission of Pearson Education, Inc., Upper Saddle River, NJ.

- Is there a clear scope and sequence of skills?
- Are there assessments for prior knowledge?
- Are the content and activities developmentally appropriate?
- Is information presented on how to help children learn difficult concepts and skills?
- Are there clear connections to real-world applications that are appropriate for my children?
- Does the curriculum utilize technology?
- Does the curriculum provide detailed homework activities that are clearly explained for parents?

Table 7-1
Lesson Planning Sheet for Diverse Needs

Characteristics of Children*	Lesson Demands	Support Choice
Attention Problem	Attention throughout	<ul><li>Secure with cue</li><li>Vary voice and raise hand for important details</li><li>Ask for summary of main ideas for problem solving</li><li>Ask Jon and Jamie to summarize what to do in practice activity</li><li>Create list of steps with Jon and Jamie to complete during practice and homework</li></ul>
Memory Problem	Multiple steps for completing math problem	<ul><li>Provide Juan with card with steps to complete</li><li>Reduce number of steps Susanne has to follow by providing answers for some parts of problems</li></ul>
Impulsivity	Waiting for assistance during 20-minute seatwork time	<ul><li>Remind Jon and Jamie to use signals when need assistance</li><li>Remind Jon and Jamie of their lists of things to do while waiting for assistance</li></ul>
	Making careless errors	<ul><li>Have peers read answers or steps while Jon and Jamie correct practice problems</li></ul>
Activity Needs	Teacher-led instruction = 20 minutes, seatwork = 20 minutes	<ul><li>Allow Jamie to move toward the end of teacher-led instruction by having her pass out papers or other materials</li><li>Have Jon run the lunch count to the office before seatwork</li></ul>
Organization Problem	Homework involved	<ul><li>Complete homework sheets with Jamie, Jon, and Juan immediately following instruction</li><li>Have children pack materials needed to take home</li></ul>

*Main characteristics of children in class: attention problems, memory problems, impulsivity, activity, and organization problems.

- Extensive practice opportunities to master concepts before proceeding to the next skill.
- A representation of different cultural backgrounds and different learning needs.
- Opportunities for active student involvement.
- Information in writing that is at a level that matches the level of most students.
- Frequent and simple evaluation opportunities.
- Recommendations for how to make modifications for students.
- Materials that use student-mediated instructional strategies such as cooperative learning.
- Validity data to support the effectiveness of the curriculum.

Figure 7-7
Curriculum Considerations for Diverse Classrooms

Source: From *The Inclusive Classroom: Strategies for Effective Instruction,* 2nd Edition, by Margo A. Mastropieri and Thomas E. Scruggs, 2004, Upper Saddle River, NJ: Pearson Education. Copyright © 2004 by Pearson Education, Inc. Adapted by permission.

Mastropieri and Scruggs (2004) outlined additional curriculum considerations for classrooms with diverse learners (see Figure 7-7). Teachers need to use information obtained from their curriculum review to align their instruction for children. Specifically, teachers need to determine if they are going to have to modify the curriculum considerably and/or add supplementary information for all or some learners. The amount of consideration that teachers give to aligning the curriculum with instruction will often determine whether some children are successful. Further areas to consider in planning how to maximize children's success in learning the curriculum follow.

Children's interest in the content area. Teachers need to determine how interested their students are in specific content areas. Younger students tend to be interested in learning in general (Byrnes, 2001). However, as early as second and third grade, some children's interest begins to wane due to difficulty with the content area, which will be addressed next, or because the curriculum materials are boring. If the curriculum is not very strong in terms of organization and clarity (e.g., includes difficult vocabulary that detracts from the main ideas and the content of one unit isn't clearly connected to that of the next), then teachers will have to add supplementary information. Overall, many teachers will need to determine how they can make the curriculum clearer and more engaging for their students. Guiding questions could include the following:

- How can I achieve the curriculum goals in a way that children find engaging and meaningful?
- How can I include children's input in upcoming curriculum units?

- How can I connect the curriculum units to each other in such a way that children understand the importance and interrelationship of each unit?

- How can I use different instructional strategies (such as cooperative learning) to increase children's interest?

Children's readiness for the curriculum.   Teachers also need to determine if some children are not ready to participate in specific curriculum units. If children are not ready to participate due to gaps in their knowledge, then teachers need to use this information to provide more explicit instruction and practice in specific areas (Tomlinson, 2005). Teachers can also use graphic organizers and questioning strategies, presented later in this chapter, to help students who are struggling with specific skills (Bos & Vaughn, 2006; Mastropieri & Scruggs, 2004).

Some children may not be as ready for a curricular unit because of their limited experiences outside of school. For example, some third-grade children might have seen Europe, traveled throughout the United States, conducted simple science experiments at home, balanced the family checkbook, conducted research on the Internet to learn more about the koala bear, and created a PowerPoint presentation just for fun. However, other children have never used a computer outside of school and have never been outside of their hometown. Children's prior knowledge will definitely influence how quickly they come to attention for specific units and lessons. If teachers determine that there are great differences in their children's prior knowledge, then they need to create opportunities for children to build this knowledge. For example, if children have never left their inner-city neighborhood and a curricular area is addressing farms or oceans, then teachers can provide relevant experiences prior to beginning the unit. Such experiences may include:

- Videos or audiotapes to familiarize children with certain sounds.

- Activities to familiarize children with smells from specific areas (a visit to a landscaping business will be similar to smells from a farm and a humidifier can help create an ocean feeling).

- Online interviews done by children with other children who live on farms or near oceans.

- Devoting a corner of the classroom to a specific topic with many activities or representations to explore.

When selecting literature, teachers also need to consider their children's experiences. Thus, stories should have elements such as main events, settings, characters, problems, and resolutions that children can relate to. Even when literature is selected considering children's backgrounds, teachers will still need to support some children in making personal connections to different aspects of the stories. The following example illustrates how one teacher surfaced her children's prior knowledge and then made an instructional decision to add to their knowledge.

On one particular day, when the students had finished reading a Greek myth about a princess, Ms. Devereaux asked, "How would you describe the princess?" Her question was designed to elicit responses about the princess's character, but the first student to respond began with a physical description. "She was beautiful, with long, blond hair," said the student. Nowhere in the story was there a description that matched this response. "What makes you say that?" Ms. Devereaux asked. "Because that's the way princesses always are," the student replied. "I don't have long blond hair and neither does anyone else in here. Does that mean that none of us could be a princess?" Ms. Devereaux asked. The student and several others seemed resigned to the fact that that was the case. Ms. Devereaux feigned disbelief that they were unaware of any black princesses. Slowly, without fanfare, Ms. Devereaux walked to her bookshelf and selected a book, John Steptoe's *Mufaro's Beautiful Daughters* (1987) about two African sisters, one good and one evil. After reading the fourth graders the book, Ms. Devereaux asked how many students still believed that a princess had to have long blond hair. No one raised a hand.

Determine what to differentiate. Teachers will need to differentiate content and instruction based on children's needs. Teachers can plan to individualize content, instruction, and/or the way children demonstrate that they have learned key skills, concepts, principles, or facts (Tomlinson, 1999). Especially for young children, the need for teacher flexibility in what and how children learn is incredibly important. Teachers can use some of the following planning questions for differentiating instruction:

- Are there children who are not ready for this unit?
- What can I do to enhance children's readiness for the curriculum (including strengthening prior knowledge)?
- What individualized goals, activities, and outcomes need to be developed to enhance individual children's understanding of the unit? For example,
  - How can I provide individualized supports for some children to promote their understanding of key main ideas?
  - What additional practice opportunities will some children need (could include enrichment)?
  - How can I create flexibility for children within the unit so that children with different skills can engage in different learning activities?
  - How can I create multiple types of products or outcomes for children so that their strengths and interests can be harnessed?
  - How can I link multiple units together and create an overarching framework within these units?

Identify main ideas for units and lessons.   Teachers need to determine what they want all of their students to learn in a given unit. If the main ideas are clear to the teacher, then instruction can be designed to highlight these main ideas and minimize detail that is not as important. Teachers also need to plan to support children's mastery of the main ideas during instruction. Strategies that teachers can use to highlight main ideas are presented in Figure 7-8.

Many children will struggle with understanding the main ideas in different types of text. This is because main ideas often include abstract information that is not concretely communicated. Many children need support to assist them in developing the ability to both extract a main idea and provide supporting information. Strategies for supporting understanding main ideas include the following (Bos & Vaughn, 2006; Mastropieri & Scruggs, 2004; Meese, 2001; Mercer & Mercer, 2005):

- Show a series of pictures depicting a main idea and have children determine this idea. Having three pictures of a child involved in different sports would support a main idea of the child being athletic or liking sports. Having a child seen with three different cats would communicate the main idea that this child likes cats.

- Main ideas in pictures or written form begin at a literal level and move to involving more inferences as children are ready. When children struggle with inferential information, go back and use more literal examples and infuse questions to support inferences.

- Create sentence strips that communicate a main idea of a paragraph and supporting details. Read the paragraph to students and then have students arrange the strips. The strips can be read by the teacher and arranged in large-group instruction or children can work in diverse small groups (with readers of different levels).

- The teacher should always model think-alouds regarding the process of determining main ideas and connect supporting details to these broader ideas.

- Main ideas in text can be illustrated using specific analogies such as a table strategy. The table strategy, described by Meese (2001), includes describing the top of a table as the main idea and the legs as the supporting details. Tables can be drawn on sheets and copied for children to write or draw on directly.

- Older children who are independent readers can use the RAP strategy for determining main ideas while reading. RAP stands for Read a paragraph, Ask yourself what this paragraph was about, and Put the main idea and supporting information in their own words (Schumaker, Denton, & Deshler as cited in Meese, 2001).

Figure 7-8
Supporting Knowledge of Main Ideas

During Instruction

During instruction, teachers need to use research-based practices to present information. For all content areas, research-based practices that are appropriate for children who are struggling in the primary grades include direct instruction, cooperative learning, graphic organizers, and questioning strategies (Hall, 2005; Johnson & Johnson, 1986; Mastropieri & Scruggs, 2004; Meese, 2001; Zentall, 2005).

Regardless of the specific instructional strategy, lessons should always begin with the following:

- Securing children's attention
- A visual overview of the lesson for organization and clarity
- Surfacing prior knowledge in the area
- Connecting the content to the broader unit of the curriculum
- Supporting children in making connections to their own lives
- A review of behavioral expectations for proactive behavioral management

After instruction or activities related to surfacing the main ideas are provided, teachers need to ensure that children have sufficient practice opportunities. If direct instruction is used, children will have guided practice opportunities, and once they reach a level of mastery (80 to 90% of questions answered correctly), they will practice independently (Bos & Vaughn, 2006; Meese, 2001). When teachers use cooperative learning or other formats appropriate for the content (such as discovery learning for science content), the teacher must determine how children will receive the level of practice they need. Some children will quickly understand the main idea of the lesson. However, others will need more practice and more explicit support for learning the information. Teachers need to build these supports into the lesson.

Finally, teachers need to determine the assessment strategies they will use. How will children show that they have mastered the content? What are the big ideas that all children need to master before moving on to the next lesson? Such assessment strategies can include answering three questions, completing a probe to demonstrate mastery of a skill, or completion of another written product. Teachers can also consider giving children main idea questions and answer sheets to grade their answers. Children who struggle with the content can then ask for teacher or peer assistance in learning the material before moving onto the next lesson. In a classroom with a strong sense of community, children should feel safe saying, "I don't understand this."

After Instruction

The extension of learning in school to practicing at home is critical, especially as children get older. Children need to practice information to achieve higher levels of learning where they can apply and generalize knowledge to new settings (Bos & Vaughn, 2006; Raymond, 2004). To this end, teachers should determine what is developmentally appropriate in terms of the amount of homework and then collaborate with families to increase supervision of homework at home. Teachers should also be flexible if some families cannot supervise homework or if family members have time on the weekends but not during the week. Chapter 4 provides ideas regarding ways to accommodate children with limited or unique resources for homework assistance.

Children can also be provided with opportunities to practice prerequisite skills before learning new content. Thus, rather than securing prior knowledge, children would be practicing to strengthen their prior knowledge. Especially for math, additional independent practice right before new instruction would be beneficial for some children. If a teacher believes only a small group of children need this level of support, then this small group can be pulled to a table in the back while other children are working on something else.

Teachers also need to consider how they will support maintenance and generalization of content. Monthly reviews or assessments to ensure maintenance would be appropriate. If some children do not retain a high level of mastery of content (around 80–90% questions answered correctly), then they should be provided with more practice opportunities to strengthen their knowledge. For generalization, children can have goals for applying important skills across content areas. For example, children can have goals for handwriting, using correct spelling (as they move into third grade), and using new vocabulary words in their writing.

Overall, differentiated instruction should be guided by the following eight principles outlined by Tomlinson (1999):

1. The teacher is clear about what matters in subject matter.
2. The teacher understands, appreciates, and builds upon student differences.
3. Assessment and instruction are inseparable.
4. The teacher adjusts content, process, and product in response to student readiness, interests, and learning profiles.
5. All students participate in respectful work.
6. Students and teachers are collaborators in learning.
7. Goals of a differentiated classroom are maximum growth and individual success.
8. Flexibility is the hallmark of a differentiated classroom. (p. 48)

Direct Instruction

Direct or explicit instruction is particularly appropriate when children need more intense instruction with extensive feedback regarding students' progress. Direct instruction is a teacher-directed instructional strategy used to carefully plan, manage, and evaluate the effectiveness of instruction (Engelmann & Carnine, 1991; Hall, 2005; Meese, 2001; Wisconsin Policy Research Institute Report, 2001). A direct or explicit instruction lesson includes the following components (Gersten, Woodward, &

Darch, 1986; Hall, 2005; Lewis & Garrison-Harrell, 1999; Meese, 2001; Rosenshine & Stevens, 1986):

- Secure children's attention
- Review prior knowledge (*reteach if needed*)
- Preview main ideas of current lesson
- Provide explicit instruction on main ideas of lesson
- Model examples of main ideas
- Provide guided practice
- Provide independent practice if children were successful in guided practice
- Assess mastery and retention of content
- Provide homework

Direct instruction includes extensive monitoring of children's progress with fading levels of teacher support as children master information (from guided practice to independent practice). Many of these instructional components were described in the previous sections on differentiated instruction. Direct instruction is a unique instructional strategy that leaves little room for student error because of the ongoing interaction between children and teachers. In other more implicit types of approaches, children could be paying attention to details and not the main ideas or could be struggling to understand the connections between certain concepts. Therefore, explicit or direct instruction principles have been documented to be essential to use with learners who are vulnerable for failure (Adams, 2005; American Institutes for Research, 2005; Engelmann & Carnine, 1991; Hall, 2005). Teachers can access more information on direct instruction, direct instruction curricula, and additional research on direct instruction from the National Association for Direct Instruction website (www.adihome.org).

Strategies to Enhance Organization and Meaning

Graphic Organizers

Children benefit from having structure to help organize main ideas and to compare and contrast different information (Baxendell, 2003). "Graphic organizers help students see how ideas are organized within a text or concept. Learners can then apply this structure to their own ideas" (Baxendell, 2003, p. 47). Baxendell (2003) stressed that teachers should make sure graphic organizers are used consistently and creatively and arranged coherently. For consistent use, teachers should select a few types of graphic organizers and then plan specific routines for implementation. For example, teachers can always use a specific type of main idea and details chart for reading expository text and a specific type of story web for narrative text. For coherent use, teachers should emphasize big ideas, provide clear labels and illustrations of how main concepts are related, and choose a small

Graphic organizers help children understand the organization of main ideas and supporting details.

number of ideas to cover. Creative use of organizers can include using them with illustrations, student-mediated instruction, homework, and exam reviews (Baxendell, 2003).

Graphic organizers have typically been used for text enhancement so that children can comprehend more of what they read (Mastropieri & Scruggs, 2004). There are many types of graphic organizers. Story maps and webs are common in primary grades and are used to help orient students to familiar components of narrative text (stories). Story maps organize these components visually and may include written prompts and spaces for children to write the setting (main character, place, time), the goal of the character, the problem, the action, and the outcome (Meese, 2001; Mercer & Mercer, 2005). For younger children, teachers can use different terminology and complete a large story map on the board or another large space. As older children are able to read more independently, they can be provided with their own maps to use when reading a story.

Teachers can also use Venn diagrams to help children compare and contrast different information or concepts. A common use in primary grades involves comparing and contrasting elements in two stories. When completing Venn diagrams, children place what is different or unique in each story on the sides that do not overlap, and place the common features on the part that does overlap. Another type of organizer one first-grade teacher uses to help her children structure their stories is

Name Preston   Date 30 2002

Beginning   Middle   End

Figure 7-9
Preston's Organizer

a beginning-middle-ending graphic. Figure 7-9 presents a child's beginning-middle-ending organizer, and Figure 7-10 illustrates the story he generated using the organizer.

Other organizers include sequence charts, cause-and-effect diagrams, and main idea and detail charts. Sequence charts organize a sequence of main events and can

---

A first grader wrote a story about his dog from his beginning-middle-end graphic organizer. He then read this story to his teacher.

By Preston. Bo Ran Away. (next page)

I was petting him. His name was Bo. He is my dog. (next page)

He ran away. (next page)

We looked on the street. We can't find him. (next page)

All the police trying to catch him. There's a speech bubble that says "We're going to take Bo if you don't catch him. There's Bo. He's chewing a mailbox but we aren't by him. (next page)

We looked everywhere. Dog catcher mad because Bo ate stop sign. Dog catcher almost hit this kid but the kid made it. Dog catcher was going fast. (next page)

Bo's gone. We have to go home. (next page)

He. . . I can't read these words. I'll erase them. He came back. (next page)

I love Bo. You know what? He's a big baby! I'm going to add this! Watch me use finger spaces.

Figure 7-10
Preston's Story

Figure 7-10
Continued

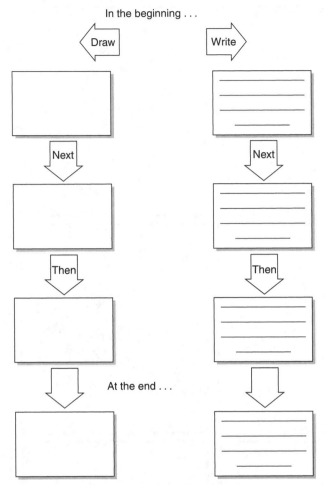

Figure 7-11
Plot Story Map

Source: From *Teaching Students with Learning Problems in the Inclusive Classroom* (p. 296), by Lisa Freund and Rebecca Rich, 2005, Upper Saddle River, NJ: Pearson Education. Copyright © 2005 by Pearson Education, Inc. Reprinted by permission.

be applied to narrative or expository text (Freund & Rich, 2005; see Figure 7-11). An example of a first-grade child's use of a sequence chart to generate a story about himself is provided in Figure 7-12. Figure 7-13 presents the first draft of the story the child generated from his sequence chart. Sequence charts can be used in creative ways to illustrate the steps in solving a math problem or completing a task (Baxendell, 2003). Figure 7-14 provides an example of how a sequence chart can be used with older children to support homework completion and organization.

Figure 7-12
Rio's Sequence Chart

163

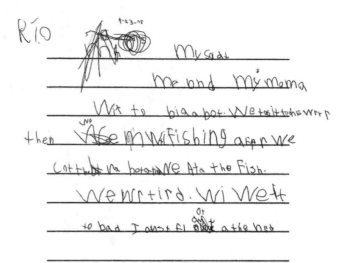

My Sailboat

Me and my mama went to buy a boat. We took it to the water. Then, we went fishing. After we caught the four fish we ate the fish. We were tired. We went to bed. I almost fell out of the bed.

Figure 7-13
Rio's Story

Cause-and-effect organizers display how different events lead to a main event and the outcomes of this event. Main idea and detail charts can be used to support reading and writing about any type of text, which makes this a very appealing strategy to use young children. Children can also use simple graphic organizers to organize information for with oral or written reports. For example, children can be provided with a web for creating an oral report about themselves. The teacher can provide a list of topics for their webs and children can then choose what they want to talk about.

Children can also be supported in generating their own topics to write about at the beginning of the year, which can be displayed in a graphic organizer to be referred back to over the course of the year. Figure 7-15 includes a list of potential topics a first grader wanted to write about. Figure 7-16 includes a list of topics a first-grade class generated as interesting topics for their future writing projects.

Questioning Strategies

Children can be taught to impose predictable questions to increase comprehension of material, to remind themselves of specific components to address in their writing, and to help them organize an approach to solving problems. There are many different

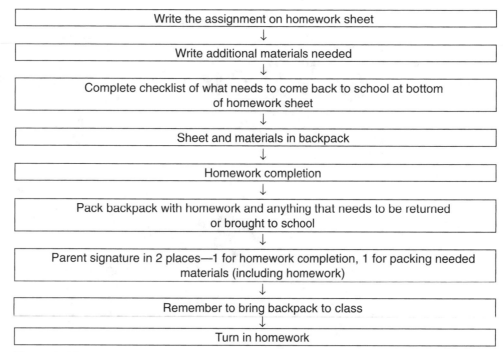

Write the assignment on homework sheet
↓

Write additional materials needed
↓

Complete checklist of what needs to come back to school at bottom of homework sheet
↓

Sheet and materials in backpack
↓

Homework completion
↓

Pack backpack with homework and anything that needs to be returned or brought to school
↓

Parent signature in 2 places—1 for homework completion, 1 for packing needed materials (including homework)
↓

Remember to bring backpack to class
↓

Turn in homework

Figure 7-14
Sequence Chart for Homework Completion

types of strategies across all content areas that have been supported by research. A few very versatile strategies for reading and writing, which are appropriate for primary grades, include the K-W-L strategy, the RAP strategy, think-alouds and questioning, and collaborative strategic reading. The K-W-L strategy supports approaching reading or researching an area with a purpose (Ogle, 1986). Children are taught to ask three questions related to a particular area—what they Know about a topic, what they Want to know, and what they Learned (Ogle, 1986). The RAP strategy is a questioning strategy that children can use for determining the main ideas in text (refer to Figure 7-8).

Many children need to have specific questions to impose on reading as they do not engage in questioning strategies independently. Children can be taught to predict what different stories will be about, to ask questions during reading, and to summarize main ideas and supporting details. Young children can be guided through this process with teacher think-alouds. Teachers can help children understand the process of reading for meaning when they stop often, summarize, support predictions, determine if predictions were accurate, and make meaningful connections (Vaughn & Klingner, 1999).

Collaborative strategic reading is a specific strategy for increasing comprehension of text through previewing information and making predictions, interacting with content during reading (monitoring for understanding and summarizing the main idea) and using self-questioning to help summarize the content.

I can write about...

NAME Alejandra

Figure 7-15
Alejandra's Topics to Write About

(Back of Page)

my dog	my family
a fish	my birthday cake
my piano	a mermaid
my house	fireworks
jump rope	my castle toy
pizza	a dolphin

Figure 7-15
Continued

Table 7-2 summarizes the three strategies utilized in collaborative strategic reading. These three phases are taught separately over a period of 2 to 3 weeks (Vaughn & Klingner, 1999). This strategy can be modified for children as young as third grade and has been documented to be very effective for children who underachieve in reading.

These reading strategies can also help students create written summaries of stories or information. The K-W-L format can be organized into a simple paragraph for first and second graders and as three paragraphs for third graders. The RAP and collaborative reading strategies can be used to form outlines for a written summary. Another example of an organizer that can be used for children in the third grade and above is provided in Figure 7-17. The Basic Reaction Frame can be used to provide structure for children who struggle in writing by having children respond to predictable statements (Mercer & Mercer, 2005).

As children move to upper elementary grades, there is more of an emphasis on the mechanical aspects of writing. Many children struggle in the area of spelling. If

Writing Ideas

my bike	ABC story
recess games	5 Expectations Safe Kind Respectful Peaceful Responsible
friends	a dream
weather	a wish
favorite sports	favorite book
animals	a vacation
teachers	a scary time
when I was a baby	toys

Figure 7-16
A Class-Generated List of Topics for Writing Projects

Table 7-2
Using Collaborative Strategic Reading

Reading Phase	Steps
Preview and Predict	■ Children are given 2–3 minutes to scan the reading selection, looking for key features and ideas in narrative or expository text.
	■ Children are told to think about what they know about this area (connections).
	■ Children are prompted to make predictions.
	■ Children are given 6 minutes to share their connections and to form predictions together.
Monitor During Reading	■ Teach students how to determine success and problems they are having when reading.
	■ Teach the Click and Clunk strategy: A click is something that the students really connect with and understand. A Clunk is the opposite. A clunk stops you quickly and interrupts your reading.
	■ Students are first taught to recognize clicks and clunks and then are taught how to "de-clunk."
	■ "De-clunking" strategies can be placed on a card (clunk card) to remind students of what to do when they get stuck reading.
	■ Students are also taught how to summarize main ideas using the "Get the Gist" strategy. Students create gist statements that include the most important points or elements (and no irrelevant details).
	■ Students can form gist statements in groups and determine the best gist statement. Groups can compare gist statements and vote on the best and discuss why a specific "gist" is the best for communicating the main idea.
Wrap Up	■ Students are taught to review the story or reading selection and answer specific questions. For younger students, question stems can be used to support higher-level questions, including comparing and contrasting elements of the selection.
	■ Students can wrap up in groups and form their own questions for other groups to answer regarding the selection. Teacher support is needed to make sure the questions are related to main ideas and not less important details.

Source: Summarized from "Teaching Reading Comprehension Through Collaborative Strategic Reading" by S. Vaughn and J. K. Klingner, 1999, *Intervention in School and Clinic, 34,* pp. 284–292.

Basic Reaction Frame

I learned some interesting facts about _____ from reading

this section. First,_____

_____

Second, _____

_____ .

Third, _____

_____ .

However, the most interesting thing I learned was _____

_____ .

Contrast Frame

Insects differ from spiders in several ways. First, insects, _____

_____ , while spiders _____ .

Second, insects, _____ , while

spiders _____ .

I think the easiest way to tell an insect from a spider is _____

_____ .

Figure 7-17

Basic Reaction Frame: A Strategy to Support Written Expression

Source: From *Teaching Students with Learning Problems,* 7th Edition (p. 330), by Cecil D. Mercer and Ann R. Mercer, 2005, Upper Saddle River, NJ: Pearson Education. Copyright © 2005 by Pearson Education, Inc. Reprinted by permission.

teachers spend 10 to 15 minutes a day and teach children specific ways to study their words, children's spelling can improve greatly (Fulk & Stormont-Spurgin, 1995). Some simple questioning strategies that have been documented to improve spelling include the following:

- **What do I know?** Give pretests to children to determine words they already know how to spell so they don't spend time studying these.

- **How many should I study?** Reduce the number of spelling words children are supposed to study at one time. Children can study two or three words until they have mastered the words.

- **How should I study?** Have children use a strategy for studying the words. An example is the three-step strategy where children "copy a word, write it from memory and compare the word with the correct word" (Fulk & Stormont-Spurgin, 1995, p. 18). Children can use small pieces of paper to copy a word and then turn the paper over while they write the word from memory on another piece of paper. Then they can turn over the model (correct spelling) and compare. If they misspelled the word, then they can complete the steps again.

- **Who should I study with?** Teachers can use peer tutoring to help children practice their spelling and receive immediate feedback from peers.

There are also specific questioning strategies that children can impose on math problems. Mercer and Mercer (2005) provide a mnemonic for students to use to help them remember both how to solve problems and how to relate numbers to quantities. The DRAW (Mercer & Mercer, 2005) stands for:

D—Discover the sign $(+, -, \times, \div)$

R—Read the problem ("four plus three equals blank")

A—Answer, or "DRAW" a conceptual representation of the problem, using lines and tallies, and check

W—Write the answer $(4 + 3 = 7)$ (p. 439)

Miller, Strawser, and Mercer (1996) provide another strategy for solving math word problems:

1. Read the problem.
2. What question is in the problem?
3. What do I have to do to answer the question?
   Add _____ Subtract _____
   Divide _____ Multiply _____
4. Is any information not needed?
5. Use numbers to write out problem.
6. Solve problem.
7. Check answer.

Overall, questioning strategies help children apply structure for solving math problems, determine main ideas and key points when reading, and attend to specific skills needed to complete a written product (editor role). These strategies are particularly important to teach young children who have difficulty creating their own strategies to support their learning.

Student-Mediated Instruction

Examples of student-mediated instruction include cooperative learning, peer tutoring, and self-management. Self-management was presented in Chapter 6 as it is also often used to support appropriate behavior. These child-mediated strategies are particularly beneficial for children who struggle with self-regulation and who need structured opportunities to manage their learning and behavior (e.g., Fulk & King, 2001; Hall, 2005; Tournaki & Criscitiello, 2003; Williams, 2003). In each of these instructional formats, children play a more active role in their learning. Peer-mediated instruction includes cooperative learning and peer tutoring. Hall (2005) identified four characteristics of peer-mediated instruction:

1. Students are assigned roles and specific responsibilities are taught.
2. Students serve as teachers for each other.
3. Teachers play an active role by monitoring and facilitating.
4. Students benefit academically and socially.

Cooperative Learning

In diverse classrooms, cooperative learning is an essential instructional strategy for building relationships among students (Johnson & Johnson, 1986). Teachers form cooperative learning groups by arranging small groups of students (typically 3 to 6) to work together on specific tasks (Hall, 2005). Cooperative learning differs from group work in that specific structures are set up to ensure accountability among members. In a cooperative learning environment, each member of the group is responsible for learning the information and for helping other group members learn the information. Specific elements of cooperative learning include (Johnson & Johnson, 1986; Johnson, Johnson, & Stanne, 2000):

- *Positive Interdependence.*   Students depend on each other to learn the content. Interdependence can be established in many ways, including having group members:
  1. Share resources.
  2. Wait for one member to finish a part of the activity before another can begin his/her part.
  3. Earn rewards contingent upon group completion of tasks.
  4. Have a specific job each is responsible for.
- *Individual Accountability.*   Each individual member is responsible for learning the material and meeting the learning goals.
- *Student Interactions.*   Students interact with each other and assist each other.
- *Group Processing.*   Students evaluate how they are doing in their groups. When students feel certain obstacles are present, which are inhibiting their progress, then they reflect on what to do. The teacher guides this process and helps students understand behaviors that help them learn and behaviors that detract from learning.

Cooperative learning, which includes the above basic elements and heterogeneous grouping, has extensive research support when used with primary grade children and does not include a competitive element (Hall, 2005). Questions teachers can ask when setting up cooperative learning groups for young children are presented in Figure 7-18.

1. Form groups: 3 to 6 children with diverse backgrounds
2. Teach social skills needed before starting
3. Select a form of group interdependence: ■ Material—share sheet/resources/create one product ■ Role—each member has a job ■ Task—one member has to finish, then another begins ■ Reward—each receives reward based on group performance ■ Other: _____
4. Choose assessment for individual accountability ■ Interview each member for "big ideas" ■ Give individual quizzes ■ Other: _____
5. Promote child interactions ■ Structure environment for interactions—face to face ■ Monitor groups—make sure everyone is participating ■ Other:_____
6. Support group processing ■ Help children monitor progress throughout ■ Give questions to ask (e.g., Is everyone working?) ■ Help solve problems among members ■ Provide words to help discuss social behaviors ■ Other: _____
7. Take notes throughout to inform future use ■ What worked well: ■ Changes for future:

Figure 7-18
Cooperative Learning Groups in Primary Grades Checklist

Peer Tutoring

Peer tutoring is another useful tool for working on specific academic skills because it includes multiple practice opportunities with immediate feedback. Peer tutoring has been documented to be effective with students who are vulnerable for failure (Fulk & King, 2001; Hall, 2005). Especially with young children, teachers will need to provide support for the tutor and tutee. When using peer tutoring, teachers will need to prepare materials for clear presentation (Bos & Vaughn, 2006). For example, teachers can have a flashcard with a letter on one side and, on the other side, a word that begins with that letter and the letter. Teachers can then prepare the tutor by providing specific instructions. For example, a teacher can support Taylor's tutor by providing the following instructions:

- Show Taylor the side of the card with the letter; you have the side with the letter and the word
- Ask Taylor, "What sound does this make?"
- Wait 5 seconds and ask again, "What sound does this make?"
- If she says the right sound say, "Correct"
- If she says the wrong sound say, "The right sound is a as in apple."
- Go to the next card.

The teacher stays with this pair, first modeling, then allowing tutors to practice and providing feedback until both master the process. Children of diverse abilities can be supported in learning skills even if the tutor is at a lower level. For example, if Taylor is a second grader working on letter–sound correspondence and Jon, her partner, is working on building vocabulary to use in writing, then Taylor can be supported in quizzing Jon. Taylor can have pictures representing words on her side of the flashcard and Jon can have the word on his side. He then says the word and Taylor matches the picture to the word. To further support Taylor in her tutoring role, the teacher should make sure Taylor knows all of the words.

Children can serve as tutors to help build academic skills.

Fulk and King (2001) provide an excellent summary of additional ways to use peer tutoring, including using peer coaches for oral reading practice with the less proficient peer serving as the coach first, which allows the child to hear the selection once before reading aloud.

Similarly, children of varying abilities can quiz each other in math or spelling. Even when a peer is slightly below or ahead in math skills, children can benefit from hearing the problems or words. There are multiple resources on peer tutoring at the website for the National Center for Accessing the Curriculum (www.cast.org). Again, research has strongly supported the role of peer tutoring in raising the achievement of children who are vulnerable for failure (Fuchs, Fuchs, Mathes, & Simmons, 1997; Fulk & King, 2001; Hall, 2005).

Case Examples Revisited

Recall the case examples at the beginning of this chapter. What supports would you put in place for their different characteristics? What intervention strategies would you use for each child? Table 7–3 provides a summary of Destiny's characteristics and possible assessment and intervention choices. Prepare a similar chart in which you outline your specific intervention plan for Martin or Jon.

Table 7-3
Assessment and Intervention Plan for Destiny

Characteristics	Supports/Intervention Choices
■ Limited reading vocabulary	■ Define vocabulary words with Destiny prior to writing tasks
■ Attention problems	■ Use cues to secure attention
	■ Have her restate directions and important main ideas for assignments
	■ Break assignments into smaller chunks and have her check in before beginning next part
■ One year behind in reading	■ Use assessment system linked to standards or a criterion-referenced measure to determine specific reading abilities
■ Difficulty generating ideas for written expression	■ Use graphic organizers to help generate ideas for writing tasks
	■ Allow tape recording of writing assignments to support literacy
■ Popular with peers, leader	■ Collaborate with second-grade teacher and have Destiny serve as a peer tutor for a child who is slightly below her reading ability (build fluency and self-esteem)

8

Fostering Resilience Through Partnerships

Long before children knock on the kindergarten door—during the crucial period from birth to age five when humans learn more than any other five-year period—forces have already been put in place that encourage some children to "shine" and fulfill their potential in school and life while other forces stunt the growth and development of children who have just as much potential. (Hodgkinson, 2003, p. 1)

Many children are vulnerable for failure due to early experiences in their home environments; others, however, are vulnerable due to conflicts between their characteristics and their school environments. Gloria Ladson-Billings (1994) describes one teacher's perspective (Patricia Hilliard) regarding the negative impact that school can have on children:

> I've taught all kinds of kids, rich ones, poor ones, white ones, black ones. Some of the smartest youngsters I've worked with have been right here in this community, but a lot of the time they don't believe in themselves. School saps the life out of them. You want to see intelligence walking around on two legs? Just go into a kindergarten class. They come to school with fresh faces, full of wonder. But by third grade you can see how badly school has beaten them down. You can really see it in the boys. I sometimes ask myself what it is we're doing to these children. (p. 89)

In Chapter 1, systems theory was used to provide a framework for understanding risk factors that create vulnerability for negative outcomes. This chapter will similarly apply systems theory components to explain how teachers and families can foster resilience in children (McWayne, Hampton, Fantuzzo, Cohen, & Sekino, 2004; O'Donnell et al., 2002; Pianta & Walsh, 1998; Shumow et al., 1999;

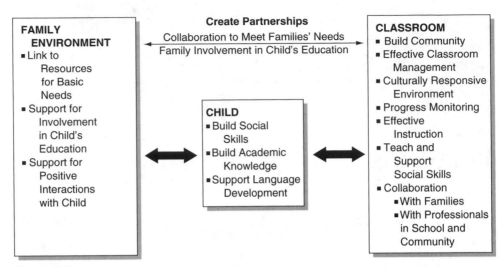

Figure 8-1
Characteristics and Interactions That Create and/or Sustain a Context for Resilience

Tiegerman-Farber & Radziewicz, 1998). Children who are vulnerable for failure typically have multiple characteristics in their lives that impede their success in school. The importance of collaboration with families to foster resilience in children cannot be overstated. This chapter will provide strategies to create contexts where families and professionals in schools can form partnerships to better meet the needs of children and their families (McWayne et al., 2004; see Figure 8-1).

Forming Partnerships with Families

By forming partnerships, teachers can develop an understanding of families' values and beliefs regarding education. After teachers develop partnerships with families, they can work to increase family involvement in children's learning and assist families in meeting their basic needs. These three areas are discussed in detail in the following sections. The following competencies are essential for forming partnerships with families (Esler, Godber, & Christenson, 2002; Ortiz & Flanagan, 2002; Overton, 2005; Turnbull et al., 2006):

- Demonstrating sensitivity to family composition
- Communicating respectfully and positively
- Demonstrating professional competence and commitment
- Establishing trust

Building partnerships with families is essential to supporting children.

Demonstrating Sensitivity to Families' Characteristics

To establish meaningful relationships with families, professionals need to first understand children's family compositions (Berger, 2000; Overton, 2005; Tiegerman-Farber & Radziewicz, 1998; Turnbull et al., 2006). Any biases professionals have related to a more "traditional" conceptualization of family (e.g., children and a mother and father) should be surfaced, acknowledged, and tempered. Families today can be defined as ". . . two or more people who regard themselves as a family and who carry out the functions that families typically perform" (Turnbull et al., 2006, p. 7). Thus many people may be part of children's families, including siblings, cousins, one or two parents, stepparents, aunts, uncles, grandparents, church members, friends, spiritual advisors, etc. The parents in a child's family may be a single parent, a mother and a father, two mothers, two fathers, grandparents, or an aunt.

Children may also be placed in foster care or temporary crisis care, and teachers need to understand the current family dynamics of their children. For example, some children may be in an emergency foster care placement whereas others may be awaiting adoption by their foster parents.

When teachers know more about the members of a child's family, they can involve those members in the child's educational activities (Tiegerman-Farber & Radziewicz, 1998). It is essential to include family members who support young children's daily care needs when they get home from school (older sister or brother, grandparent, aunt) in partnerships. However, research shows that many important family members are not solicited for such relationships. For example, many grandparents who are full-time caregivers for their grandchildren report that they have not received information to help them support their grandchildren's development and learning at home (Turnbull & Turnbull, 2001).

Communicating Respectfully and Positively

Effective parenting requires knowledge, energy, patience, problem solving, and life management skills (Berger, 2000). Yet, many parents face the demands of parenting with limited educational and economic resources. Parents may have stressors in their lives, such as divorce, unemployment, or impending homelessness if they do not pay their rent (Stormont, 2004). It is important that professionals understand each family's unique characteristics, consider any current demands they are facing, and then demonstrate respectful communication regarding children's needs related to school.

For example, understanding the different demands and challenges faced by single parents is important and often overlooked by educators (Epstein, 1987). Further, if a family is facing severe economic struggles and health concerns and a young child's homework is not being done or the child's reading log is not being signed by a family member, it is vital that educators see this concern in context. Collaborating with families to try to address their more pressing needs for security and well-being by establishing links with community agencies should be the first concern of teachers. During or after the process of trying to establish links with community agencies is completed, professionals should collaborate with families and explore options to support homework completion including (refer to Chapter 4):

- Completing homework in the classroom setting during designated times (not recess),
- Completing homework before or after school (at school),
- Completing homework with an extended family member on the weekends.

Being sensitive and respectful of families also requires listening to families' preferences and then honoring these preferences (Tiegerman-Farber & Radziewicz, 1998; Turnbull et al., 2006). What are their preferences regarding homework completion and/or supporting their children's learning at home? Perhaps they would like to have teachers demonstrate more flexibility so they could have their children complete the bulk of their homework on the weekends. Or perhaps they feel comfortable with the teacher involving the grandmother to supervise homework for a set time every day after school.

It is also important to understand families' cultural beliefs and how these impact educational partnerships (Barbour, Barbour, & Scully, 2005; Esler et al., 2002; Espinosa, 2005; Ortiz & Flanagan, 2002; Turnbull et al., 2006). For example, families from many cultural backgrounds may want to get to know an educator better before they begin to discuss personal matters (Barbour et al., 2005; Turnbull et al., 2006). Thus, if family members are slotted for a 10-minute meeting and feel pressure to "hurry up" and not get "off track," then opportunities for creating true partnerships will be missed. Ortiz and Flanagan (2002) also illustrate how cultural beliefs may affect teachers' relationships with families:

> For example, families from many Hispanic and Latino backgrounds typically view the school system as entirely capable of handling any and all situations with their children. They generally seek not to interfere and when called upon by the school or school staff, even for innocuous or positive reasons, Hispanic families are likely to suspect that they are actually being summoned because of problems with their child . . . the respect for educators within Hispanic families is quite large, and they are unlikely to provide much discussion or feedback . . .

Thus, it is important for educators to understand these beliefs and how they may impact relationships with families and to not misinterpret a family's value of respect for teachers as a sign of disinterest in their child's education.

In addition to being respectful, families also want professionals to use specific types of communication styles in their interactions (Berger, 2000; Ortiz & Flanagan, 2002; Swick, 1995; Turnbull et al., 2006). Families want professionals to be friendly, avoid jargon, be honest, and use ongoing communication systems that are family friendly and flexible (Barbour et al., 2005; Tiegerman-Farber & Radziewicz, 1998; Turnbull et al., 2006). Other ideas for communicating positively include the following (Berger, 2000; Esler et al., 2002; Swick, 1995; Turnbull et al., 2006):

- Determine families' preferences for communication and have multiple modes available including Internet based, weekly folders, phone calls, and tape-recorded messages on answering machines for weekly schedules and important topics.
- Share positive information with families regarding children's successes.
- Establish informal settings where information can be shared and relationships can be built, such as family nights, lunches, and weekend pancake breakfasts.
- Be flexible about where events take place.
- Follow up when families do not attend conferences, open houses and other events; problem solve with them how to overcome barriers.
- Have interpreters available.
- Listen to families' concerns, write them down, and restate them back to families. Follow up on their concerns as soon as possible.
- Stress that families' input is very important and create an environment where their input is valued.

First-grade teacher Deanna Bickel provides two examples of how simple positive communication helped open doors to partnerships with families.

I had a student last year who was not performing at grade level, and I was concerned about him. I scheduled a meeting to discuss my concerns. The principal attended, too, and the parent immediately questioned why the principal needed to sit in on this meeting. I showed the parent work samples and running record scores so she could see that her son was performing significantly below grade level. She was not very pleasant throughout the meeting. My main concern was that he had attended preschool and half-day kindergarten prior to attending first grade (rather than full-day kindergarten), which explained why he was performing below his peers. We met for approximately 45 minutes and the parent then walked around my room and questioned everything that was hanging up in my room—she wanted an explanation for things she saw in the room. She left the meeting by walking out of the room, not friendly at all. A few weeks passed, and I felt there was a lot of tension between us. Finally, one day I decided that I was going to share something positive with her about her son. So, when she picked him up from school I simply said to her, "I just want to tell you how polite your son is . . . and what a joy he is to have in class. He always says 'Please' and 'Thank You,' which I rarely hear from my other students." From that day on, she was very pleasant to me and helped her son every night on reading, writing and/or his math homework . . . which I always thanked her for.

At "Meet the Teacher Night" I had a parent tell me she was NOT going to pay the $4.00 I was asking all students to bring to purchase their Scholastic News Subscription for the year. The parent told me they didn't want it, and I told her how we use them every Friday in first grade. After the first full week of school, I put a note in the child's Friday Folder about what a great start she was off to in first grade. On Monday, the parent wrote back "I'll send her $4.00 on Tuesday. I received the child's money on Tuesday, too."

Demonstrating Professional Competence and Commitment

It is important for families to feel that teachers are committed to providing the best educational opportunities for their children. Teachers should hold high expectations for themselves and their students and believe it is their responsibility to make sure every child learns (Resnick & Glennan, 2002; Turnbull et al., 2006). Teachers can demonstrate their commitment and competence to families by (Fish, 2002; Resnick & Hall, 1998; Swick, 1995; Turnbull et al., 2006):

- Being lifelong learners who strive to improve their abilities
- Being good problem solvers

- Being a person who seems to "go above and beyond"
- Finding or creating new resources to meet identified needs
- Demonstrating strong collaborative skills with other professionals on their children's behalf
- Soliciting and being open to feedback from families
- Demonstrating flexibility regarding when, where, and how communication with families occurs
- Using setbacks as ways to learn
- Seeking input from families

When teachers are not committed to being lifelong learners and to improving their capacity to meet the needs of all learners, they often discourage parental input. "When teachers are uncertain or insecure about their own teaching skills, they fear criticism of how they do their job and discourage parent participation in their classrooms" (Barbour et al., 2005, p. 319).

Establishing Trust

Trust is the essential element for sustainable relationships between people (Esler et al., 2002; Fish, 2002; Ortiz & Flanagan, 2002; Turnbull et al., 2006). When families trust teachers, they feel that teachers are acting in the best interests of their children (Turnbull et al., 2006). It is important for professionals to understand that many families do not naturally trust educators and they should not assume that families believe that they are acting in their children's best interests. Many factors influence how challenging it may be to develop trust with families including family members' past experiences with administrators and teachers, and their experiences in society (Barbour et al., 2005; Turnbull et al., 2006).

When teachers demonstrate the characteristics discussed earlier in their interactions with families (e.g., sensitivity to families), and are also confidential and reliable, they are showing families that they are trustworthy (Turnbull et al., 2006). Carla Berg describes how she established trust with families by demonstrating several of these characteristics:

> I also try to establish trust by daily or frequent communication. I prefer to use daily communication notebooks. When language or literacy are challenges for families, I use the phone or picture communication, or I find a reliable translator. However we determine works best to communicate, I always share positive messages about their child. No matter how small the progress CELEBRATE! It may be a new experience for parents to get good news from school about their child. Parents appreciate that someone else values their child's good qualities. I also rely on open communication to share when I am uncertain, and I ask for their input, I respect their suggestions, and tell them about the outcomes of our combined efforts. (Turnbull et al., 2006, p. 169)

It is important to strive to develop trusting relationships to foster resilience in children and their families. When such partnerships are formed with families, teachers can also work to increase family involvement in education and to help link families to resources.

Increasing Family Involvement

"Every school will promote partnerships that will increase parent involvement and participation in promoting the social, emotional, and academic growth of children." (Goal 8 from Goals 2000: Educate America Act, Wiley, 1994). Clearly, this goal has not been met but efforts to disseminate the importance of family involvement for all children and ways to overcome potential barriers continue.

Parent involvement in school has a large impact on children's success. Parent involvement reduces the impact that living in at-risk neighborhoods has on children's academic performance and engagement in antisocial behaviors (O'Donnell et al., 2002; Shumow et al., 1999). Further, parents of kindergarten children who were more involved in supporting learning opportunities at home had children with greater abilities to self-regulate and to use appropriate social behavior in school and at home (McWayne et al., 2004). The reason for lesser involvement include children's challenging behavior and family stressors. Other factors that inhibit parental involvement in children's learning may include (McWayne et al., 2004):

- Work responsibilities
- Limited time to talk with other families
- Attention to household tasks

Finding ways for families to become more involved in school is important.

- Stress related to parenting
- Stress related to meeting their families' basic needs

Thus, oftentimes, the parents who are least involved are the ones who could use professional support the most. Given the importance of families in supporting children's education and development, it is vital that educators take the initiative to increase family involvement (Esler et al., 2002). Most families want to be involved in supporting their children's education and feel a level of stress when they do not have time to balance all of their responsibilities (McWayne et al., 2004). Teachers can help families overcome barriers to involvement.

There are different types of family involvement and different ways that professionals can foster involvement (Epstein, 1987, 1998; Landsverk, 1995; Swick, 1995; Turnbull et al., 2006). According to Epstein (1991, 1995), families and educational professionals can form partnerships to enhance children's development and learning in the following areas:

- Parenting
- Learning at home
- Home–school communication
- School involvement
- Decision making
- Community connections

Communicating positively has already been addressed, and securing community resources is addressed later in the chapter. The next section will further expand on the remaining opportunities for involvement, including support for parenting, learning at home, and involvement in classroom or school activities. Ways to involve parents in decision making will be addressed within the context of the other involvement opportunities.

Support Parenting

Of all the family characteristics that are linked to children's vulnerability for failure, negative parenting practices is the most significant (Rutter, 2000). Resilient children often have families who utilize effective parenting strategies, such as providing consistent routines and rules in the context of a warm, nurturing, and encouraging environment. Moreover, resilient children are often provided support to help them manage developmental challenges (Bauman, 2002).

Parents who use ineffective parenting strategies may not understand their children's behavior within a developmental context (Horning & Rouse, 2002). Thus, without an understanding of how long 5-year-olds can sit and attend, parents may have unrealistic expectations for their children, which may lead to punitive or harsh punishment. Parents may also not be aware of the countless environmental influences on children's behavior, including their own parenting behaviors (Horning & Rouse, 2002).

For example, parents may not understand the importance of setting reasonable expectations and rules and then being consistent in enforcing the rules. As an educator, it is important to understand the need to provide parents with information on children's development and the challenges that children face at specific ages. Parents can also be provided with information to foster supportive parenting practices (Berger, 2000; Horning & Rouse, 2002).

Schools can directly involve families in determining their needs for information by conducting needs assessments (Berger, 2000). Information on the greatest concerns or needs for parents can be obtained through surveys, interviews, or in small-group discussions. Topics of interest can also be obtained through (Berger, 2000):

- *Brainstorming* ideas and then listing the most interesting topics. If parents are having difficulty thinking of ideas, they can be provided with specific prompts such as "One problem I have at home with my child is . . ."
- *Annoyance tests* can be used to determine areas that parents are most interested in learning more about. Essentially, with or without prompts, parents share the behaviors of their children that annoy them the most.
- *Understanding community and school resources* may also be of great interest to parents.

Topics of interest may include how to:

- Get children to do chores or their homework
- Resolve conflicts between siblings
- Support children's development
- Deal with teasing
- Support or establish routines

Once topics are targeted, schools should organize their resources, solicit professionals to work with parent groups, and help families overcome barriers to participation.

Support Learning and Development at Home

There are many activities families can utilize to support their children's learning at home. Most families who are asked by teachers to support their children's homework comply (Epstein, 1987). Teachers need to reach out and try to involve *all* families (Epstein, 1986; Landsverk, 1995). When teachers put forth the initiative and sustained effort to encourage family involvement, families become more involved in different activities, including reading aloud to children, signing children's homework, taking children to the library, and visiting the classroom (Epstein, 1986). Parents overwhelmingly report that they believe home involvement in children's education is important and desire teacher support in understanding how they could help their children at home (Epstein, 1986, 1987).

Especially for young children, extending school activities to home can begin with simple activities. Teachers may assign a home activity that includes children sharing information about their school day (Epstein, 1986; McWayne et al., 2004). Teachers can support children in providing more specifics by having time at the end of the day to reflect on their day. For example, during the last 15 minutes of school, children can draw or write answers to the following written prompts (with pictures for early grades):

- My favorite part of the day was:
  _____ :-)
- Something I thought was hard today was:
  _____ :-(
- At recess I played with:
  _____ :-)

Occasionally, teachers can include a parent interview where parents ask children these questions. It is also important for teachers to involve families in other activities. Families should be involved in determining their role for supporting homework and other educational activities (Landsverk, 1995). Teachers could interview parents over the phone, in person, or send home a written survey to determine activities that the family typically engages in, challenges related to completing educational activities at home, and their opinions regarding homework (see Figure 8-2).

By understanding families better, teachers can design appropriate educational activities that could be used in a natural context, which is especially appropriate for young children (Riley, 1994). For example, if families indicate that they often go to the store, then language and literacy activities could be linked to the store. If a family with a kindergarten-aged child frequently goes on walks and to the park, assigned activities may include picking out objects with different colors or shapes, counting objects, or drawing a picture at home to represent the activity.

Children could also practice social goals and expectations in all contexts and teachers could extend working on social behavior to the home setting. For example, teachers could indicate a specific skill children are working on (e.g., finding something to do while waiting, keeping cool when upset, asking politely for help) and describe how to structure the home and community environments to be supportive of this skill. An example of how a teacher could support this collaboration is provided in Figure 8-3. This form would need to be individualized by inserting appropriate skills and times when families could be asked to work on skills (see examples in Figures 8-4 and 8-5). A discussion with families about why working on such social behaviors is important is a vital component of extending support for social development at home. Teachers can share developmental struggles that children of specific ages face and common social problems for a given age. This can help families see their children's behavior within a developmental context. Information can also be provided in weekly folders on ways families can support their children's education.

Home Learning: We like to do the following together:

- Go to the library
- Go to parks
- Take walks
- Go to the store
- Visit friends and relatives
- Read books
- Sing
- Go to the mall
- Listen to music
- Watch TV
- Play video games
- Find information on Internet
- _____
- _____

If home learning activities were connected to the types of things you like to do together, would that make "homework" easier?

- Yes
- No

What are some challenges that you have related to your child's homework?

- None
- Directions are not clear
- Time
- Child forgets to tell me
- Don't believe children this young should have homework
- Other: _____

How much homework do you think is appropriate for your child:

- 30 minutes a day
- 20 minutes a day
- 10 minutes a day
- 5 minutes a day
- 10 to 15 minutes a few times a week
- None

Figure 8-2
Survey on Parents' Opinions of Homework

Dear family of _____

You child is working on: _____

The specific behaviors related to this skill include:

Please work on this skill when you _____

At school, I do the following when working with your child:

- **Remind** him/her of what he should do—see above.
- **Watch** his/her behavior.
- **Remind** of what he/she should be doing if he/she makes a mistake.
- **Praise** him/her when he/she uses the skill correctly!
- **Understand** that this is something that requires teaching and support just like academics.

Figure 8-3

Homework on Social Behavior—General Format

Dear family of **De Quan**

You child is working on: ***Asking for help***

The specific behaviors related to this skill include:

- Understanding when he needs help (can't complete a problem, gets stuck when writing or reading, when doing chores)
- Keeping cool (calm)
- Thinking of who to ask for help (who is not busy and can help)
- Asking for help with kind words
- Saying "thank-you"

Please work on this skill when you are home and he is working on chores or on his homework

At school, I do the following when working with your child:

- **Remind** him of what he should do—see above.
- **Watch** his behavior.
- **Remind** of what he should be doing if he makes a mistake.
- **Praise** him when he uses the skill correctly!
- **Understand** that this is something that requires teaching and support just like academics.

Figure 8-4

Homework for Social Behavior—De Quan's

Dear family of **Rebecca**

You child is working on: ***Walking (instead of running)***

The specific behaviors related to this skill include:

- Understanding when she needs to walk
- Keeping feet on ground
- Walking at a slow and steady speed

Please work on this skill when you are at a store or anywhere you would like your child to consistently walk.

At school, I do the following when working with your child:

- **Remind** her of what she should do—see above.
- **Watch** her behavior.
- **Remind** of what she should be doing if she makes a mistake.
- **Praise** her when she uses the skill correctly!
- **Understand** that this is something that requires teaching and support just like academics.

Figure 8-5
Homework for Social Behavior—Rebecca's

Involvement in School

Families also need to be supported in being more involved in the school setting. Given different past experiences with school, some parents may be more or less inclined to sign up for different activities and events (Barbour et al., 2005). Other parents may have significant barriers that impede their ability to participate, even though they want to be more involved. Teachers should be creative and involve all families who desire involvement and attempt to involve those who do not want to be involved. Figure 8-6 lists multiple options for family involvement and potential barriers to involvement. By understanding more specific influences on involvement and the ways in which families would like to be involved, teachers can work to involve more families and remove as many barriers as possible.

Assisting in Meeting Basic Needs

All families struggle to meet their needs; however, when family contexts include stressors, the family's ability to meet the needs of all members may be compromised (Turnbull et al., 2006). Educational professionals need to increase their understanding of the various demands on families today and their ability to assist families. Families try to meet the needs of their members in various ways. The most important

---

I would like to be involved in my child's school in the following ways:

School Fund-Raising:
- Making something to be sold
- Coming up with some ideas for future fund-raising
- Giving some of my time to raise funds
- Coming to school to participate in activities

Classroom Activities:
- Helping supervise a class party
- Coming to hear project presentations
- Making something for a class party
- Visiting child at lunch
- Sharing with class (job, interest area, culture)
- Helping on special days (read-a-thon, etc.)

Potential Problems I May Have Include:
- Transportation
- Getting off work
- Child care
- Financial
- Time

Figure 8-6
Ways for Family Members to Be Involved

need that families fulfill for their members is sharing affection and demonstrating unconditional love (Turnbull et al., 2006). However, many factors can create a context for negative interactions in families. Teachers can encourage affection toward children through sharing positive communication about children and designing homework activities that are sensitive to current family dynamics.

Educational professionals can also support more positive family interactions by assisting families in meeting other basic needs. Many families struggle financially and work hard to secure things that other people take for granted, such as housing, food, health care, school supplies, clothing, education, and employment. School professionals, including teachers, should strive to link families with community resources (Fowler & Corley, 1996; Turnbull et al., 2006). Educators can make a list of support services available in the community and then support the establishment of a family support person, team, or family center to disseminate this information and link families with resources (Fowler & Corley, 1996). Table 8-1 provides an example of a list of community resources available to support families. Some communities will be very limited in resources they could provide to families, and schools should problem solve ways that they could be involved in providing more resources to support families by sponsoring food drives, clothing drives, fund-raisers, etc.

Table 8-1
Community Resources Available to Meet Families' Needs

Family Need	Community Resources
Economics	Salvation Army
	Special utility fund
	Social Security office
	Volunteer support center
	Place of worship
	Local food bank
Health Care	Local community center
	Medicaid
	Physicians with sliding pay scale
	Dental care support
Continuing Education	Local community college
	High school with day-care center for teenage parents
	Online support possibilities offered through library
	Adult literacy programs
Employment	Temporary employment agency
	Community job counselors
	Public library assistance for accessing information about jobs
	School postings for employment possibilities, including recess monitors and instructional aides
Parenting Stress	Local crisis centers for children
	Parents' day- or night-out programs offering free respite
	Easter Seals—Child care at free or reduced cost
	Parent support group

Note: This is not an exhaustive list of resources. This is an example of the type of information that schools would collate.

After professionals collaborate and determine resources available in their community to meet families' basic needs, they need to develop contact information sheets. Where appropriate, these sheets should be available in multiple languages. The contact information should include specifics about the agency, the types of

Community Agency:
_____

Services Provided:

Times of Operation:

Who to Contact:

Must Meet the Following Criteria to Qualify:

Figure 8-7
Community Resource Information Sheet

services provided, times of operation, person to contact, and any criteria used to determine if families qualify (see Figure 8-7). Once this information is obtained and shared with families, professionals should also determine if there are any barriers to accessing the services. Professionals may need to assist families in overcoming barriers to securing resources by:

- Having interpreters available.

- Assisting in paperwork and time frames to complete paperwork. Often one mistake can cause significant delays in receiving services or financial support. For some families, this can mean losing their housing.

- Locating resources available in the community to assist with child care, clothing, transportation and other barriers to securing employment and continued education.

Summary

Especially when children are facing conditions that create vulnerability for failure, families and teachers need to work together to support resilience in children. Families and teachers should support children's growth in positive environments filled with encouragement and warmth. Teachers need to form partnerships with families to be able to increase their involvement in supporting their children's development and learning at home.

Furthermore, as discussed in this text, teachers need to use effective teaching practices to build community, manage the classroom, be culturally responsive, monitor progress, support social development, and support academic development (refer to Figure 8-1). According to Resnick and Hall, we need to "honor every child's educational right to expert instruction . . ." (1998, p. 108). By utilizing practices that create a context for success, teachers can play a large role in supporting resilience in children (Bauman, 2002; Resnick, 1995).

References

Abedi, J. (2003). *Impact of student language background on content-based performance: Analyses of extant data (CSE Report)*. Los Angeles: National Center for Research on Evaluation, Standards, and Student Testing.

Adams, J. B. (2005). What makes the grade? Faculty and student perceptions. *Teaching of Psychology, 32*(1), 21–24.

Adelman, H. S., & Taylor, L. (1993). *Learning problems & learning disabilities: Moving forward*. Pacific Grove, CA: Brooks/Cole Publishing.

Airasian, P. W. (1996). *Assessment in the classroom*. New York: McGraw-Hill.

Alberto, P., & Troutman, A. C. (2003). *Applied behavior analysis for teachers* (6th ed.). Upper Saddle River, NJ: Merrill/Prentice Hall.

Alexandrin, J. R. (2003). Using continuous, constructive, classroom evaluations. *Teaching Exceptional Children, 36,* 52–57.

American Institute for Research. (2005). *An educator's guide to school-wide reform*. Arlington, VA: Educational Research Service.

American Psychological Association. (2000). *Diagnostic and statistical manual of mental disorders* (text revision). Washington, DC: Author.

Arnold, D. H. (1997). Co-occurrence of externalizing behavior problems and emergent academic difficulties in young high-risk boys: A preliminary evaluation of patterns and mechanisms. *Journal of Applied Developmental Psychology, 18,* 317–330.

Barbour, C., Barbour, N. H., & Scully, P. A. (2005). *Families, schools and communities: Building partnerships for educating children* (3rd ed.). Upper Saddle River, NJ: Merrill/Prentice Hall.

Barkley, R. (1995). *Taking charge of ADHD: The complete authoritative guide for parents*. New York: The Guilford Press.

Barkley, R. (1998). *Attention-deficit hyperactivity disorder: A handbook for diagnosis and treatment* (2nd ed.). New York: The Guilford Press.

Bass, J. L., Brennan, P., Mehta, K. A., & Kodzis, S. (1990). Pediatric problems in a suburban shelter for homeless families. *Pediatrics, 85*(1), 33–38.

Bassuk, E. L., & Rosenberg, L. (1988). Why does family homelessness occur: A case-control study. *American Journal of Public Health, 78*(7), 783–788.

Bauman, S. S. M. (2002). Fostering resilience in children. In C. L. Juntunen & D. R. Atkinson (Eds.), *Counseling across the lifespan: Prevention and treatment* (pp. 41–55). Thousand Oaks, CA: Sage Publications.

Baxendell, B. W. (2003). Consistent, coherent, creative: The 3 C's of graphic organizers. *Teaching Exceptional Children, 35*(3), 46–53.

Belfiore, P. J., Auld, R., & Lee, D. L. (2005). The disconnect of poor-urban education: Equal access and a pedagogy of risk taking. *Psychology in the Schools, 42*(8), 855–863.

Bello, M., Fajet, W., Shaver, A. N., Toombs, A. K., & Schumm, J. S. (2003). Basal readers and English language learners: A content analysis study. *Reading Research and Instruction, 42*(2), 1–15.

Belsito, L., Ryan, B. A., & Brophy, K. (2005). Using behavioral and academic indicators in the classroom to screen for at-risk status. *Psychology in the Schools, 42*(2), 151–158.

Berger, E. H. (2000). *Parents as partners in education: Families and schools working together* (5th ed.). Upper Saddle River, NJ: Merrill/Prentice Hall.

Bloomquist, M. L., August, G. J., Cohen, C., Doyle, A., & Everhart, K. (1997). Social problem solving in hyperactive-aggressive children: How and what they think in conditions of automatic and controlled processing. *Journal of Clinical Child Psychology, 26*(2), 172–180.

Bos, C. S., & Vaughn, S. (2006). Strategies for teaching students with learning and behavior problems (6th ed.). Boston: Allyn and Bacon.

Bredekamp, S., & Copple, C. (Eds.). (1997). *Developmentally appropriate practice in early childhood programs* (Rev. ed.). Washington, DC: National Association for the Education of Young Children.

Bronfenbrenner, U. (1979). *The ecology of human development: Experiments by nature and design.* Cambridge, MA: Harvard University Press.

Bronfenbrenner, U. (1989). Ecological systems theory. In R. Vasta (Ed.), *Annals of child development: Vol. 6. Six theories of child development. Revised formulations and current issues* (pp. 187–251). Greenwich, CT: Jai Press.

Bronfenbrenner, U., & Mahoney, M. A. (Eds.). (1975). *Influences on human development.* Hinsdale, IL: Holt Rinehart and Winston.

Burg, M. A. (1994). Health problems of sheltered homeless women and their dependent children. *Health & Social Work, 19*(2), 125–131.

Byrnes, J. P. (1996). *Cognitive development and learning in instructional contexts.* Needham Heights, MA: Allyn and Bacon.

Byrnes, J. P. (2001). *Cognitive development and learning in instructional contexts* (2nd ed.). Boston: Allyn and Bacon.

California Department of Education. (2005). *Academic performance index.* Sacramento, CA: Author.

Campbell, S. B. (1995). Behavior problems in preschool children: A review of recent research. *Journal of Child Psychology and Psychiatry, 36*(1), 113–149.

Campbell, S. B. (1998). Developmental perspectives. In T. H. Ollendick & M. Hersen (Eds.), *Handbook of child psychopathology* (3rd ed., pp. 3–35). New York: Plenum Press.

Campbell, S. B., & Ewing, L. J. (1990). Follow-up of hard-to-manage preschoolers: Adjustment at age 9 and predictors of continuing symptoms. *Journal of Child Psychology & Psychiatry & Allied Disciplines, 31,* 871–889.

Campbell, S. B., Pierce, E. W., March, C. L., Ewing, L. J., & Szumowski, E. K. (1994). Hard-to-manage preschool boys: Symptomatic behavior across contexts and time. *Child Development, 65,* 836–851.

Capuzzi, D., & Gross, D. R. (2004). Defining youth at risk. In D. Capuzzi & D. R. Gross (Eds.), *Youth at risk: A prevention resource for counselors, teachers, and parents* (4th ed., pp. 3–19). Alexandria, VA: American Counseling Association.

Capuzzi, D., & Gross, D. R. (2006). *Youth at risk: A prevention resource for counselors, teachers, and parents* (4th ed.). Upper Saddle River, NJ: Merrill/ Prentice Hall.

Choate, J. S., Enright, B. E., Miller, L. J., Poteet, J. A., & Rakes, T. A. (1995). *Curriculum-based assessment and programming* (3rd ed.). Boston: Allyn and Bacon.

Cohen, L., & Spenciner, L. J. (2005). *Teaching students with mild and moderate disabilities: Research-based practices.* Upper Saddle River, NJ: Merrill/ Prentice Hall.

Coie, J. D., & Dodge, K. A. (1988). Multiple sources of data on social behavior and social status in the school: A cross-age comparison. *Child Development, 59,* 815–829.

Colvin, G., Kameenui, E., & Sugai, G. (1994). Reconceptualizing behavior management and schoolwide discipline in general education. *Education and Treatment of Children, 16,* 361–381.

Correa, V. I., Jones, H. A., Thomas, C. C., & Morsink, C. V. (2005). *Interactive teaching: Enhancing programs for students with special needs* (4th ed.). Upper Saddle River, NJ: Merrill/Prentice Hall.

Cunningham, C. E., & Siegel, L. S. (1987). The peer interactions of normal and attention deficit disordered boys during free play, cooperative task, and simulated classroom situations. *Journal of Abnormal Child Psychology, 15,* 247–268.

Dail, P. W. (1993). Homelessness in America: Involuntary family migration. *Marriage & Family Review, 19,* 75.

Dalton, J., & Watson, M. (1997). *Among friends: Classrooms where caring and learning prevail.* Oakland, CA: Developmental Studies Center.

Deno, S. L. (1985). Curriculum-based measurement: The emerging alternative. *Exceptional Children, 52,* 219-232.

Derman-Sparks, L. (2003a). Markers of multicultural/antibias education. In C. Copple (Ed.), *A world of difference: Readings on teaching young children in a diverse society* (pp. 171-172). Washington, DC: National Association for the Education of Young Children.

Derman-Sparks, L. (2003b). Developing antibias, multicultural curriculum. In C. Copple (Ed.), *A world of difference: Readings on teaching young children in a diverse society* (pp. 173-178). Washington, DC: National Association for the Education of Young Children.

Derman-Sparks, L., & The A.B.C. Task Force (2003). Creating an anitbias environment through visual materials. In C. Copple (Ed.), *A world of difference: Readings on teaching young children in a diverse society* (p. 45). Washington, DC: National Association for the Education of Young Children.

Diener, M. B., & Milich, R. (1997). Effects of positive feedback on the social interactions of boys with attention problems. *Journal of Clinical Child Psychology, 26*(3), 256-265.

Eber, L., Sugai, G., Smith, C. R., & Scott, T. M. (2002). Wraparound and positive behavior interventions and supports in the schools. *Journal of Emotional & Behavioral Disorders, 10*(3), 171-180.

Education Development Center. (2003). *Ubiquitous learning: How technology is expanding learning opportunities in U. S. homes, schools, and communities.* Newton, MA: Author.

Eliason, C. F., & Jenkins, L. T. (1999). *A practical guide to early childhood curriculum* (6th ed.). Upper Saddle River, NJ: Merrill/Prentice Hall.

Engelmann, S., & Carnine, D. (1991). *Theory of instruction: Principles and applications.* Eugene, OR: ADI Press.

Epstein, A. S. (1998). Is the High/Scope® educational approach compatible with the revised Head Start performance standards? *High/Scope Resource, 17*(2), 1, 8-11.

Epstein, J. L. (1986). Parents' reactions to teacher practices of parent involvement. *The Elementary School Journal, 86*(3), 277-294.

Epstein, J. L. (1987). Parent involvement: What research says to administrators. *Education and Urban Society, 19*(2),119-136.

Epstein, J. L. (1991, January). Paths to partnership: What we can learn from federal, state, district, and school initiatives. *Phi Delta Kappan, 72*(5), 344-349.

Epstein, J. L. (1995, May). School/family/community partnership: Caring for the children we share. *Phi Delta Kappan, 76*(9), 701-712.

Esler, A. N., Godber, Y., & Christenson, S. L. (2002). *Best practices in supporting home-school collaboration.* In A. Thomas & J. Grimes (Series Eds.), *Best practices in school psychology IV, Vol. 1* (pp. 389-411). Bethesda, MD: National Association of School Psychologists.

Espinosa, L. M. (2005). Curriculum and assessment considerations for young children from culturally, linguistically, and economically diverse backgrounds. *Psychology in the Schools, 42*, 837-853.

Espinosa, L. M., & Laffey, J. M. (2003). Urban primary teacher perceptions of children with challenging behaviors. *Journal of Children & Poverty, 9*(2), 135-156.

Favazza, A. R. (2001, June). Spirituality, ethics, and relationships in adulthood. *American Journal of Psychiatry, 158*(6), 980.

Fish, M. C. (2002). Best practices in collaborating with parents of children with disabilities. In A. Thomas & J. Grimes (Eds.), *Best practices in school psychology IV, Vol. 1* (pp. 363-376). Bethesda, MD: National Association of School Psychologists.

Fowler, R. C., & Corley, K. K. (1996). Linking families, building community. *Educational Leadership, 53*(7), 24-26.

Fox, L., Dunlap, G., Hemmeter, M. L., Joseph, G. E., & Strain, P. S. (2003). The teaching pyramid: A model for supporting social competence and preventing challenging behavior in young children. *Young Children, 58*(4), 48-52.

Freund, L., & Rich, R. (2005). *Teaching students with learning problems in the inclusive classroom.* Upper Saddle River, NJ: Merrill/Prentice Hall.

Fuchs, D., Fuchs, L., Mathes, P. H., & Simmons, D. C. (1997). Peer-assisted strategies: Making classrooms more responsive to diversity. *American Educational Research Journal, 34,* 174-206.

Fuchs, L. S. & Deno, S. L. (1994). Must instructionally useful performance assessment be based in the curriculum? *Exceptional Children, 61,* 15-24.

Fulk, B. M., & King, K. (2001). Classwide peer tutoring at work. *Teaching Exceptional Children, 34*(2), 49-53.

Fulk, B. M., & Stormont-Spurgin, M. (1995). Fourteen spelling strategies for students with learning disabilities. *Intervention in School and Clinic, 31*(1), 16-20.

Gagnon, S. D., & Nagle, R. J. (2004). Relationships between peer interactive play and social competence in at-risk preschool children. *Psychology in the Schools, 41,* 173–190.

Garcia, S. B., & Ortiz, A. A. (2004). *Preventing disproportionate representation: Culturally and linguistically responsive prereferral interventions.* Denver, CO: National Center for Culturally Responsive Educational Systems.

Gartrell, D. (2003). Bridging differences. In C. Copple (Ed.), *A world of difference: Readings on teaching young children in a diverse society* (pp. 163–166). Washington, DC: National Association for the Education of Young Children.

Gersten, R., & Chard, D. (1999). Number sense: Rethinking arithmetic instruction for students with mathematical disabilities. *The Journal of Special Education, 33*(1), 18–28.

Gersten, R., Woodward, J., & Darch, C. (1986). Direct instruction: A research-based approach to curriculum design and teaching. *Exceptional Children, 53,* 17–31.

Gonzalez, M. L. (1990). School + home = a program for educating homeless students. *Phi Delta Kappan, 71,* 785–787.

Graue, M. E., & DiPerna, J. C. (2000). Redshirting and early retention: Who gets the "gift of time" and what are its outcomes? *American Educational Research Journal, 37*(2), 509–534.

Grenell, M. M., Glass, C. R., & Katz, K. S. (1987). Hyperactive children and peer interaction: Knowledge and performance of social skills. Journal of Abnormal Child Psychology, 15, 1–13.

Gunter, P. L., & Coutinho, M. J. (1997). Negative reinforcement in classrooms: What we're beginning to learn. *Teacher Education and Special Education, 20*(3), 249–264.

Haley, M., & Sherwood-Hawes, A. (2004). Children having children: Teenage pregnancy and parenthood. In D. Capuzzi & D. R. Gross (Eds.), *Youth at risk: A prevention resource for counselors, teachers, and parents* (4th ed., pp. 211–242). Alexandria, VA: American Counseling Association.

Hall, L. A. (2005). Teachers and content area reading: Attitudes, beliefs and change. *Teaching and Teacher Education: An International Journal of Research and Studies, 21*(4), 403–414.

Herring, M., & Wahler, R. G. (2003). Children's cooperation at school: The comparative influences of teacher responsiveness and the children's home-based behavior. *Journal of Behavioral Education, 12*(2), 119–130.

Hodgkinson, H. L. (2003). *Leaving too many children behind: A demographer's view on the neglect of America's youngest children.* Washington, DC: The Institute of Educational Leadership.

Horner, R., Sugai, G., & Vincent, C. (2005). School-wide positive behavior support: Investing in student success. *Impact, 18*(2), 4–5.

Horning, L. E., & Rouse, K. A. G. (2002). Resilience in preschoolers and toddlers from low-income families. *Early Childhood Education Journal, 29*(3), 155–159.

Howse, R. B., Lange, G., Farran, D. C., & Boyles, C. D. (2003). Motivation and self-regulation as predictors of achievement in economically disadvantaged young children. *Journal of Experimental Education, 71,* 151–174.

Hubbard, J. A., & Newcomb, A. F. (1991). Initial dyadic peer interaction of attention deficit hyperactivity disorder and normal boys. *Journal of Abnormal Child Psychology, 19,* 179–195.

Huitt, W. (2003). The information processing approach to cognition. *Educational Psychology Interactive.* Valdosta, GA: Valdosta State University. Retrieved November 29, 2005, from http://chiron.valdosta.edu/whuitt/col/cogsys/infoproc.html

Johnson, D., Johnson, R., & Stanne, M. (2000). Cooperative learning methods: A meta-analysis. Retrieved September 4, 2002, from http://www.clcrc.com/pages/cl-methods.html

Johnson, D. W., & Johnson, R. T. (1986). Mainstreaming and cooperative learning strategies. Exceptional Children, 52(6), 552–561.

Johnson, L. J., & Pugach, M. C. (1990). Classroom teachers' views of intervention strategies for learning and behavior problems: Which are reasonable and how frequently are they used? *The Journal of Special Education, 24*(1), 69–84.

Jones, V. F., & Jones, L. S. (2001). *Comprehensive classroom management: Creating communities of support and solving problems.* Boston: Allyn and Bacon.

Juntunen, C. L., & Atkinson, D. R. (2002). *Counseling across the lifespan: Prevention and treatment.* Thousand Oaks, CA: Sage Publications.

Kaiser, A. P., Hancock, T. B., Cai, X., Foster, E. M., & Hester, P. P. (2000). Parent-reported behavioral problems and language delay in boys and girls enrolled in Head Start classrooms. *Behavioral Disorders, 26*(1), 26–41.

Kaiser, A. P., & Hester, P. P. (1997). Prevention of conduct disorder through early intervention: A social-communicative perspective. *Behavioral Disorders, 22,* 117-130.

Kartub, D., Taylor-Greene, S., March, R., & Horner, R. H. (2000). Reducing hallway noise: A systems approach. *Journal of Positive Behavior Interventions, 2*(3), 179-182.

Kauffman, J. M. (2005). *Characteristics of emotional and behavioral disorders of children and youth* (8th ed.). Upper Saddle River, NJ: Merrill/Prentice Hall.

Kea, C., Campbell-Whatley, G. D., & Richards, H. V. (2004). *Becoming culturally responsive educators: Rethinking teacher education pedagogy.* Denver, CO: National Center for Culturally Responsive Educational Systems.

Kim, O. H., & Kaiser, A. P. (2000). Language characteristics of children with ADHD. *Communication Disorders Quarterly, 21*(3), 154-165.

Kokkinos, C. M., Panayiotou, G., & Davazoglou, A. M. (2005). Correlates of teacher appraisals of student behaviors. *Psychology in the Schools, 42*(1), 79-89.

Kozol, J. (1991). *Savage inequalities: Children in America's schools.* New York: Crown Publishers.

Ladson-Billings, G. (1994). *The dreamkeepers: Successful teachers of African American children.* San Francisco: Jossey-Bass.

Lake, R. (1990). An Indian father's plea. *Teacher Magazine, 2*(1), 48-53.

Lampi, A. R., Fenty, N. S., & Beaunae, C. (2005, Fall). Making the three Ps easier: Praise, Proximity, and Precorrection. *Beyond Behavior, 15*(1), 8-12.

Landau, S., & Milich, R. (1988). Social communication patterns of attention-deficit-disordered boys. *Journal of Abnormal Child Psychology, 16,* 69-81.

Landau, S., & Moore, L. A. (1991). Social skill deficits in children with attention-deficit hyperactivity disorder. *School Psychology Review, 20,* 235-251.

Landsverk, R. A. (1995, Spring). *Families, communities, schools, learning together 2: Families in education packet.* Madison, WI: Wisconsin Department of Public Instruction.

Lee, D. L., Belfiore, P. J., Scheeler, M. C., Hua, Y., & Smith, R. (2004). Behavioral momentum in academics: Using embedded high-p sequences to increase academic productivity. *Psychology in the Schools, 41*(7), 789-801.

Lehr, C. A., & Christenson, S. L. (2002). Best practices in promoting a positive school climate. In A. Thomas & J. Grimes (Eds.), *Best practices in school psychology IV, Vol. 1* (pp. 929-948). Bethesda, MD: National Association of School Psychologists.

Lembke, E. S., & Stormont, M. (2005). Using research-based practices to support students with diverse needs in general education settings. *Psychology in the Schools, 42*(8), 761-763.

Lerner, J. W., Lowenthal, B., & Lerner, S. R. (1995). *Attention deficit disorders: Assessment and teaching.* Pacific Grove, CA: Brooks/Cole Publishing.

Levin, J., & Nolan, J. F. (2004). *Principles of classroom management: A professional decision-making model.* Boston: Allyn and Bacon.

Lewis, T. J. (2005). Implementing school-wide positive behavior supports. *Impact, 18*(2), 26-27.

Lewis, T. J., & Garrison-Harrell, L. (1999). Effective behavior support: Designing setting-specific interventions. *Effective School Practices, 17*(4), 38-46.

Lewis, T. J., Powers, L. J., Kelk, M. J., & Newcomer, L. L. (2002). Reducing problem behaviors on the playground: An investigation of the application of school-wide positive behavior supports. *Psychology in the Schools, 39*(2), 181-190.

Lewis, T. J., Powers, L. J., & Newcomer, L. L. (2001, October). *Positive behavior support at the school-wide level.* Paper presented at the Fourth International Conference on Children and Youth with Behavioral Disorders. Atlanta, GA.

Lewis, T. J., & Sugai, G. (1999). Effective behavior support: A systems approach to proactive schoolwide management. *Focus on Exceptional Children, 31*(6), 1-24.

Lin, H. L., Lawrence, F. R., & Gorrell, J. (2003). Kindergarten teachers' views of children's readiness for school. *Early Childhood Reaserch Quarterly, 18*(2), 225-237.

Logan, T. (1998, March). Creating a kindergarten community. *Young Children, 53*(2), 22-26, 30-35.

Maag, J. W. (2001). Rewarded by punishment: Reflections on the disuse of positive reinforcement in education. *Exceptional Children, 67*(2), 173-186.

Marshall, K. (2003). Recovering from HSPS (Hyperactive Superficial Principal Syndrome): A progress report. *Phi Delta Kappan, 84*(9), 701-709.

Mastropieri, M. A., & Scruggs, T. E. (2004). *The inclusive classroom: Strategies for effective instruction* (2nd ed.). Upper Saddle River, NJ: Merrill/ Prentice Hall.

McClurg, L. G. (1998, March). Building an ethical community in the classroom: Community meeting. *Young Children, 53*(2), 30–35.

McGinnis, E., & Goldstein, A. P. (1997). *Skillstreaming the elementary school child: New strategies and perspectives for teaching prosocial skills* (Rev. ed.). Champaign, IL: Research Press.

McKinley, L. A. (2003). *Educational accommodations adopted by general and special education teachers for students with attention deficit-hyperactivity disorder.* Unpublished doctoral dissertation, University of Missouri-Columbia.

McWayne, C., Hampton, V., Fantuzzo, J., Cohen, H. L., & Sekino, Y. (2004). A multivariate examination of parent involvement and the social and academic competencies of urban kindergarten children. *Psychology in the Schools, 41*(3), 363–377.

Meese, R. (2001). *Teaching learners with mild disabilities* (2nd ed.). Belmont, CA: Wadsworth.

Mercer, C. D., & Mercer, A. R. (2005). *Teaching students with learning problems* (7th ed.). Upper Saddle River, NJ: Merrill/Prentice Hall.

Merrell, K. W., & Wolfe, T. M. (1998). The relationship of teacher-rated social skills deficits and ADHD characteristics among kindergarten-age children. *Psychology in the Schools, 35*(2), 101–109.

Miller, S., Strawser, S., & Mercer, C. (1996). Promoting strategic math performance among students with learning disabilities. *LD Forum, 21*, 34–40.

Mindes, G. (2003). *Assessing young children* (2nd ed.). Upper Saddle River, NJ: Merrill/Prentice Hall.

Missouri Department of Elementary and Secondary Education. (2004). *The impact of the new Title I requirements on charter schools' non-regulatory guidance.* Jefferson City, MO: Author.

Nakasato, J. (2000). Data-based decision making in Hawaii's behavior support effort. *Journal of Positive Behavior Interventions, 2*(4), 247–251.

National Center on Accessing the General Curriculum. *Limited English proficient students and special education.* Retrieved October 19, 2004, from http://www.cast.org/publications/ncac/ncac_limited.html

National Coalition for the Homeless (1999). *Making the grade: Challenges and successes in providing educational opportunities for homeless children and youth.* Washington, DC: Author.

National Council of Teachers of Mathematics. (2005). *A family's guide: Fostering your child's success in school mathematics.* Reston, VA: Author.

O'Donnell, D. A., Schwab-Stone, M. E., & Muyeed, A. Z. (2002). Multidimensional resilience in urban children exposed to community violence. *Child Development, 73*(4), 1265–1282.

Ogle, D. M. (1986). KWL: A teaching model that develops active reading of expository text. *Reading Teacher, 39*(6), 564–570.

Okagaki, L., & Diamond, K. E. (2003). Responding to cultural and linguistic differences in the beliefs and practices of families of young children. In C. Copple (Ed.), *A world of difference: Readings on teaching young children in a diverse society* (pp. 9–15). Washington, DC: National Association for the Education of Young Children.

Olson, J. L., & Platt, J. C. (2004). *Teaching children and adolescents with special needs* (4th ed.). Upper Saddle River, NJ: Merrill/Prentice Hall.

Olson, M. (2001). Painting tiles. *Teaching Children Mathematics, 7*(7), 426–427.

Olympia, D., Farley, M., Christiansen, E., Pettersson, H., Jenson, W., & Clark, E. (2004). Social maladjustment and students with behavioral and emotional disorders: Revising basic assumptions and assessment issues. *Psychology in the Schools, 41*(8), 835–847.

Ortiz, S. O., & Flanagan, D. P. (2002). Best practices in working with culturally diverse children and families. In A. Thomas & J. Grimes (Series Eds.), *Best practices in school psychology IV, Vol. 1* (pp. 337–351). Bethesda, MD: The National Association of School Psychologists.

Otto, B. (2006). *Language development in early childhood* (2nd ed.). Upper Saddle River, NJ: Merrill/Prentice Hall.

Overton, S. (2005). *Collaborating with families: A case study approach.* Upper Saddle River, NJ: Merrill/Prentice Hall.

Pianta, R. C. (1999). *Enhancing relationships between children and teachers: School psychology book series.* Washington, DC: American Psychological Association.

Pianta, R. C., & Walsh. D. J. (1998). Applying the construct of resilience in schools: Cautions from a developmental systems perspective. *School Psychology Review, 27*(3), 407-417.

Piotrkowski, C. S., Botsko, M., & Matthews, E. (2000). Parents' and teachers' beliefs about children's school readiness in a high-need community. *Early Childhood Research Quarterly, 15*(4), 537-558.

Ramsey, P. G. (2003). Growing up with the contradictions of race and class. In C. Copple (Ed.), *A world of difference: Readings on teaching young children in a diverse society* (pp. 24-28). Washington, DC: National Association for the Education of Young Children.

Raymond, E. B. (2004). *Learners with mild disabilities: A characteristics approach*. Boston: Allyn and Bacon.

Resnick, L. B. (1995). From aptitude to effort: A new foundation for our schools. *Journal of the American Academy of Arts and Sciences, 124*(4), 55-62.

Resnick, L. B., & Glennan, T. K. (2002). Leadership for learning: A theory of action for urban school districts. In A. M. Hightower, M. S. Knapp, J. A. Marsh, & M. W. McLaughlin (Eds.), *School districts and instructional renewal* (pp. 160-172). New York: Teachers College Press.

Resnick, L. B., & Hall, M. W. (1998). Learning organizations for sustainable education reform. *Journal of the American Academy of Arts and Sciences, 127*(4), 89-118.

Richards, H. V., Brown, A. F., & Forde, T. B. (2004). *Addressing diversity in schools: Culturally responsive pedagogy*. Denver, CO: National Center for Culturally Responsive Educational Systems.

Riley, R. W. (1994). Ingredient for success: Family involvement. *Teaching PreK-8, 25*, 12.

Rosenshine, B., & Stevens, R. (1986). Teaching functions. In M. C. Wittrock (Ed.), *Handbook of research on teaching* (3rd ed., pp. 376-391). New York: Macmillan.

Rutter, M. (2000). Resilience reconsidered: Conceptual considerations, empirical findings, and policy implications. In J. P. Shonkoff & S. J. Meisels (Eds.), *Handbook of early childhood intervention* (2nd ed., pp. 651-682). New York: Cambridge University Press.

Salend, S. J., & Sylvestre, S. (2005). Understanding and addressing oppositional and defiant classroom behaviors. *Teaching Exceptional Children, 37*(6), 32-39.

Salvia, J., & Ysseldyke, J. E. (1991). *Assessment* (5th ed.). Boston: Houghton Mifflin.

Sanson, A., Smart, D., Prior, M., & Oberklaid, F. (1993). Precursors of hyperactivity and aggression. *Journal of the American Academy of Child and Adolescent Psychiatry, 32*(6), 1207-1216.

Scott, T. M. (2001). A schoolwide example of positive behavioral support. *Journal of Positive Behavioral Interventions, 3*, 88-94.

Shane, P. G. (1996). *What about America's homeless children? Hide and seek: Sage sourcebooks for the human services series* (Report No. ED402373). Thousand Oaks, CA: Sage Publications.

Shonkoff, J. P., & Meisels, S. J. (Eds.). (2000). *Handbook of early childhood intervention* (2nd ed.). New York: Cambridge University Press.

Shumow, L., Vandell, D. L., & Posner, J. (1999). Risk and resilience in the urban neighborhood: Predictors of academic performance among low-income elementary school children. *Merrill-Palmer Quarterly: Journal of Developmental Psychology, 45*(2), 309-331.

Skinner, C. H., Neddenriep, C. E., Robinson, S. L., Ervin, R., & Jones, K. (2002). Altering educational environments through positive peer reporting: Prevention and remediation of social problems associated with behavior disorders. *Psychology in the Schools, 39*(2), 191-202.

Slavin, R. E. & Cheung, A. (2003, December). *Effective reading programs for English language learners: A best evidence synthesis* (Report: No-66). Baltimore, MD: Johns Hopkins University, Center for Research on the Education of Students Placed At Risk.

Smith, T. E. C., Polloway, E. A., Patton, J. R., & Dowdy, C. A. (1995). *Teaching students with special needs in inclusive settings*. Boston: Allyn and Bacon.

Stecker, P. M., Fuchs, L. S., & Fuchs, D. (2005). Using curriculum-based measurement to improve student achievement: Review of research. *Psychology in the Schools, 42*(8), 795-819.

Stone, J. G. (2003). Communicating respect. In C. Copple (Ed.), *A world of difference: Readings on teaching young children in a diverse society* (pp. 41-42). Washington, DC: National Association for the Education of Young Children.

Stormont, M. (1998). Family factors associated with externalizing disorders in preschoolers. *Journal of Early Intervention, 21*(3), 232-251.

Stormont, M. (2001a). Social outcomes of children with AD/HD: Contributing factors and implications for practice. *Psychology in the Schools, 38*(6), 521-531.

Stormont, M. (2001b). Preschool family and child characteristics associated with stable behavior problems in children. *Journal of Early Intervention, 24*(4), 241-251.

Stormont, M. (2002). Externalizing behavior problems in young children: Contributing factors and early intervention. *Psychology in the Schools, 39*(2), 127-138.

Stormont, M. (2004). Nowhere to turn: Homeless youth. In D. Capuzzi & D. R. Gross (Eds.), *Youth at risk: A prevention resource for counselors, teachers, and parents* (4th ed., pp. 401-424). Alexandria, VA: American Counseling Association.

Stormont, M., Beckner, R., Mitchell, B., & Richter, M. (2005). Supporting successful transition to kindergarten: General challenges and specific implications for students with problem behavior. *Psychology in the Schools, 42*(8), 765-778.

Stormont, M., Covington, S., & Lewis, T. J. (2006, spring). Using data to inform systems: Assessing teacher implementation of key features of program-wide positive behavioral support in Head Start classrooms. *Beyond Behavior, 15*(3) 10-14.

Stormont, M., Espinosa, L., Knipping, N., & McCathren, R. (2003, Fall). Supporting vulnerable learners in the primary grades: Strategies to prevent early school failure. *Early Childhood Research & Practice, 5*(2). Retrieved January 21, 2004, from http://ecrp.uiuc.edu/v5n2/stormont.html

Stormont, M., Lewis, T. J., & Beckner, R. (2005, July/August). Possitive behavior support systems: Applying key features in preschool settings. *Teaching Exceptional Children, 37*(6) 42-49.

Stormont, M., Smith, S. C., & Lewis, T. J. (2006). *Teacher implementation of precorrection and praise statements in Head Start classrooms as a component of a program-wide system of positive behavior support.* Manuscript submitted for publication.

Stormont, M., & Stebbins, M. S. (2005). Preschool teachers' knowledge, opinions, and educational experiences with attention deficit/hyperactivity disorder. *Teacher Education and Special Education, 28*(1), 52-61.

Stormont-Spurgin, M. (1997). I lost my homework: Strategies for improving organization in students

with ADHD. *Intervention in School and Clinic, 32*, 270-274.

Stormont-Spurgin, M., & Zentall, S. S. (1995). Contributing factors in the manifestation of aggression in preschoolers with hyperactivity. *Journal of Child Psychology and Psychiatry, 36*(3), 491-509.

Sugai, G., Horner, R. H., Dunlap, G., Hieneman, M., Lewis, T. J., Nelson, C. M. et al. (2000). Applying positive behavioral support and functional behavioral assessment in schools. *Journal of Positive Behavioral Interventions, 2*, 131-143.

Sugai, G., Horner, R., Lewis, T. J., & Cheney, D. (2002, July). *Positive behavioral supports.* Invited presentation at the OSEP Research Project Directors' Conference, Washington, DC.

Sugai, G., & Lewis, T. J. (1996). Preferred and promising practices for social skills instruction. *Focus on Exceptional Children, 29*(4), 1-16.

Swick, K. J. (1995). What parents really want from family involvement programs. *Day Care & Early Education, 22*(3), 20-23.

Tabors, P. O. (2003). What early childhood educators need to know: Developing effective programs for linguistically and culturally diverse children and families. In C. Copple (Ed.), *A world of difference: Readings on teaching young children in a diverse society* (pp. 17-23). Washington, DC: National Association for the Education of Young Children.

Taylor-Greene, S., Brown, D., Nelson, L., Longton, J., Gassman, T., Cohen, J., et al. (1997). School-wide behavioral support: Starting the year off right. *Journal of Behavioral Education, 7*, 99-112.

Tiegerman-Farber, E., & Radziewicz, C. (1998). *Collaborative decision making: The pathway to inclusion.* Upper Saddle River, NJ: Merrill/Prentice Hall.

Tomlinson, C. A. (1999). *The differentiated classroom: Responding to the needs of all learners.* Upper Saddle River, NJ: Merrill/Prentice Hall.

Tomlinson, C. A. (2005). *How to differentiate instruction in mixed-ability classrooms* (2nd ed.). Upper Saddle River, NJ: Merrill/Prentice Hall.

Tournaki, N., & Criscitiello, E. (2003, November/December). Using peer tutoring as a successful part of behavior management. *Teaching Exceptional Children, 36*(2), 22-25.

Turnbull, A., & Turnbull, R. (2001). *Families, professionals, and exceptionality: Collaborating for empowerment* (4th ed.). Upper Saddle River, NJ: Merrill/Prentice Hall.

Turnbull, A., Turnbull, R., Erwin, E., & Soodak, L. (2006). *Families, professionals, and exceptionality: Positive outcomes through partnerships and trust* (5th ed.). Upper Saddle River, NJ: Merrill/Prentice Hall.

Umbreit, J., & Blair, K. S. (1997). Using structural analysis to facilitate treatment of aggression and noncompliance in a young child at-risk for behavioral disorders. *Behavioral Disorders, 22*(2), 75–86.

Van Acker, R., Grant, S. H., & Henry, D. (1996). Teacher and student behavior as a function of risk for aggression. *Educational and Treatment of Children, 19*, 316–334.

Vanderbilt, A. A. (2005, Full). Designed for teacher: How to implement self-monitoring in the classroom. Beyond Behavior, *15*(1), 21–24.

Vaughn, S., & Klingner, J. K. (1999). Teaching reading comprehension through collaborative strategic reading. *Intervention in School and Clinic, 34*(5), 284–292.

Vitaro, F., Tremblay, R. E., Gagnon, C., & Biovin, M. (1992). Peer rejection from kindergarten to grade 2: Outcomes, correlates, and prediction. *Merrill-Palmer Quarterly, 38*, 382–400.

Vitaro, F., Tremblay, R. E., Gagnon, C., & Pelletier, D. (1994). Predictive accuracy of behavioral and sociometric assessments of high-risk kindergarten children. *Journal of Clinical Child Psychology, 23*, 272–282.

Walker, H. M., Colvin, G., & Ramsey, E. (1995). *Antisocial behavior in school: Strategies and best practices.* Pacific Grove, CA: Brooks/Cole Publishing.

Walker, H. M., Ramsey, E., & Gresham, F. M. (2004). *Antisocial behavior in school: Evidence-based practices* (2nd ed.). Belmont, CA: Thomson/Wadsworth.

Ward, A. W., & Murray-Ward, M. (1999). *Assessment in the classroom.* Belmont, CA: Wadsworth Publishing.

Warnes, E. D., Sheridan, S. M., Geske, J., & Warnes, W. (2005). A contextual approach to the assessment of social skills: Identifying meaningful behaviors for social competence. *Psychology in the Schools, 42*(2), 173–187.

Watson, M. (2003, July). Attachment theory and challenging behaviors: Reconstructing the nature of relationships. *Young Children, 58*(4), 12–20.

Watson, M., & Ecken, L. (2003). *Learning to trust: Transforming difficult elementary classrooms through developmental discipline.* San Francisco, CA: Jossey-Bass.

Webster-Stratton, C. (1997). Early intervention for families of preschool children with conduct problems. In M. J. Guralnick (Ed.), *The effectiveness of early intervention* (pp. 429–453). Baltimore, Maryland: Brookes.

Weinstein, C. S., & Mignano, A. J. (2003). *Elementary classroom management: Lessons from research and practice* (3rd ed.). New York: McGraw-Hill.

Werner, E. E. (1990). Protective factors and individual resilience. In S. J. Meisels & J. P. Shonkoff (Eds.), *Handbook of early childhood intervention* (pp. 97–116). New York: Cambridge University Press.

Wiley, A. L. (1994). Measurement of performance, productivity, and quality. *Journal of the Society for Technical Communication, 41*(2), 360–364.

Williams, J. P. (2003, March). Incorporating partner practice and writing and self-regulation into the theme scheme program. *Teaching Exceptional Children, 35*(4), 70–73.

Wisconsin Policy Research Institute Report (2001, March). *Direct instruction and the teaching of early reading.* Thiensville, WI: Author.

Witt, J. C., Elliott, S. N., Kramer, J. J., & Gresham, F. M. (1994). *Assessment of children: Fundamental methods and practices.* Madison, WI: Brown & Benchmark Publishers.

Wood, D. L., Valdez, R. B., Hayashi, T., & Shen, A. (1990). Health of homeless children and housed, poor children. *Pediatrics, 86*(6), 858–866.

Wortham, S. C. (2005). *Assessment in early childhood education* (4th ed.). Upper Saddle River, NJ: Merrill/Prentice Hall.

Yell, M. L., & Drasgow, E. (2005). *No child left behind: A guide for professionals.* Upper Saddle River, NJ: Merrill/Prentice Hall.

Zentall, S. S. (1993). Reaserch on the educational implications of attention deficit hyperactivity disorder. *Exceptional Children, 60*(2), 143–153.

Zentall, S. S. (2005). Theory- and evidence-based strategies for children with attention problems. *Psychology in the Schools, 42*, 821–836.

Zentall, S. S. (2006). *ADHD and education: Foundations, characteristics, methods, and collaboration.* Upper Saddle River, NJ: Merrill/Prentice Hall.

Zentall, S. S., Harper, G. W., Stormont-Spurgin, M. (1993). Children with hyperactivity and their organizational abilities. *Journal of Educational Research, 87*(2), 112–117.

Zentall, S. S., & Stormont-Spurgin, M. (1995). Educator preferences of accommodations for students with attention deficit hyperactivity disorder. *Teacher Education and Special Education, 18*(2), 115–123.

Index